DAVID YOUNG

INSIDE THATCHER'S LAST ELECTION

DIARIES OF THE CAMPAIGN THAT SAVED ENTERPRISE

Biteback Publishing

First published in Great Britain in 2021 by
Biteback Publishing Ltd, London
Copyright © David Young 2021
Copyright in the foreword © Charles Moore 2021

ISBN 978-1-78590-683-1

10 9 8 7 6 5 4 3 2 1

A CIP catalogue record for this book is available from the British Library.

Set in Adobe Caslon Pro and Futura

Printed and bound in Great Britain by
CPI Group (UK) Ltd, Croydon CR0 4YY

To Lita, my wife and partner of sixty-five years, without whom none of the adventures in my life would have happened nor would life have been so enjoyable.

CONTENTS

FOREWORD
BY CHARLES MOORE

Composing the final volume of my authorised biography of
Margaret Thatcher, I had the great benefit of reading David
Young's diary of the 1987 general election, in which he played
such a key role. At that stage it was unpublished, so David was
giving me a head-start. Now, backed up by a crisp introduction
and a reflective postscript, it can be studied by scholars and read
with enjoyment by all.

That election was a very strange one. It was the third victory
on the trot for the Conservatives under Mrs Thatcher, and there
was never strong rational evidence that the Labour Party, only
just beginning to recover from its years of division and weak
leftist leadership, was at all likely to overturn the vast majority
she had won for her party in 1983.

Somehow or other, it did not feel quite like that at the time.
The Tories were very jumpy – none more so than Mrs Thatch-
er herself. Rightly, she never took election results for granted.
Wrongly, she placed too little trust in her top lieutenants on

that occasion. Faction-fighting and disharmony were the consequence, although in truth they did not trouble the actual voters much.

It is probably the case that Mrs Thatcher was feeling the strain of having been so long in office. 'The tiredness; ah, the tiredness,' recalls Lord Young in relation to himself. It applied to her too. As Willie Whitelaw, Thatcher's former deputy, remarked at the time: 'There's a woman who is not going to fight another general election.' Although she triumphed at the poll, she perhaps had some slight foretaste of the end which came – without consultation with the electorate – more than three years later. She felt insecure.

Lord Young was perfectly placed as a diarist of that time. As one of the most important managers of the campaign, he was right in the thick of it. As a non-career politician, however, he could observe proceedings with a degree of detachment which is denied to those fighting to get re-elected themselves. He tells his side of the story clearly, entertainingly and frankly – and is not frightened of admitting to moments of panic or bad temper. He felt vindicated by the result but does not conceal that it was a bumpy ride.

David Young did not disappear. As well as experiencing much business success after leaving office, he continued to serve. When David Cameron became Prime Minister, he gave Lord Young an office in 10 Downing Street, so he could advise him about reviving the entrepreneurism which he has done so much to encourage throughout his working life. As the most business-minded practitioner of Thatcherism in politics, David Young has a unique perspective. The exciting tale told in this book takes the reader into the eye of the storm.

Charles Moore
February 2021

INTRODUCTION

In her time Margaret Thatcher won three elections. The first was the election that broke the mould and saw a woman as Prime Minister for the very first time in our history. But Thatcher was far more than the first woman to lead the Conservative Party, remarkable as that may be. She was a woman with a purpose in life, and that was to restore the economy of the United Kingdom. But even more than that, she wanted to restore the self-respect of the individual, as well as of the nation, and to return to the prudent shop-keeping skills she had learnt at her father's dinner table, over their shop in Grantham.

But at the beginning it was not easy. The country had barely recovered from the 1978–79 Winter of Discontent, when all the public sector unions had been on strike for many weeks and the change from a Labour government to a Conservative one hardly improved their tempers. Her first Cabinet was still an uneasy balance between the 'wets' and the 'dries': her supporters were not in the majority and she was learning on the job. The economy was not going well, and the nationalised industries were proving a disastrous drain upon the government. After exchange control was finally abolished the pound shot to record heights, putting further strain on the economy. Unemployment continued its relentless advance. The country continued to be beset by strikes, and when she gave way, once again, to the miners' union headed by Scargill, I nearly resigned on the spot. But she was far cleverer and more far-seeing than was I!

Murmurings and mutterings began in the back benches and occasional coded speeches were being made when she was rescued by General Galtieri. His invasion of the Falkland Islands and South Georgia and the response that she led restored the island to the Commonwealth. It was a decision she alone made – and, in turn, it made her.

It is difficult now, all these years later, to remember the shot in the arm that the Falklands gave to the entire nation. For decades we had been in decline: a once great nation looking for a role, we were still smarting from the debacle of the Suez Crisis, when the United States, once our junior cousins, told us to go home and start behaving ourselves. Now, when part of our Commonwealth had been invaded by a dictator, we had reached out over 8,000 miles with our Armed Forces and fought and died to free our people.

Suddenly, we were back again. She had put the Great back into Britain, and she became the Iron Lady – a title she never lost. For the first time she had control of the party and could begin to shape the government as she desired.

The second election crushed the most left-wing manifesto the country had yet seen; a manifesto that afterwards was described as the longest suicide note in history. She won the election so decisively, with a majority of 144, that there was not to be another hard-left manifesto from the Labour Party for thirty-four years, until 2017 (and even then, the Conservative Party, with indifferent leadership supported by a completely forgettable manifesto, showed that there was still no place in British public life for hard-left policies).

A great deal happened over the four years before the third election in 1987. The stranglehold the trade unions had held over the British economy for the post-war decades was finally relaxed by the simple expedient of giving their membership a democratic and secret vote before any decision to strike.

The third, the only election in which I have played any part in my life, was one which I believe consolidated the course of the nation until today. They say that distance lends enchantment, yet after many decades I can still feel the sheer horror of the last weeks of that election and what would have happened to all we had done over the previous eight years if we had lost.

To understand why I feel this way, you have to go back to the first election I ever remember: the 1945 post-war election. I am not sure whether I am a member or not of the wartime generation. I was thirteen when the war ended, but young people grew up very quickly in those days, as we lived in the centre of London, and so the Blitz, the V1s and the V2s were no strangers.

I was an enthusiastic supporter of the first post-war Labour government. It seemed to me, in those days of innocence, that it was entirely logical to plan resources so they may be put to best use for the nation, to use taxation as a means of redistribution, to eliminate inequalities and to enable workers to have a say in the direction of the business that employed them through their union.

I left school at sixteen to work in a solicitors' office in the City, and over the next half a dozen years I not only learnt a little law and became a solicitor but also had the scales stripped from my eyes. What I saw evolve was not a world of greater equality but a world of greater regulation. Everything, almost everything in life, required the consent of some authority or other. There was even a time when you could not spend more than £5 on home decoration without a licence.

The government began a great programme of nationalisation of all of our run-down industries, and with every industry they nationalised they increased the burden on the exchequer. I had little concept of taxation at that time, but in years to come I realised that the confiscatory level of taxation that would be justified at a time of all-out war was simply carried on in the days of peace.

The years passed, and to the mild surprise of my firm I duly qualified, married and realised I did not enjoy the law. I was offered a job in Great Universal Stores (GUS), the largest mail-order and retail firm of the day, and after a year or so I became PA to the chairman, Sir Isaac Wolfson. Before long I was engaged in buying a medium-sized firm a week. It was not as if this required any ability to negotiate – they would queue up to be sold and the work entailed was merely, would they fit in, if so where and what should we offer.

After a while I realised why the queue was so long. Taxation on earned income reached 83 per cent very quickly and was then

98 per cent on interest and dividends, so the black economy flourished. There was no capital gains tax, yet death duties were cripplingly high, and the death of a large shareholder in a private company would put the very company's existence in peril.

Over the next decade or two a large part of our economy, the Mittelstand, simply disappeared and was absorbed into larger companies, and it only made sense to run a small firm for the living expenses you could draw from it. More and more, you would come across 'lifestyle' companies, where the owners would play golf or go fishing whenever they wanted, as it was simply not worth putting in more effort when any additional reward would be taken away in tax.

Even in larger businesses there was a limit to the effort management would put in since their take-home pay was severely limited by tax. In truth, their main interest was getting shares in the company they worked for, and when they reached the top ensuring that the company would be taken over so they could cash in.

I realised only too well during those years how taxation could shape and cripple an economy. Yet the Conservative Party, whenever it was their time in office, changed little and left the economy largely unreformed by the time they lost office. Indeed I, who had little interest in politics, felt that their only ambition lay in delaying, rather than stopping, an eventual socialist society.

By the early '60s I had left my employment and gone on my own. Why did I do so? Well, partly for the challenge – I was probably constitutionally unfit to work for anybody – and partly to create the opportunity to maybe make some capital. I built distribution estates at the junctions of the new motorway networks that were then being built, founded a plant-hire and civil engineering business and by 1970 had sold out to Town and City Properties, the second largest property company of the day.

The '70s was a decade seared in the memories of all who worked through it. For me, the secondary banking crisis ensured that I had to start all over again, which I did through a joint venture with Manufacturers Hanover Trust, a leading New York bank, to engage in international property lending.

I was briefly enamoured with Ted Heath, the very first British politician I had heard who articulated the need for enterprise but who, alas, retracted at the first hint of opposition once in power and retreated to his comfort zone in a corporatist society.* But the real problem of the government did not lie with politicians but with the unequal balance of power that was enjoyed by the trade unions over employers and even the government themselves.

Even in my early years, when I worked for GUS and was briefly responsible for all the company's trade union negotiations, I realised the nature of many of these discussions. Our main union was the Union of Shop, Distributive and Allied Workers, the shopworkers' union, and we would meet and quickly agree a few pence an hour increase, and then they would ask us to stay on for some beer and sandwiches for a couple of

---

* Corporatism is a political culture closely related to fascism, the adherents of which hold that the corporate group which forms the basis of society is the state.

hours, so they could impress their membership with how hard they had to work to gain an agreement. Since the leadership of the unions were invariably very left wing, they saw that their responsibility was to redress the imbalances of society, and the source of their authority with the membership was their ability to gain more money for their members, irrespective of the health of the employer. Indeed, the post-war Labour government had added many statutory protections to the unions, which future governments of either party did not take away.

This reached a peak during the early years of the '70s, when the unfortunate combination of the oil-price rise, which followed the 1973 Arab–Israeli War, and substantially increased union militancy left Ted Heath with no alternative but to introduce a three-day week. We were all allocated three days each week when we could work. A year later, when the statistics were finally published, productivity was shown to have actually increased over this period, which was a fitting commentary on just how inefficient our economy had become. Eventually, in desperation, Heath called an election to decide who should run the country: the government or the unions.

Unfortunately for him, the country decided that he should not, and a surprised Harold Wilson was unexpectedly returned to office, without any clear idea of what to do nor how to restore the increasingly fragile economy. The government was rapidly running out of money and the economy, overtaxed and over-regulated, was beset by strikes. Instead of the number of strikes reducing with the change to a far more sympathetic government, the very political, left-wing leadership of the Trade Union

Congress saw this as their opportunity and applied immediate and increasing pressure upon the government.

The number of strikes continued to increase as the economy continued to decline, and by 1975 the government had completely run out of money and was forced to ask the IMF for a loan. We were now well and truly the sick man of Europe and even my at times limitless optimism was subdued – my wife and I even toyed with the idea of emigration. However, a short trip to Boston, where we hit the school bussing riots, quickly cured us of the idea.

By then, such was the desperate state of the nation that Margaret Thatcher became the leader of the Conservatives. It is difficult now to convey the shock and surprise of the Conservative Party, of all parties, choosing a woman leader: the first not only in the UK but of a major country in Europe as well.

I, by now, was completely disenchanted with British politics, but slowly it became apparent that the Conservatives were on their way to becoming a very different party when I heard Sir Keith Joseph* make speeches about the need for an enterprise economy. At that time I was still bruised by Ted Heath's sudden conversion to corporatism, but after a while I thought I should take the party at face value. I went to see Joseph after I first met him when he was a guest of honour at a dinner I chaired, and I so agreed with his speech that I volunteered to work for him on the spot and began to work for him. I became a director of

---

* Sir Keith Joseph (Baron Joseph of Portsoken after 1987), 1918–94. Conservative MP, 1955–87; Minister of Housing, Local Government and Welsh Affairs, 1962–64; Secretary of State for Health and Social Services, 1970–74; Trade and Industry, 1979–81; Education and Science, 1981–86.

the Centre for Policy Studies, the free market think tank, where we were all taken with the idea of monetarism: the control of money supply advocated by Prof. Friedman.

In the meantime, strikes continued unabated. The economy continued in freefall and Harold Wilson retired and was replaced by Jim Callaghan. By the autumn of 1978 we thought things could not possibly get any worse, but they did. All the public sector unions came out on strike in what came to be known as the 'Winter of Discontent', when for six full weeks everything closed and even the bodies lay unburied. That winter, some American friends rang and tentatively enquired whether they could organise some food parcels for us! At the height of the strike, Keith Joseph came to dinner and I agreed that when the Conservatives won the next election, I would give up my business interests and take two years off as a volunteer to work for him in the next government.

The strike eventually petered out and the government tried to pick up what was left of the economy. I always had extensive outside interests, including as the chair of British ORT, a branch of a worldwide Jewish vocational training organisation. I had asked Mrs Thatcher to come to speak at our yearly lunch. It was the first time we had met, and her speech was electrifying, saying all the right things about the need for an enterprise economy. After she left, a number of guests came up to me and said wistfully, 'If only…'

The election duly took place, and the Conservatives were declared winners with a majority of forty-three seats. Keith Joseph entered the Cabinet and became Secretary of State for Industry, and I was his first appointment on his first day of office when I was duly made his special adviser. At that time there were only four other special advisers in the whole of government, and I suspect I increased the average age by many years.

I only realised it years later, but Keith put me through a very tough training programme. I was given an assistant secretary's office with all the standard equipment: a desk, three chairs, a hatstand, a carpet square and a dictation machine with instructions how to send the tapes to the typing pool. I reported to a deputy secretary and did not see Keith once during the first three months, and after that only occasionally, but I learnt the hard way how to navigate my way through the mysteries of the civil service. After a year, Keith must have thought I was sufficiently house trained, and I moved up to the top floor.

The biggest mystery of all was the way that the nationalised industries were run. They all went through an annual cycle of preparing budgets and targets, which they all invariably missed. If they lost too much, over too long a period, the chairman was duly sacked and sent to the House of Lords! The biggest problem of all was that when they predictably lost money, they applied to the Treasury for more, but at each Budget, the Chancellor, faced with the choice between the industries and pensions, thought of the next election and inevitably ignored the industries. As a result, all were under-resourced; being nationalised, they could not go to the market for funds, since that was more expensive than issuing government bonds. Despite all this, people still call for nationalising industries to this day.

I was busily engaged with preparations for the eventual

privatisation of British Telecom when I received a visit from officials from the small firms department. They told me that for the previous twenty years there been an annual decline in the number of small firms and that they were now down to under 650,000 firms in the country. I could well believe them, remembering my time with GUS, and I started to devise the first of the programmes designed to help small firms. But we were the wrong department to help people start working for themselves, as I was told quite firmly that that was the province of the Employment Secretary.

After about eighteen months, by which time I had become properly established in the industry department, Keith moved to become Education Secretary and Patrick Jenkins became the new Secretary of State. He asked me to continue as his special adviser, while a few weeks later Keith asked me if I could advise him as well, and for a time I did both. However, there were dark clouds on the horizon, for unemployment had started to rise and was becoming a serious political issue.

In the meantime, Norman Tebbit,* with whom I had developed a good working relationship when he had been the minister of state in the industry department, had been promoted to Employment Secretary. Norman was one of a number of those shadow ministers I had taken to Paris to see the ORT schools and at the time had been very impressed by what I had seen. He has a gift for expressing ideas and concepts in language that people not only understand but adopt. He was great to work for, for he would

---

* Norman Tebbit (Baron Tebbit of Chingford since 1992), 1931–. Conservative MP, 1970–92; junior minister, Department of Trade, 1979–81; Industry, 1981; Secretary of State for Employment, 1981–83; Trade and Industry, 1983–85; Chancellor of the Duchy of Lancaster and chairman of Conservative Party, 1985–87.

delegate responsibility, trust his subordinates and back them no matter what the outcome. More than that, he made it all great fun.

Around this same period, the chairman of the Manpower Services Commission (MSC), which was under the employment department and by far the largest government agency dealing with all the unemployment and training matters, retired, and I put my cap in the ring. I was appointed, and at the beginning of '82 I became chairman. Over the next two years, I moved the focus of the commission, in addition to all the retraining, to helping the unemployed to start to work for themselves or start their own businesses.

Within months of the '79 election, the government began to take steps, tentative at first, to deal with the continual strikes and the unbalanced advantages that trade unions had in law. The Employment Act 1980 introduced the idea of secret ballots, if only for the election of union officials; removed immunity from the secondary action; restricted lawful picketing; and introduced the first limits on the closed shop.

This did not do much to reduce the incidence of strikes, so in 1982 the second Employment Act continued the process by removing the legal immunities which trade unions had enjoyed; outlawing political strikes; and further reducing secondary action. Although the cumulative effect of both acts was to further reduce strikes, they were still a great drain on the economy.

The first really important steps towards the restoration of an enterprise economy were taken by Geoffrey Howe* as Chancellor

---

* Geoffrey Howe (Baron Howe of Aberavon after 1992), 1926–2015. Conservative MP, 1964–66, 1970–92; Chancellor of the Exchequer, 1979–83; Foreign Secretary, 1983–89; Leader of the House of Commons, 1989–90.

in 1980, reducing the top rate of tax from 83 per cent to 60 per cent and cutting the basic rate of tax from 33 per cent to 30 per cent. Taxes were still far too high, but further reductions would have to wait for a few more years, until the economy improved.

In the midst of all of this the government called a new election. Now I was a full-time civil servant and under strict instruction not to say or do anything that could affect the election. Unemployment was becoming one of the big issues of this election, and we took steps to ensure that no officials said anything and that if there were any enquiries about unemployment, national or local, it was dealt with centrally.

As I was under instructions to say or do absolutely nothing, I went down to the West Country and had a few days fishing. Michael Foot, the leader of the Labour Party, produced his infamous manifesto, and when the results were in the government had won its landslide majority.

After the election I went back to the MSC, and, painfully, we tried to slow the rise in unemployment. That was more easily said than done. Our industries, run down during the war years, had been deprived of sufficient capital to modernise, and, anyway, post-war planning, which would put new nationalised industry plants in the centres of high unemployment rather than where they would be most efficient, served to ensure that they would not be able to compete with all the rebuilt industries of Europe and the fast-upcoming Japan and Far East.

Finally, in the summer of 1984, the Prime Minister invited me to join the Cabinet as Minister Without Portfolio, with responsibility for employment measures. We were able to start a number of programmes, helping, for example, the tourism and hostelry industries, but it wasn't until the following year, when I became Secretary of State for Employment, that I was able to employ a number of measures which began to make a real difference.

Amongst them was the Enterprise Allowance Scheme, a very simple system whereby, in essence, if someone unemployed wanted to go and work for themselves and could produce £1,000, we would agree to pay them unemployment benefit for a year while he or she set up their new firm. Over the next few years 350,000 new firms started under this scheme and, in time, two even made the FTSE 100.

But we still had much to do to restore a proper balance between companies and their trade unions. So, in 1984, the Trade Union Act introduced secret pre-strike ballots and an apparently innocent requirement that a trade union could only start industrial action if the action had been approved by a simple majority of the workers in a secret ballot not more than four weeks before any action. We also ensured that all voting members of the union's executive committee were directly elected by secret ballot at least once in every five years.

The results were spectacular. The trade unions found, to their dismay, that it was not that easy to persuade their members to go out on strike and jeopardise their own employment. Conversely, employers who were faced with a positive strike vote took the union demands seriously, particularly as they were likely to be more temperate in order to gain a positive vote. No more were there pithead ballots and ridiculous or excessive demands made in order to simply create strife. A strike was a serious matter and over the next year or two the number of strikes dropped precipitously until we were experiencing the lowest level of strikes since the war and the economy as a whole started to grow.

But while all this was positive and boded well for the future, we were approaching an election, and Labour had a new leader in Neil Kinnock. Under his leadership, the party, apparently modernised and certainly using up-to-date marketing techniques in presentation, was fundamentally just as left-wing as it had been under Michael Foot, only it was repackaged in a more subtle and contemporary manner.

Their proposals on industrial action, for example, gave members the right to have secret ballots on decisions relating to strikes, but not before any strike could take place, meaning we could see ways in which the old mayhem would return. Then they wanted to reverse all the income tax cuts we had introduced over the previous eight years and to go further with the introduction of a wealth tax on top. Instead of promising nationalisation, a word much discredited by the performance of the nationalised industries, they were promising 'social' ownership by a variety of means and to take a socially owned stake in high-tech industries, as well as social ownership of all basic utilities, including the 49 per cent of British Telecom now held in private hands.

Unemployment was no longer the big political issue. Although it was still far too high, it was now slowly going down, and all the polls showed that people thought the government was now dealing with the issue. In October, the Chancellor introduced a massive deregulation of the City, which quickly became known as the 'Big Bang' and in time led to London regaining its position as the global financial centre.

So, as we surveyed the scene at the beginning of 1987, we could see that the seeds of all that we had done over the previous eight years were beginning to grow; on the other hand, they were far too young to come out of the greenhouse.

Winning three elections in a row would always be a challenge, for by the time of the third election, the government is largely defending its past actions, while the opposition is free to promise the world. The spectacular victory we had enjoyed in 1982 was partially due to the personal glory Margaret enjoyed as a result of Falklands and partially because of the particularly inept campaign run by Labour. By 1987, though, the Falklands bounce had quite dissipated; much of what we had done was still in its early stages; and this time we were faced by a much more attractive opposition, who could well run a much better campaign than could we.

From my own point of view, I had spent the past eight years taking time out of my normal life, and I could see the beginnings of an enterprise society. All the things I had talked about with Keith in the early days were now possible. Yet, as pleased as I was with the beginning, it was only a beginning. When I listened to what Labour were saying, to what they were promising, I realised that it was far easier to undo something than to create it in the first place. I began to worry that if we did not win this third election, much of what we had done would be undone and all would have been wasted.

Some of the principal players who will appear in the pages ahead are no longer around or have retired from public life. They include Peter Morrison. When I first became a special adviser, I reported to Peter, who was a larger-than-life character, the parliamentary undersecretary of state and therefore the junior minister in the department. He came from a great political family: his father had been a fabled chairman of the 1922 Committee, while his brother Charles was a rather wet backbencher. Peter, in contrast, was not only a 'dry' but had been one of the very first to recognise the potential in Margaret and had worked for her from the beginning of her leadership campaign. He was a devil for detail and delved deep into the workings of the department. It was he who coined the term 'Martian' for civil servants, for he always asserted that they came from another world. At the beginning he was more than unpopular and stories about him were legion. Before he moved on, he became one of the most loved of ministers. He went on to the Department of Trade and Industry (DTI) and ended his political career as the Prime Minister's parliamentary private secretary (PPS) at the time of her fall.*

Howell James also looms large in my tale. In my early days as a minister, I was unhappy with my press. The reasons are now long forgotten, but Tim Bell suggested that I meet with Howell, who had just left TV-am, working, as he put it, for Roland the Rat. I took him on at our first meeting. Howell's advice transformed my relationship with the media in weeks. He came with

---

* The sad circumstances of Sir Peter's death are mentioned in Gyles Brandreth, *Breaking the Code* (London: Biteback, 2015), p. 308.

me to Employment, where he became special adviser. Some months after the election, he was stolen away from me by the BBC, where he became the director of corporate affairs. He has an ability to get on with people from all walks of life: civil servants, politicians, business people and the media. Born with a highly developed instinct for politics, time after time he would gently point out to me where I was about to blunder and steer me in the right direction. We were to work together again in later years.

Tim Bell was introduced to me by Norman Tebbit during my MSC days. He worked for the Saatchis during their early years, but by 1987 he felt that his contributions to the company were not being recognised and he left and went on his own. That was the equivalent of a declaration of war, and from then onwards the Saatchi brothers refused to work with him. This gave us immense problems, for he had worked with Margaret during all her elections and had earned and retained her trust as few others had – with good cause, for I know of no one else who can so quickly get to the heart of a situation and suggest a way forward.

It is difficult to recreate the sense of frenetic activity of daily life during a general election. There is a sense of destiny, that the events of the next few weeks really matter in the life of the nation – and in your life, too. As a result, there is the deeply ingrained pessimistic belief in every word of the opposition's claims and a tendency to discount all your own good news. Then there is the tiredness; ah, the tiredness. Day after day, from before seven in the morning until the early hours of the next day and then starting all over again, for week after week. The whole time driven by the belief that we could lose and that all we had accomplished in the past few years would be lost. I say all this not to assert it as true, but to give some indication of the sheer pressure and stark terror that those weeks held for all the players.

In times like these we are not our normal selves. I know that I was not. The niceties of civilised life dissolve under unnatural pressures. I now blush at the way I then behaved. But I suspect that I would have behaved exactly the same if I had ever found myself in similar circumstances.

As it turned out, by the time of the 1992 election I was a spectator again. I am writing these words with all the advantages of hindsight, a gift that I have successfully practised all my life. The words of my diary that follow are those I dictated at the end of each day, when I was tired and fearful of the future, now over thirty-three years ago. This in no way purports to be a complete history of that time. Rather, it is a tale of some of the players and how we coped under the day-to-day stresses and strains of an election around one of the most important political figures of the past century. It is said that no man remains a hero to his own valet. I worked for Margaret Thatcher, either directly or indirectly, for a decade. She remains a hero to this very day. But she is also a very human hero.

So much has changed over the ensuing years that it is not easy to think back and put yourself in the same frame of mind, in that far more innocent age before social media and all the horror that that is wreaking upon the quality of life today. Yet what happened over those few weeks of the election laid the foundations for the decades to come. It ensured that when the Conservative government eventually lost an election, it would be marked by a change in personalities rather than policies.

But that was a long way ahead.

DIARIES

INVITATION

I've never kept a diary before. There is always a first time. But this is a diary I'm going to keep on tape and just put away for some time in the distant future. It will be the story of my 1987 election. Today is 7 April, but I will go back to 15 March when it all started.

That weekend we'd gone down to Fairacres.* I think it was only the second time we'd been down there since November. All Saturday I thought about the stories that I had been running for weeks about Conservative central office – about how ready they were for an election, how they were a superb fighting machine – but I knew from inside how unprepared things really were. On Sunday morning, I phoned the Prime Minister. When she came through, after some pleasantries I said: 'Prime Minister, I'd just like you to know that I'm concerned about things at central office. I don't really think we are prepared … I'm coming in to

---

* My home in Graffham, West Sussex.

see you on Tuesday morning, and then I would like to talk to you about ways in which I would help you and the campaign.'

I said my work is nearly completed in the employment department – at least, all the important things that I want to do can only be done after the election. She agreed with some enthusiasm and said yes, she'd been concerned about central office, and yes, please let us talk.

The other reason that I had rung was to tell her that the unemployment figures, due on the following Thursday, were by far the best unemployment figures since records were first kept. Seasonally adjusted, they were 44,000 down. I was the first holder of my office since Maurice Macmillan in 1973 to have had unemployment lower during his term of office than the day he was appointed.* Of course she was totally delighted about the unemployment figures and she seemed enthusiastic at the prospect of our talk.

On the Monday morning, after some reflection, I arranged to call in and see Norman Tebbit on my way to the Prime Minister. Norman, as Chancellor of the Duchy of Lancaster, was occupying the set of rooms in the Cabinet Office that I used to have when I was Minister Without Portfolio.† He was very friendly and warm, for we always got on well. I told him that I was on my way to see the Prime Minister to talk about the ways I could help during the election, and he seemed quite agreeable. He told

---

* Maurice Macmillan (later Viscount Macmillan of Ovenden), 1921–84, Secretary of State for Employment between April 1972 and December 1973. When Macmillan left office, unemployment was less than 500,000. This, however, roughly coincided with the 'Barber Boom' (much derided by Thatcherites), and his term of office ended a few days before the Heath government was induced by industrial action to impose a three-day working week.
† September 1984–September 1985.

me in considerable detail about a campaign he wanted to run to expose the Lib–Lab alliance for their part in the 'Winter of Discontent', and how little their pact had actually accomplished. He felt that he had to show that a hung parliament was not quite the boon that some people thought.

I left Norman and went down to see the Prime Minister. There was a very convenient door between the Cabinet Office and No. 10, the key of which was always held in the private office of Robert Armstrong, the Cabinet Secretary.[*] When I came through into No. 10, Norman Blackwell[†] was waiting for me. Norman was part of the Policy Unit at No. 10 and was responsible for employment matters.

'Norman, look, I hope you don't mind, but today there's very little department business, this is mainly political.' With that I gave him a broad grin, so he excused himself. I went upstairs to see Margaret in her study.

At the start, I dealt with one or two small matters at the department; the figures; and how I would deal with them. After that the private secretary left, leaving just the Prime Minister, myself and Stephen Sherbourne.[‡] I launched in without any preamble. 'Prime Minister, I can really stop work now, I can leave my department for the next few weeks – it will make very

---

[*] Robert Armstrong (Baron Armstrong of Ilminster after 1988), 1927–2020. Civil servant; spent early career in the Treasury; principal private secretary to the Prime Minister, 1970–75; Home Office, 1975–79; Cabinet Secretary 1979–87; head of Home Civil Service, 1981–87.
[†] Norman Blackwell (Baron Blackwell of Woodcote since 1997), 1952–. Special adviser, Downing Street Policy Unit, 1986–87; head of Downing Street Policy Unit, 1995–97; chairman, Centre for Policy Studies, 2000–09. In those innocent days, as a civil servant Norman had to make himself scarce whenever party-political matters were discussed.
[‡] Steven Sherbourne CBE, 1945–. Conservative Research Department, 1970–75; head of Edward Heath's private office, 1975–76; political secretary to the Prime Minister, 1983–88.

little difference. I am far more worried about the election, about the state of the campaign. It is not for me to choose when the election will be, but I just want to make sure that early in May, when you see the local election results, if you want to push the button then we're ready to go. I can clear my decks and be of help.'

'Yes,' she replied, 'you must. You must first help with the presentation of the manifesto – the way it looks.' She then made some very flattering remarks about my Action for Jobs campaign* and then told me that John MacGregor† was now writing the draft of the manifesto. We spent a few minutes on what it should look like. I said it should have a few charts to make it visual as well. She was very keen on 'before and after' photographs.

Then Stephen mentioned the tour. 'Prime Minister, I believe that there is only one way to run the tour,' I said. 'Politics now is only about television – not even the press – just television. You should have a campaign in which you are seen as being met by adoring crowds, if possible on the *One O'Clock News*, but certainly the *5.45*, *Six*, *Seven*, *Nine* and *Ten O'Clock News*.'

Stephen said that central office had prepared an initial plan, which wasn't very good and had the Prime Minister going to a number of marginal constituencies. They had identified seventy-two marginal seats which were crucial if the party were to retain

---

* The campaign that brought all the employment department's programmes together.

† John MacGregor (Baron MacGregor of Pulham Market since 2001), 1937–. Special adviser to Alec Douglas-Home, 1963–64; Conservative Research Department, 1964–65; head of Edward Heath's private office, 1965–68; Conservative MP, 1974–2001; chief secretary to the Treasury, 1985–87; in various Cabinet posts until 1994.

its parliamentary majority. I exploded: 'Prime Minister, whether you go to a marginal constituency or not doesn't make nearly as much impact as you being seen on television in the best light. Quite frankly, we've got to select the right places – if you go to the north-west, go to Chester, not Merseyside. I'm sure we can find the places you can visit to get the right reception.'

We discussed for a few minutes how best to achieve this. She felt that the election agents would not be the best people – she wanted to rely upon members to choose the best locations. I suggested that she ask Michael Alison (her PPS)[*] to write to about thirty members asking them for three names each. That would help with the security, and we could then choose amongst them.

By then it was time for the Budget Cabinet to start, and so we went downstairs. On the way down the Prime Minister said that she wanted to meet with Norman and me immediately after Cabinet.

Nigel[†] had so much good economic news that the proposed Budget received a marvellous reception. We broke up after fifty minutes in a very good mood. On the way out I looked at the Prime Minister and she nodded. 'Oh yes,' she said, 'ask Norman to come back.'

We stayed on in the Cabinet room. The Prime Minister

---

[*] Michael Alison, 1926–2004. Conservative MP, 1964–97; several junior ministerial posts; PPS to the Prime Minister, 1983–87.

[†] Nigel Lawson (Baron Lawson of Blaby since 1992), 1932–. Worked on *Financial Times*, 1956–60; *Daily Telegraph*, 1961–63; special adviser to Alec Douglas-Home, 1963–64; editor of *The Spectator*, 1966–70; special political adviser in Conservative central office, 1973–74; Conservative MP, 1974–92; financial secretary to the Treasury, 1979–81; Secretary of State for Energy, 1981–83; Chancellor of the Exchequer, 1983–89.

started the conversation: 'Norman, I've been thinking about the campaign. I think David's got some free time now; I'd like him to come and help.'

Norman looked only slightly surprised and said, 'Well, of course that's no problem, I'd love that.'

I remarked that it was the old team again – referring to Peter Morrison, who had been made the deputy chairman of the party a few months before. Peter, Norman and I had all worked together when Norman was Employment Secretary, Peter was junior minister and I was chairman of the Manpower Services Commission.

We chatted for a few minutes about the sort of work to be done, and the Prime Minister left us to it. As I went out with Norman I said, 'Norman, I would like to work with you – what you would like me to do – because I am here to help you?' Norman replied that he was very busy for the next week and then taking a week's holiday the week after. He suggested that I have a good look round, get to meet the people at central office and then we'll have a chat. Right, said I, and that is how we left it.

I went back to the office and told Howell James all about it, and I must say the news caused a certain amount of surprise and pleasure. Then I started worrying a little about how we'd get the word out. The summer before there had been a very fraught period in which the newspapers had, day after day, been playing the Prime Minister against Norman, and in early August, speculation of a rift between the two reached its height. Eventually, there was a well-publicised phone call in which the Prime

Minister rang Norman at his Devon home, and they appeared to make up. I was very anxious that no further stories would go out about their relationship. Over the next few days, through Michael Dobbs,* Norman's chief of staff at central office, and Peter, I tried to find a way to get the new arrangement out in the press in a way that would not start hares running about the Prime Minister checking up on Norman through me.

The following Sunday we were in London, so I invited Peter for dinner. Howell came in at 6.30 to show me a new advertising campaign for the Job Training Scheme (JTS).† He was in full flood when Peter arrived. Peter seemed rather relieved when he found out that Howell was leaving. As soon as Howell had gone, he told me that he wanted to have a private chat – although he liked Howell very much, there were one or two things he wanted to say to me alone.

Over a good dinner, we talked, and Peter told me that after the election he would like to be considered not for Chief Whip, which I'd always assumed he'd wanted, but either for Northern Ireland Secretary or for chairman of the party. He said that Norman was not the same Norman we both worked for three years back, for since the bomb‡ he was a different person. I

---

* Michael Dobbs, 1948–. Deputy chairman, Saatchi & Saatchi, 1983–86 and 1988–91; chief of staff to chairman of Conservative Party, 1986–87; joint deputy chairman of Conservative Party, 1994–95; presenter, *Despatch Box*, 1998–2001; author of several successful books, including the televised *House of Cards* (1989), *To Play the King* (1992) and *The Final Cut* (1994).
† The Job Training Scheme was a key element of the government's strategy to reduce unemployment. It offered training to people who had been out of work for more than six months and was aimed particularly at the under twenty-fives.
‡ The IRA attack on the Grand Hotel, Brighton, during the 1984 Conservative Party conference. Norman Tebbit and his wife had been very seriously injured.

began to get from Peter the same feeling that I was getting from people outside the party about the state of central office.

We spent a few minutes on getting the story out about my role in central office. I did not want to make an appearance in Smith Square before that, as otherwise it would leak in a very uncontrolled way. Yet I only had that week and the week after to get my feet under the table, for if the election date was early, I would have little time to get things organised.

On Monday morning, I agreed with Norman that he would mention my new role casually over a press lunch while he was giving out his new line on the Lib–Lab pact. The following day nothing came out; the line about the Lib–Lab pact went like a lead balloon and was quite heavily criticised. There was no mention about my job. Later Norman told Peter that he did not get round to mentioning it. Eventually he spoke to Paul Potts of the *Daily Express*. Paul immediately rang Howell, who readily confirmed the story. We had a sensible mention in the *Express*, and I was now free to go into central office.

I met with Michael Dobbs on Thursday. After a pleasant chat, we talked about the election being called for June or October. I repeated the problems I had outlined at a recent 'political' Cabinet. We were constrained from going in much of October because of the conference season early in September – the SDP conference first, followed by the TUC Congress and then the Liberals. A mid-October election would also mean starting the campaign on August Bank Holiday. I had suggested that we should hold a manifesto conference in the first or second week of September, which would really snooker the SDP conference.

In the end, we worked out that there was a window on 1 October which would be suitable for an election.

Michael promised that he would have a word with Norman. On the Friday I was due in Milton Keynes to open a hotel for Charles Forte* (I had taken Tourism and Small Firms with me when I went to Employment, and this was the more pleasant side of my job) and to come back straight after lunch to spend three hours with Harvey Thomas† to improve my television manner.

The lunch went rather well, with a very receptive audience, although we ended up with a rather interesting return journey. There had been tremendous gales that day, the car rolling from side to side in an alarming manner on our way up the M1. I had arranged for Norman Dodds (my driver) to take us to Milton Keynes for the lunch and afterwards to drop us at the railway station so I could catch the 2.17 fast train back to London. That way I could be in central office shortly after three.

I left the lunch promptly and Norman dropped us off at the station. We found that the power lines had blown down and there were no trains expected for the rest of the day. Unfortunately, Howell had taken the telephone out of the car, so we had no way to contact Dodds. 'Don't worry,' said a porter. 'There's a coach leaving now for Bletchley station, and you can get a train to London from there.' So we hopped on the coach, and in ten

---

*   Charles Forte (Baron Forte of Ripley after 1982), 1908–2007. Hotelier; chief executive, Trust House Forte Group 1971–78; chairman from 1982.
†   Harvey Thomas CBE, 1939–. Director of press and communications, Conservative Party, 1985–86; consultant director of presentation, 1986–91. Harvey was responsible for all party conferences and many of the set-piece events. He had spent many years with Billy Graham and, in my book, was the greatest presenter of them all.

minutes we were at Bletchley station. We found no trains and no other coaches there either.

I rang the office to arrange for a government driver and then had a brainwave. I asked the office to ring the hotel in Milton Keynes. Within ten minutes, a chauffeur-driven Rolls-Royce – I found out later Charles Forte's own car – picked us up. We went back to London in great style, but, alas, too late, far too late to do my television training.

When I got back, I went into central office to see Michael Dobbs. I found to my great joy that Norman had reacted enthusiastically to our ideas for the election and told Michael to go away and work it up. That was a very good start indeed, and I went home happy.

I GO INTO CENTRAL OFFICE

During the following week I spent much of my time in central office. It was a rather surprising time for a number of reasons. I found Michael Dobbs enormously agreeable. One day, rather gingerly, I raised the subject of the manifesto. I found to my horror that no detailed plans – in fact, no work at all – had been done to produce it. The more I probed, the worse it became. On Tuesday, Howell came in to see me. He had been speaking to Michael on the phone and the latter had suggested that perhaps the best thing would be for me to take over the actual production of the manifesto.

'Hold on,' I said to Howell. 'This sounds too good to be true. Let me try it out when I see Michael tomorrow.'

When we met, he renewed his suggestion with considerable enthusiasm. Slightly sensibly (for once), I said that we should wait until Norman came back. We spent some time talking about the Prime Minister's tour. I saw the first draft of the schedule and it was actually not bad at all – but it still needed a certain amount of work.

Later that week, I met Harvey Thomas, who reacted more than enthusiastically to my being there. He had been at the big Action for Jobs breakfast, which I had run for the Prime Minister at the Queen Elizabeth II centre. He cheered me up by being rather nice about the way we had organised the occasion and the publicity it achieved. I discussed with him how he was going to organise the advance guards of the Prime Minister's tour, and he asked me for some names. I thought perhaps Daniel Janner,* who had been in to see me and despite being the son of a Labour MP was an enthusiastic supporter, would be useful, as well as David Soskin.† He told me about the people I should deal with and who I should or shouldn't see in central office.

Howell had also arranged for me to have a quick drink with Rod Tyler,‡ who had worked with the Prime Minister in the '83 election. He brought along a copy of Carol Thatcher's book, *The Diary of an Election*, which gave in considerable detail – at least as seen by the daughter, if no one else – exactly how the campaign was actually run. I started reading as soon as I got it. Rod also told me that the Prime Minister had asked him to do

---

* Daniel Janner QC, 1957–. Member of the Board of Deputies of British Jews since 2000. Son of Lord Janner of Braunstone, Labour MP 1970–97.
† The son of a very old friend of mine, Renee Soskin.
‡ At that time acting political editor of the *News of the World*.

some work on the campaign for her. Howell afterwards suggested to me that we should really see what it was he was going to
do, because he might well end up writing something about the
campaign itself.[*]

Norman, I knew, was going to see the Prime Minister at
2.30 p.m. on the following Monday. I worked up a paper during
the course of the week, outlining in some detail how a manifesto
conference should be organised. I had also suggested to Michael
Dobbs that we should have a different form of candidates' meeting if, in fact, we did go in June. A message or two came back to
me from my PPS, Robert Atkins,[†] who had become very enthusiastic about this idea. One or two items appeared as leaks in the
papers, and I suspected that was because Robert was speaking
to and sounding out a number of backbenchers. He told me
that one or two people were not too happy – in particular Peter
Morrison, which I must say surprised me greatly.

I then thought that perhaps I was rushing things a bit too
much, and I began to get more than slightly nervous about
Norman. On the Thursday night, I worked late and wrote a long,
chatty letter to Norman, with which I included the detailed
plans for the autumn manifesto conference. I gave the letter to
his private office to go out to be given to him on the plane.

On Friday, I departed for a long but very pleasant day in the
Isle of Wight. Ever since I had entered the Cabinet, I had got
into the routine of taking Fridays away from the office and

---

[*] His account was published as *Campaign!: The Selling of the Prime Minister* (London: Grafton Books, 1987).

[†] Robert (since 1997 Sir Robert) Atkins, 1946–. Conservative MP, 1979–83; junior minister in various departments, 1987–94; Conservative MEP, North West Region, 1999–2014.

visiting different parts of the country. When I was at the Manpower Services Commission, I had a big map of the UK on the wall in the private office, and we would stick different coloured pins to show where we had been: blue for a party engagement, white for MSC etc. When I became Minister Without Portfolio, I would spend the Fridays on party engagements, often speaking at lunch and dinner and numerous times in between. This time it was a department engagement in the Isle of Wight, although in the run up to an election, every engagement had political overtones. When I met with party workers for tea or coffee and biscuits, my officials would wait ostentatiously outside. It was a good day, and I was very interested in the small aircraft manufacturing facility on the island. However, the best part was that, at the end of the day, I finished up in Fairacres for the weekend. This time, I had the whole weekend off – except for my briefing boxes – until Sunday, when I had to drive to Newport to be there first thing on Monday morning for another Action for Jobs breakfast.

Norman was arriving back on Sunday evening at 7 p.m. In my note, I had suggested that I would ring him in the car on the way back from Newport, and I would try to see him before lunch.

Sunday 5 April

Just before I set off for Newport on the Sunday afternoon, Robert Atkins rang me – he always rang me at five or five-thirty on a Sunday afternoon. What he said really made me think. Evidently Norman was spitting blood about my appointment. He didn't know anything about it in advance, it had caused him a great deal of trouble and he thought it was all wrong. Secondly, although it was welcomed by many in the back benches, Robert detected a certain amount of reservation from Cranley Onslow,[*] who, conscious as ever of his position, said that he would only deal with the party about the candidates' conference. I had to calm Robert down to make sure he didn't say too much. Then he mentioned the enthusiastic reception I had had from some on the left of the party. Richard Needham[†] wanted to have a chat with me, as did Ian Lang,[‡] and I said I would see them. But it certainly got me worried about Norman.

During the week, when Norman was away, the Prime Minister had been to Moscow. Day after day the television news had been full of the amazing reception the Russians had given her, and the commentators were full of the progress she had made with Gorbachev. That contrasted with the very public visit that Neil Kinnock had made to Washington in late March, when Ronald Reagan had given him less than twenty minutes. He looked so inadequate, the contrast so great, that it became more and more obvious that the Labour Party could sink out of sight.[§]

---

* Cranley Onslow (Baron Onslow of Woking after 1997), 1926–2001. Conservative MP, 1964–97; Minister of State, Foreign Office, 1982–83; chairman of 1922 Committee, 1984–92.

† Richard Needham (since 1997 Sir Richard; 6th Earl of Kilmorey, though he does not use the title), 1942–. Conservative MP, 1979–97; junior minister in various departments, 1983–92.

‡ Ian Lang (Baron Lang of Monkton since 1997), 1940–. Conservative MP, 1979–97; Whips' Office, 1981–86; undersecretary, Department of Employment, 1986; Scottish Office, 1986–90; Secretary of State for Scotland, 1990–95; president of the Board of Trade, 1995–97.

§ Reagan was hardly likely to welcome Kinnock with open arms, given Labour's stance on nuclear disarmament. In August 2003, *The Guardian* published details of US diplomatic correspondence underlining the extent of misgivings in Washington at the prospect of a Labour victory in the election (see 'Revealed: Reagan's secret plans to snub Kinnock if he won the 1987 election', *The Guardian*, 4 August 2003).

That morning the *Sunday Times* said we had a 12 per cent lead in the polls and that Labour were down to third place. I had one or two calls from lobby correspondents during the morning. David Hart[*] had rung to say that he had tried to speak to Margaret but she was taking the day off. That did not stop him saying that this, that and the other should be done.

In the afternoon, before travelling back to Newport, I put a call in to Chequers.[†] I told the Prime Minister I was making good progress, but I was concerned about Norman. At the moment I was walking on eggshells, and I reminded her that he was coming in to see her on Monday afternoon. She should just react carefully, and I would explain all on Tuesday morning.

She said, 'Well, of course Norman should welcome you. It's the old team, it should be perfectly all right.'

I said, 'Prime Minister, I will explain.' I also told her that one or two other things weren't exactly perfect, either.

Monday 6 April

The week started off with a minor crisis in the department. For the past few days, industrial action had been building up – both the Society of Civil and Public Servants and the Civil and Public Services Association (the two main civil service unions) had voted heavily in favour of strike action. Disruption had already started in the north-west and in Wales, where I had to go for the Action for Jobs breakfast with Nick Edwards[‡] in Newport. I walked into

---

[*] One of a small number of outsiders who would call the PM with occasional advice.

[†] The official country residence of the Prime Minister, in Buckinghamshire.

[‡] Nicholas Edwards (Baron Crickhowell after 1987), 1934–2018. Conservative MP, 1970–87; Secretary of State for Wales, 1975–79.

the exhibition centre, where the breakfast was being held, past pickets who hadn't even recognised me – their own Secretary of State! A few minutes later, Nick came in laughing because the pickets hadn't recognised the Secretary of State for Wales either.

The breakfast went well, and I was able to get away on time. In the car on the way back, I rang John Turner,* my private secretary, and asked him to put a call through to Norman Tebbit's office to say I was going to be back at about 11.30 and could I see him at twelve. The drive dragged on, seemingly interminable. Half an hour, three quarters of an hour passed. I thought of another pretext for ringing the office. John said casually, 'Oh, yes, that appointment's fine. Mr Tebbit's got EA [economic Cabinet subcommittee] but then he will be back in his office.' Little did he realise how much I wanted that message. As luck would have it, I arrived in London early. I had a chat with Howell – who had heard nothing – dealt with one or two papers, and then went over to central office.

When I walked into Norman's room, Peter was there with Michael Dobbs. Peter made some joke and left almost immediately, saying that I was not the reason he was leaving; he had to go to another meeting. Norman looked bronzed but was very quiet – in fact almost sullen. I said, 'Norman, did you have a good holiday? How's Margaret?'

'Yes, yes everything's fine.'

'I wanted to have a chat with you to see how we can work together.'

---

* John Turner CBE, 1946–. Principal private secretary to DY, 1986–87; deputy chief executive, employment service, 1989–94; member of the civil service appeals board since 2000.

'Oh, it's very difficult,' he said.

'Norman,' I said, 'I'm only here to help *you*. If you want me to push off, just say the word and I'll go.'

Then followed the most difficult forty-five minutes since I'd tried to persuade a bank manager to give me my first overdraft – it really was very difficult. I said, 'Norman, what did you think of the paper I sent you about the manifesto conference in September?'

'Well, it's a funny thing, David,' he said. 'It may surprise you to know that actually, before I went away, I asked for the conference to be booked. Just shows you', he went on, 'that two great minds think alike.'

I laughed it off. But Norman obviously had forgotten our earlier conversations – not that I was going to remind him. It was enough that he had adopted the idea. We talked about other ways in which I thought I could help. I mentioned the production of the manifesto and my idea for a manifesto meeting, at which point he started to perk up. I then mentioned the Prime Minister's tour.

Norman said, 'We've produced the tour, but she doesn't like it.'

'Norman, you know what human nature's like, and you know what she's like … If you produce the tour it's no good; if I produce the same tour it'll be fine, you just see.' I think the point went home, and as we went on we had another joke and a laugh. I said, 'Look, let me just show you some work I've done on a timetable.' This was a critical path network for the manifesto. I went through the dates, which included calling the election as late as 25 June.

Norman said, 'Hold on, hold on, not so fast, not so fast. 4 June is when it's going to be – not 11 June; we must have a short campaign.'

'I know,' I said, 'but I was told by No. 10 that in fact we can't have the 4th; we can only have the 11th. You see, to have 4 June we have to call the election by 7 May – and we can't decide then, as that is the day of the local elections. We certainly cannot decide until we know those results.'

'Oh, that's nonsense,' said Norman. 'I cleared with the Chief Whip that we could certainly go on 4 June.'

He then called back Michael Dobbs, who had made himself scarce as soon as Peter left. Michael came in rather cautiously, I thought, wondering what he would find. Norman asked for the election book. He started jumping up and down. It appears that the advice we've got does point to 11 June. I must confess, I was totally amazed that here was the chairman of the party and his chief of staff – here we are in April – and they still had not done the detailed work as to when the first possible date to call the election would be after the May elections, and that he should still be thinking of the 4th. There was no question: wherever I looked round central office, there was a great deal of talking but no detailed work.

Norman then asked his secretary to fix for Murdo Maclean[*] of the Whips' Office to see him. The more we talked, the more it became clear that we would have to prorogue Parliament on

---

[*] Murdo (since 2000 Sir Murdo) Maclean, 1943–. Civil servant in the Board of Trade 1964–65; Prime Minister's office, 1967–72; Department of Industry, 1972–78; private secretary to government Chief Whip, 1978–2000.

18 May. If the PM decided to go to the Palace on the 11th, that would give us the few days necessary to clear up the remaining parliamentary business.

I then had to leave for a lunch engagement. Before I left, Norman told Michael that I was going to deal with the manifesto and the tour. I told Michael that I would come in on Friday afternoon.

After lunch, I was in the Lords for the report stage of the Banking Bill; a tedious and rather long afternoon. I had arranged for Howell to see me at the end of the day so I could bring him up to date, but I had a message that he'd been called to a meeting with Norman Tebbit. When the debate was over, I had two more messages. Peter Morrison said he would ring me just for a chat (but didn't in fact ring). Howell did ring, to say he'd heard from Stephen Sherbourne. They'd had a very good meeting indeed at No. 10, and evidently Norman was very happy with my being there. So maybe it will work out. We'll just have to wait and see.

Tuesday 7 April

After I finished last night's boxes, I prepared three copies of a critical path network, a detailed timetable and an agenda in order to prepare the manifesto. My first appointment this morning – after a haircut – was to see the Prime Minister, at 9.30. She had just finished the review of the papers and was in a relaxed mood. She said she'd had a good meeting with Norman and asked how was I getting on. I said it was difficult, but I was making resaonable progress. I had agreed with Norman some areas that I would cover, including the manifesto.

Only now had I got clearance to deal with the three items: the manifesto, the tour and now Norman had invited me to look at party-political broadcasts. I had been working on the tour and would get the details to her.

I then went through my critical path network in some detail. I finished by saying that I wanted to have a special candidates' conference. She burst out laughing. 'Oh,' she said, 'it was your idea, was it?' Then I showed her the timetable for the manifesto, and we also went through my note for a 'special autumn conference'. As I had only now got clearance, I was going to go away with Howell to start on the detailed charts and graphs and look at the artwork. I promised to have it all for her – at least the first sight of everything – by Easter.

She wanted to have a special meeting to discuss campaign issues on the Thursday before Easter, and of course on the Tuesday after Easter, when she wants me to be all day at No. 10. I suggested we make it at Chequers, because she will be less bothered by the private office. This was agreed.

Originally she wanted me there in the morning to discuss the manifesto, and then after lunch for the tour. At one time she didn't want Norman there the whole day. I said in some desperation, 'No, please, whatever you do, please, I don't want to be there unless Norman is.' We agreed a fairly small cast of characters, including Norman.

The date of the election came up, as she was rather concerned about the dates of Jewish festivals. She asked me for the dates, and to my shame I had to confess that I was not too sure! In the end Michael Alison had to go and get a letter she'd had from a constituent with all that information. Happily, I had already told her – and the letter subsequently proved me right – that 4 June was in fact ruled out by the Jewish holidays. 11 June looks good because of the local government elections on 7 May. The first analysis of the results will only become available on the Friday and Saturday, 8 and 9 May, and then we can decide on the basis of the results over the rest of the weekend. We can start the process on Monday 11 May, but we will not be able to prorogue Parliament until the following Monday, as we have to get through the Finance Bill and finish off the Scottish Rating Bill. That means that the first practical day for the election must be 11 June, with the disadvantage that the very good unemployment results are due to come out on the 18th.

As for an October election, apart from the disadvantage of the Jewish festivals, if we really want to stymie the SDP conference then we have to think about calling it in the first few days of Bank Holiday week – the first few days in September – and thus 1 October becomes the first really practical date. So, it looks as if the choice is narrowing to those two dates.

We talked for a while about themes. The Prime Minister said that she wanted to see the Saatchis and was very keen that Tim Bell should work with them. She had great confidence in Tim. When Tim left Saatchis two years ago, he had an agreement with them that he would continue to advise the government. Stephen and I said we would look at the contract, and I would speak to Tim. I think she was concerned generally about the administrative arrangements, and I told her – just to put her mind at rest – to forget about it. I would undertake to make sure that everything was delivered.

Having gone through the detailed dates and the principle of the manifesto – not the actual words – and agreed that we could have a popular version of it, I also told her that I was planning in my department to have a big poster campaign round the country, which would start on 1 May for two months. We would be able to arrange, as the government had to give up the posters in the event of an election being called, that the party would be able to use the sites. The Prime Minister said she wanted a longer chat with me when things were less rushed, as Willie Whitelaw* was waiting for her. We agreed that I would get a date fixed and subsequently we organised this for 5 o'clock on Friday afternoon.

The rest of the day carried on being pretty horrendous. I gave the keynote address at the Human Resources Development Week at the Barbican and then went upstairs and launched the prospectus of the Open College with Michael Green.† On the way back from the Barbican, Howell was with me, and I agreed with him that we would ask Tim Bell to help with the artwork and the layouts.

I dashed back to the office for a variety of different engagements, including a slightly fraught meeting with the TUC. I

---

* William Whitelaw (Lord Whitelaw of Penrith after 1983), 1918–99. Conservative MP, 1955–83; Conservative Chief Whip, 1964–70; Cabinet minister, 1970–74, 1979–83. At this time Leader of the House of Lords.
† Michael Green, 1947–. Chairman, Carlton Communications, 1983–2004, and Independent Television News (ITN), 1993–2004.

have been invited to do ITN television for the election night, which is happily some way ahead still.

That evening there was a marvellous dinner to celebrate the thirtieth anniversary of the Institute of Economic Affairs (IEA),* at which the Prime Minister was one of many speakers. There were many good contributions, including one from Keith Joseph, who was so warmly received and obviously loved. Great tributes were paid to him. The PM was the eleventh speaker. Now that wasn't quite as horrendous as it sounds because most of the contributions were reasonably short and all were entertaining. She ended up her short contribution saying: 'I may be the eleventh speaker but I want to remind you all: the cock may crow, but only the hen can lay an egg.' She brought the house down – there's no doubt that in this company she was a great hit.

Incidentally, one of the other speakers was Lord (Jo) Grimond,[†] and I found it very odd that he should be a speaker, since he had given me so much trouble earlier that week in the Lords on the Banking Bill. He had come out with the most protectionist speech imaginable, in which he said that everything was all right as long as Scottish companies could not be taken over by anybody else, particularly by the English! It really was rather odd that he should speak at the IEA.

Peter Morrison rang me, and we agreed to meet tomorrow.

---

* A bastion of economic liberalism, the IEA was founded in 1955 to contest the growing trend of state intervention.
† Jo Grimond (Baron Grimond of Firth after 1983), 1913–93. Leader of Liberal Party, 1956–67 (and briefly in 1976). Notwithstanding his intellectual gyrations, Grimond was a long-standing contributor to IEA publications.

And on Wednesday, I'm due to have a meeting – the first of the real meetings – about the Prime Minister's tour, and then we'll have to take it from there.

Generally speaking, the whole scene looks reasonably interesting – the polls are good, and the pace is certainly hotting up. Whenever it is now, I'm well and truly in it.

Wednesday 8 April

Last night I was so tired I really couldn't do any of my boxes. But today I had to be in early, at 8.30, because we had a Public Expenditure Survey (PES) meeting. Kenneth Clarke,* Michael Quinlan† and all the officials were there. I was singularly uninterested in the whole thing. We had planned such big changes in our programmes that whatever this three-year expenditure period was forecasting would be totally changed. After the meeting, I came back to the office and tried to catch up with my boxes.

Later I went off to launch a career service conference with Kenneth Baker‡ and to deal with some other matters. When I came back to the office, Ian Lang had come in to see me, because

---

*   Kenneth Clarke QC (Baron Clarke of Nottingham since 2020), 1940–. Conservative MP 1970–2019; assistant government whip, 1972–74; junior minister, 1979–85; Paymaster General and Minister for Employment, 1985–87; Chancellor of the Duchy of Lancaster and Minister for Trade and Industry (with special responsibility for inner cities), 1987–88; Secretary of State for Health, 1988–90; Education, 1990–92; Home Secretary, 1992–93; Chancellor of the Exchequer, 1993–97.
†   Michael (after 1985 Sir Michael) Quinlan, 1930–2009. Permanent secretary, Department of Employment, 1983–88; permanent undersecretary, Ministry of Defence, 1988–92.
‡   Kenneth Baker (Baron Baker of Dorking since 1997), 1934–. Conservative MP, 1968–97. PPS to Edward Heath, 1974–75; junior minister, 1981–85; Secretary of State for Environment, 1985–86; Education and Science, 1986–89; chairman of Conservative Party, 1989–90; Home Secretary, 1990–92.

I think he was concerned about the position of Scotland. Then Howell came in, very full of life, to report on his meeting with Tim Bell. He told me that by Friday – certainly by next Monday – we would have mock layouts and diagrams and everything necessary for the manifesto.

It was a remarkably busy day. I came back from a lunch of foreign economic representatives in London to have my first meeting with Roger Boaden* at central office. He seemed quite pleasant – very pleasant, actually – and efficient. I dashed back for another meeting at No. 10, then came back for the first of the meetings on the PM's tour, with Roger Boaden, myself, Peter Morrison and Peter's private secretary. Michael Dobbs was away somewhere. Peter let me chair the meeting, and we ran through I suppose about 80 per cent of it.

It appears now that my idea for having a candidates' conference has run up against Norman, who is losing enthusiasm for it – that's something I'll have to work out. But I certainly was able to reintroduce my idea for finishing her tour back in the Isle of Wight, framing it against that marvellous backcloth of the great Union Jack. I made sure we have got a few good televisual items in it – for example, on Election Day minus three or four, I think we'll go to Alton Towers. All said and done, I thought it was rather a good meeting.

It now looks as if I have managed not only to get the tour underway, but also, I was told today that the Prime Minister would like to see me 5 o'clock on Friday for a quiet chat to see how the

---

* Official in the Employment Department.

work is progressing. I have now received my formal invitations both for Maundy Thursday and for the Tuesday after Easter. The pace is hotting up, but one thing I must do is get a bit more rest, because it's quite difficult to run a fairly busy department as well as gear up a general election campaign. At least, I think it is!

Anyway, with a bit of luck, tomorrow I shall spend a little more time in central office, then up to the Midlands – to Ashby Castle for a fundraising dinner – then to speak to a conference at lunchtime on Friday and finish up at central office. Whatever we're doing, it's a busy life!

Thursday 9 April

I came into the department in order to get a letter to the Chancellor about our policy for the manifesto. But I suddenly realised that if we weren't careful the announcement of the unemployment figures – and the count day was today – would be delayed by the threatened industrial action. I could not think of anything worse than the figures being delayed during an election, with the allegation that we had delayed them for political ends – particularly when they were likely to be so good!

I immediately called a meeting as soon as I came in. Roger Dawe* was there – in fact, the whole crowd turned up. Leigh Lewis† (my former private secretary, who knew me so well) had drafted a splendid press release about the industrial action – it was so way-out that even I didn't have the gall to use it! I

---

* Roger Dawe CB OBE, 1941–. Deputy secretary, Department of Employment, 1985–87.

† Leigh (now Sir Leigh) Lewis KCB, 1951–. Parliamentary private secretary to DY as Minister Without Portfolio and Secretary of State for Employment, 1984–86; chief executive, Jobcentre Plus, Department for Work and Pensions, since 2001.

think he had his leg pulled quite a lot by most people in the department.

After a long discussion, I toned down the wording of the press statement and then decided that, as I'd had a message that the Prime Minister wanted to discuss the minute I'd sent to her, I would come back after the meeting. I had also made up my mind that I would have a first sight of the unemployment figures before deciding when the statement would go out – either the Sunday night, embargoed for Monday, or else on the Wednesday, when the figures were due. There were many counter-arguments, for if I issued a fairly provocative hardline statement now, I might trigger off the strike itself. The essence of what we are getting at is simply this: because of the industrial action, there is a very good chance that many thousands of people – particularly unemployed people in Scotland – would not get their benefit money over Easter.

In what turned out to be a very hectic schedule that day, I approved the new Action for Jobs advertising, and then just before Cabinet, Peter Morrison rang and made my blood run cold. He told me that over a dinner with Ian Gow,* he had heard that Robert Atkins, my PPS, had been going round saying some rather odd things. First, that I was working for a half-mad chairman, then that I'd found a terrible state of morale in central office and all sorts of other allegations. Right away I called Howell in and asked him if he could pass a message to Robert

---

* Ian Gow, 1937–90. A soldier and solicitor before entering politics; Conservative MP, 1974–1990; PPS to Prime Minister, 1979–83 (he earned the nickname 'Supergrass' because of his devoted service to Mrs Thatcher); junior minister, 1983–85 (resigned in protest at Anglo-Irish Agreement); assassinated by the IRA.

to tell him to be very careful. No doubt about it, the one thing that could stop me doing my job would be these stories. It would only start Norman getting worried about me.

I went off to Cabinet. This was eventful only because the Prime Minister was in fighting mood about Japan, and the more we discussed the problem the more it became quite apparent that there was nothing we could do about it.* She then asked if there were any other matters. I looked at her and raised the matter of my industrial dispute. I got clear approval for my line, but she wanted it agreed with the Treasury and with Norman Fowler.† After Cabinet, instead of going over to central office and seeing Peter as I had agreed, we all met and got the line approved. Apparently, the announcement is set to go ahead for the Sunday night.

After my meeting at the Treasury, Howell and I left to go up to the fundraising dinner at Ashby Castle. In the car, Howell showed me the latest work for the manifesto. He also had a copy of Tim Bell's contract with Saatchis, from which it was quite clear that Tim was retained to advise the Prime Minister or the Conservative Party during the election. I told Howell that I would show this to the Prime Minister at my meeting with her on Friday afternoon.

---

* At this time, there was a long-running trade dispute with protectionist Japan, triggered in part by that country's attitude to the intrusion of Cable & Wireless into its telecommunications market. During Prime Minister's Questions on 9 April, Neil Kinnock had taunted Mrs Thatcher about the row, which had led to a visit to Japan by the Minister for Consumer Affairs, Michael Howard.

† Norman Fowler (Baron Fowler of Sutton Coldfield since 2001), 1938–. Conservative MP, 1970–2001; Secretary of State for Transport, 1979–81; Social Services, 1981–87; Employment, 1987–90. Resigned to spend more time with his family, but returned to office as chairman of the party, 1992–94; Lord Speaker, 2016–2021.

John Turner telephoned me once or twice in the car – evidently a number of very good media bids are coming in, including a meeting with the entire editorial board of *Forbes* magazine – so it looks very encouraging for my visit to the States. I'm due tomorrow to have a slightly tedious day travelling around, ending up with the Prime Minister at the end of the day.

Friday 10–Sunday 12 April

We had a rather splendid night at Ashby Castle and a marvellous breakfast cooked in a little private kitchen near our room, although we found that overnight the peacocks had done something unspeakable to our car. After breakfast we went to a very good meeting in Northampton job centre. I must say the quality of our people administering Restart[*] on the ground really has to be seen to be believed.

We went on to Tony Baldry's[†] meeting in the Cherwell Valley. Then I dashed back to the office in time to agree the precise form of the statement that I'll be making about the industrial dispute, embargoed for Monday. The more I think about it, the more worried I get about the prospect of postponing the unemployment figures during an election period. Also, we now have the very good news indeed that the unemployment headline figure will be 82,000 down and seasonally adjusted 30,000 down. This means unemployment is now at 3,043,000. It looks quite clear that, if we have a June election, unemployment will

---

[*] Restart was another element of the government's strategy for jobs. It offered interviews and help to people of all ages who had been out of work for more than six months. By the time of the 1987 general election, the government claimed that it had helped 1.3 million people.
[†] Tony Baldry, 1950–. Conservative MP, 1983–2015.

come under the 3 million just about a week too late. Still… you can't win 'em all.

Tim Bell was waiting to see me when I got back to the office, and I got his agreement to go through his contract with the Prime Minister, as she was seeing Maurice Saatchi[*] on the following Wednesday. He is very anxious indeed to work with me. I also heard a slightly scurrilous story that has evidently been put out by the Lonrho people, about Gordon Reece's[†] work for the Al-Fayeds.[‡] We then spent a few minutes just talking about the shape and form of the manifesto, what we'd actually have and what we would get for the following Monday evening. Finally, Tim told me he'd had lunch that day with Michael Dobbs, who'd been in a very low way. Michael, I think, was feeling very left out of things for a number of reasons, but in particular because the Prime Minister didn't want him at any meeting. I was told that whenever Norman asked her if Michael could come, she'd say 'No' very definitely. Then Norman would go and repeat this to Michael Dobbs, which I didn't think was too clever. I told Tim that I would raise the matter with her and let him know what she said.

I then went off to see the Prime Minister, who had Stephen Sherbourne with her and was in a quite relaxed mood. I first of all cleared the position of Tim's contract. She was quite happy with it and said she would raise it with Maurice Saatchi. I

---

* Maurice Saatchi (Baron of Staplefield since 1996), 1946–. Co-founder of Saatchi & Saatchi, 1970; chairman, 1985–94; partner, M&C Saatchi since 1995. An opposition spokesman in the House of Lords since 1999.

† Gordon (after 1986 Sir Gordon) Reece, 1929–2001. Public relations consultant and television producer; adviser to Mrs Thatcher, 1975–79; director of publicity at Conservative central office, 1978–80.

‡ This refers to the bitter takeover battle for the Harrods department store, between the Al-Fayed brothers and Lonrho, headed by Tiny Rowland.

offered to produce a letter from Tim, in which he would suggest working with her during the election, but she said, 'No, that won't be necessary. Everyone knows that Tim was there and would want to work for us.'

I then asked her if it would be possible for Michael Dobbs to come to the Easter meetings. Her immediate reaction was no – she just bridled at the thought. So I said to myself, 'Oh, I'll just leave it.' We discussed what would actually happen in the meetings on Thursday, and I said it's very important that we do follow up all our decisions. I tried again by gently suggesting that Michael Dobbs could keep notes for the chairman. She thought about it and then decided that Robin Harris,* the head of the research office, would keep the notes. Then we decided that, as we were meeting on a Thursday and then on the following Tuesday, we would just have a short note of decisions and, most importantly, a list of whose responsibility it was to follow up.

I then spent some time telling her what I was hoping to do for the manifesto, and what I would have ready for her. I quietly pointed out to her that Tim had told me that, so far as he knew, none of the campaign party election broadcasts had even been sketched out. He would raise it with her. She now accepts the sensitivities of the situation. It was agreed that I would give Stephen a list of some questions for her to raise during the course of the meeting.

I then raised some other matters for after the election. I said,

---

* Robin Harris, 1952–. In Conservative Research Department, 1978–81; government special adviser, 1981–85; director, Conservative Research Department, 1985–88; member, Downing Street Policy Unit, 1989–90; adviser to Baroness Thatcher from 1990.

'I hate mentioning them, but they would involve machinery of government. If you are to make any changes – I don't want to add to your burdens – but you have to think of them now over the Easter weekend. After Easter, before we know where we are, within a week we are in the local government elections, then in the campaign and the next thing you know you'll be back here after the election having to form a new Cabinet.'

I briefly discussed the changes that I wanted to make in my own area. I told her I was determined that the unions, who had no real place as part of the general governance of the country, really should be confined to their real interest – their members. I said I was very keen on seeing an end to the Manpower Services Commission and to – as I described them – the 'wretched' Area Manpower Boards, trying to make the system more like the private industry councils of the United States, which were at least 75 per cent local employers. Because of the corporatist nature of the MSC, they were run by board, including the unions and the employers, as well as the government, which made it extremely difficult to make effective management decisions. The PM was slightly nervous about the general drift of what I was proposing, but I said I'd let her have a note in writing through Stephen.

'But,' I said, 'Prime Minister, it's not just my changes. Can I just say two things? First of all, I'm not keen on general changes in the machinery of government. When you combine departments or split them up, it's a great opportunity for civil servants to play demarcation games for two years, whereas we've really got to get a great deal done.

'But I do think there are small changes that should be done. I should take regional policy and perhaps give up responsibility for industrial relations to the DTI – those sort of changes, involving sixty or 100 civil servants in the centre, could be done without much problem.'

She said that after electricity had gone there would be no real job left for the Ministry of Energy. Then we began to discuss one or two personalities. I put the thought in her mind that Kenneth Clarke might well make a very good Leader of the House. But this was put off for another time, and I repeated that I would let her have a note. I also told her that I would be doing something on the Sunday night about the civil service dispute, in case it built up too far.

Well, at that point we broke up. It had been about an hour's meeting and ended at 6 o'clock. It had been a long, long week and I was quite happy to see an end to it.

It was a quiet weekend – I had no political engagements at all – in fact, it seemed like I spent most of the Saturday either sleeping or being too tired to sleep. On the Sunday, I was doing my boxes – I had three that weekend – when David Hart rang. He said he'd been speaking to the Prime Minister in the morning and he would like to help. He said to her that Saatchis were no good. She said to him: 'Well, if you have any ideas, communicate them through David Young.' So, after a chat for a few minutes, I told Hart I'd be back in touch with him. It looks as if the PM is making me the contact point for all the people she occasionally likes to hear from but not the whole time.

Paul Twyman* also rang. He had been one of my original team of civil servants when I was back in the Cabinet Office as Minister Without Portfolio and had then come with me over to the Department of Employment. He had been a very successful head of the deregulation unit in its first eighteen months and had recently left the department and gone to work for central office. He made veiled noises about how difficult things were in central office and how much he'd welcome doing things for me. I said I'd be in touch with him.

I carried on working on a speech that Geoffrey Holland† had suggested I should make at the forthcoming National Economic Development Office (NEDO) conference. Then the department rang through to say there was some interest in my press release about the civil service dispute, and I would be on the *Today* programme on Monday morning. Actually, my biggest worry for weeks if not months past is to find a suitable phrase to put on the tombstone of my late father.‡ Eventually after a great deal of reading inspiration struck and I thought of the very last few verses of Ethics of the Fathers, Proverb 17 – 'The glory of children lies with the fathers.' Just finding that – which was so appropriate – made me feel so much better.

Monday 13 April

I completed my boxes, and the following morning I left early to

---

* Paul Twyman. Civil servant who first joined the Board of Trade in 1967; worked in Department of Employment, 1985; adviser to chairman of party and head of economic section of Conservative Research Department, 1987.

† Geoffrey (after 1989 Sir Geoffrey) Holland, 1938–2017. Distinguished career as civil servant; permanent secretary, Department of Employment, 1988–93; vice-chancellor, University of Exeter, 1994–2002.

‡ Within a few days of each other the previous August, I had lost both my father and my only brother, Stuart (then chairman of the BBC).

the BBC in Portland Place for my slot on the *Today* programme. It was not one of my best performances. After it was over, I went into the office for a few minutes. One or two fairly routine matters, and then over to central office to see Roger Boaden. He gave me the latest print-out of the Prime Minister's tour, and I went through it in detail. I think it is shaping up rather well, with all my suggestions incorporated. But I still think she could stop at a Happy Eater or a hotel – somewhere in order to represent tourism more.

Michael Dobbs was the only other appointment I had that morning, and I wandered down to see him. But his secretary told me he was tied up with someone. I was just speaking to the chairman's secretary when in came Norman, slightly reserved, looking very off-duty in a sports jacket and trousers. I followed him into his office and sat down. He was in a very difficult mood. Quiet – sullen, really – and I began to fear that I was going to have a repetition of last week's meeting.

He said rather abruptly: 'You know, we've got to be very careful – details of the Prime Minister's tour in Wales have leaked out.'

I wasn't quite sure if he was accusing me of having leaked it – that would be a bit much. Nick Edwards was the Welsh Secretary, and I replied: 'I was last with Nick on Monday of last week – long before I ever saw the tour.' I didn't bother to tell him that I only saw the detail of the tour for the first time just half an hour ago. I assured him that I haven't talked to anybody, then chatted for a few minutes, desperately thinking of some way to convince him. Suddenly he started to unburden himself, saying that he's not really sure if he's the one who's responsible for running the election.

'Good lord,' I said, 'you're the chairman!'

'Well,' he said, 'I'm not so sure.' It became more and more apparent that he was again having a very difficult time with the Prime Minister. He didn't like the idea of Tim Bell being involved and wanted to know where she got the idea from.

'I saw her twice last week. She just mentioned it the first time, but the second time we did discuss it. I think it makes her comfortable. I suspect that in some ways,' I went on, 'the Prime Minister probably wants to have the same team around her as last time.'

Norman then proceeded to repeat to me some slightly scurrilous tales about Tim, which I'd heard a few times before from him. I could see this was not getting us anywhere. So I said, 'Look, Norman, I'm only here to help. If you tell me to go, I'll push off straight away. I just think I can make things easier.'

He didn't seem to disagree, so we chatted for a bit longer, and towards the end he warmed up again. I was due at a lunch with Eric Sharp[*] and Keith Joseph. We went downstairs – in fact, my car hadn't turned up, so we had a joke together. He was really in quite a good mood by the time we parted. He was leaving to take his wife, Margaret, to their home in Devon. A moment or two later, my car appeared. As soon as I got in the car, I rang the office to get Stephen Sherbourne to ring me.

When Stephen came through, I said that I had just had a

---

[*] Sir Eric Sharp (Baron Sharp of Grimsdyke after 1989), 1916–94. Chairman of Cable & Wireless, 1980–90.

very difficult meeting with the chairman. 'Oh,' said Stephen, 'I thought things were looking up, because I saw him at about ten or ten-thirty and he was very relaxed indeed.'

'No,' I replied, 'I think things are very fraught for the Wednesday afternoon meeting with Maurice Saatchi.' Stephen told me that he intended to be with them for a while, to deal with the Saatchi matter, to look at one or two party-political broadcast tapes which Norman was bringing with him, to give them a drink, then to disappear. I asked him to get a message to the Prime Minister and to make sure she would handle Norman gingerly, which he promised.

I went off to lunch at the Boulestin, where I had a long-standing engagement with Keith Joseph. Eric Sharp had rung me and offered to be the host if he could raise a matter with me over lunch. Before long, it became apparent that he had a problem with some civil servants in the Department of Trade and Industry, who he thought were trying to undermine his position in his negotiations with the Japanese government about Cable & Wireless. I promised him that if he would send me a note, I would see that the Prime Minister got it straight away. After Eric left, I had a long and pleasant chat with Keith, reminiscing about the early days and looking forward to what we could do once the election was out of the way. I thought he was looking very well and very relaxed, and I gave him a lift back. On my return to the department, I found out that, in addition to the normal appointments, I had Michael Dobbs coming in to see me at 4 o'clock.

My first departmental meeting was on the forthcoming

unemployment figures to be announced on Wednesday. Wednesday was going to be another good day – the eighth fall in a row. The only cloud was the *Daily Express*, which that day ran a front-page story under banner headlines which asserted that I expect unemployment to go under 3 million. That made me realise that I must be careful not to raise expectations too soon. Howell made the surprising suggestion that I should stop issuing a statement each month with the figures. The more I think about it, the more I think it would be worth doing. But I decided I'd wait till the twelve-month anniversary of the first fall in unemployment and then do it.

After that, Basil Feldman[*] came in. Basil had unfortunately lost the National Union chairman election to Peter Lane[†] and was really looking for a job. He had been in to see the PM, and she'd asked him to see me – a bit like David Hart really. I explained to him that things were very delicate, but that I would do what I could when I could. He was going away until 3 May anyway, but I would wait to see what role could be found for him during the election itself. He has a lot of energy and is a very good organiser. The great pity is that I suspect he overplayed his hand and canvassed far too hard, missing his chance to chair the National Union.[‡]

Michael Dobbs was next. I knew from Norman that Michael

---

[*] Basil Feldman (Baron Feldman of Frognal since 1996), 1923–2019. Member of the board of Conservative Party National Union, 1975–98; chairman, 1991–96; held various senior posts within Conservative Party in London; vice-president of Greater London area since 1985.

[†] Sir Peter Lane (Baron Lane of Woking since 1990), 1925–2009. Chartered accountant; vice-chairman, National Union of Conservative Associations, 1981–83; chairman, 1983–84; chairman of the executive committee, 1986–91.

[‡] He succeeded at the next election, five years later.

was in a fairly bad way, so we had a general chat for a few minutes. Michael soon started to complain about the Prime Minister: she will not have him anywhere around her, which makes doing his job very difficult. So right away I said, 'Look, Michael, some things are important: one, we have got to win the election. Two, you've got to come out of it really well and go on to something else full of glory. Whatever the relationship is, it is something we must just keep between ourselves.'

At this point he relaxed. 'Got it in one,' he said. 'Right on the button.' He seemed vastly relieved and we carried on in a very relaxed frame of mind. He gave me the impression that Norman was slightly unhappy that I'd been brought in because it should have been arranged better, but he certainly bore no hard feelings about me being around the place. He then told me that a constituency seat was coming up and he was minded to apply for it.

'Michael,' I said, 'marvellous idea, only if you want to. But if it will help, tell Norman that I'll come along and help to do all the bits and pieces if you've got to go off and run a campaign.' And in many ways, of course, that would be the best answer. We carried on talking for quite a while. I think that now I am beginning to get through to him. It's a very great pity that she has such antipathy to him. It must be chemistry, but as a result there is nothing very much that he can do during the course of this campaign.

Earlier that day, I had seen Clive Tucker,* one of my senior civil servants in the department, and I had agreed a note about machinery of government. I saw him again before the end of the

---

* Clive Tucker CB, 1944–. Undersecretary at Department of Employment, 1987; later director of international affairs, Department for Education and Employment.

day and the note will serve the purpose very well. I will give it to the Prime Minister when we next meet.

Tuesday 14 April

Second day of Passover. This morning, at 9.15, I had a meeting with John MacGregor, ostensibly to go through the manifesto. When I came in to see John, he said things were not going too well. John O'Sullivan, who was writing part of the manifesto, had been treating it rather like an essay. MacGregor was very concerned that it was too long and really had to be cut down a lot more. I got out my critical path network and showed him what we had to do and how much time we had left. He agreed that, although the dates were tight, it would be possible. I undertook that by the Thursday I would get the outline shape of what I wanted to do – of course, what I really needed was the words, so we could fit in the graphs and the pictures. He also thought the Prime Minister was still very set on having pictures in the manifesto.

I had the departmental interest on my conscience, so I briefly raised the letter I'd written to him with the 'three guarantees' I wanted included in the manifesto [see p. 65]. I arranged that I would call him later. He saw me out, and there was Stephen Sherbourne waiting to see him. So, we both dragged Stephen back in again. He then showed me Robin Harris's draft of our achievements of the past eight years. I had the idea on the spot that we should publish our achievements along with the manifesto but in a separate book. Stephen arranged that I would get a copy of this sent over to me during the day.

Stephen said he was very worried himself about the manifesto, and that a great deal more work still had to be done on it – it was too long. We will discuss how to tackle it when we meet later on in the week.

I rushed off to do a launch of the new JTS at the Barbican with Bryan Nicholson* (my successor as chairman of the Manpower Services Commission). We did a spot on television and then I went on to *The Guardian*, where I was due to sit down with the whole editorial team and be gently cross-examined. Afterwards, they gave me lunch, and it turned out to be a very pleasant occasion. Occasionally they would ask me about the manifesto, and I would say I hadn't read it. I don't suppose any of them believed me, but little did they know how true it was.

That morning, a rather stupid letter from Prof. Layard† in the *Financial Times* had me all worked up. Barry Sutcliffe, one of the department's press people who had come with me to *The Guardian* lunch, had got the *FT* to hold the columns open, and in the car on the way back I scribbled out a robust reply. On my return to the office, I spent a few minutes with Peter Makeham,‡ Howell and John and ended up with the usual compro-

---

* Bryan (since 1987 Sir Bryan) Nicholson, 1932–. He spent many years at Rank Xerox, rising to become a director, 1984–87; MSC chairman, 1984–87; chairman and chief executive, Post Office, 1967–92.
† Richard Layard (Baron Layard of Highgate since 2000), 1934–. Professor of Economics at London School of Economics, 1980–99; economic consultant to Russian government, 1991–97; director, Centre for Economic Performance, LSE, since 1990.
‡ Peter Makeham, 1948–. Civil servant in the Treasury, 1983–84; Cabinet Office, 1984–85; Department of Employment, 1985–87; Department of Trade and Industry, 1987–90; back at Employment from 1990; latterly Director-General, performance and reform, Home Office.

mise – more or less keeping the response as my original one, but making the point that Layard was becoming more and more of a politician and less and less of an academic.

Then Tim Bell came in and brought the first mock-ups of the manifesto – one in a modern style quite similar to the last one, and one which I thought was much more attractive. I told him of my idea that we should prepare a matching pair of books, one which would be called 'Our Achievements' and the other which would be the manifesto. He became very enthusiastic about the concept, and we spent some time agreeing the format. He took the mock-ups away, and with a bit of luck I'll get them by Wednesday evening in time for the Thursday meeting.

I told Tim about my meeting last Friday with the Prime Minister. He suggested that he would be very happy to be a consultant to central office, and then he could report directly to me if needs be. I was very satisfied with all this, and I must say he's very good to have aboard.

I rang up Stephen Sherbourne and told him that I'd had a long talk a couple of days ago with Michael Dobbs, and I had just seen Tim Bell. Oddly enough, they both suggested the same thing – that when the Prime Minister sees Maurice Saatchi on Wednesday afternoon, she somehow arranges that Tim becomes a consultant to central office, which will keep everybody happy. I hope that suggestion will work out. I went on to warn Stephen once again that she should be very careful how she deals with Norman and made some suggestions about what we should do during the meetings, in particular the Tuesday afternoon meeting when we discuss the tour. I suggested that she should start off with some administrative arrangements, in particular that I act as anchor-man back in central office.

I also asked Stephen if he had received the copy of my minute to the PM about machinery of government. He said he would put it in to her without going through the system. The only other really noteworthy thing during the day that I was speaking to Nigel Wicks[*] about Eric Sharp's letter, and I hope we're beginning to get things straightened out with the Prime Minister on the Cable & Wireless deal in Japan.[†]

When I got back home there was a letter from David Hart, full of the 1987 campaign. It doesn't look bad – it's rather better, I suspect, than some of the other things that have been prepared, and I will give it to the PM on Thursday, so she can read it over the weekend.

Wednesday 15 April

The day started off quietly enough, with Michael Quinlan asking to see me for a moment or two on a confidential matter. It turned out to be that the department thought they had possibly traced the leak to the BBC in the Zircon affair.[‡] It looks

---

[*] Nigel (since 1992 Sir Nigel) Wicks CBE, 1940–. Civil servant in the Treasury, 1968–75, 1978–83, 1989–2000; private secretary to the Prime Minister, 1975–78; economic minister at the British embassy in Washington, 1983–85; PPS to the Prime Minister, 1985–88; chairman of Committee on Standards in Public Life 2001–04.

[†] Thanks to the sterling work of the Prime Minister, Cable & Wireless subsequently made a considerable breakthrough in the Japanese market, becoming the largest shareholder with Toyato and C.Itoh (now Itochu) in IDC, the second international carrier in Japan.

[‡] The Zircon spy satellite had been developed at a cost of £500 million without parliamentary authorisation. In January 1987, police in Glasgow forced the BBC to hand over material relating to a programme on the satellite, part of a series entitled *The Secret Society*.

remarkably enough as if it could be Sally Fletcher – who was the wife of Clive Ponting, the MoD assistant secretary who had a famous trial two or three years back.* She was a principal in the civil service and was transferred over to our department but was now on gardening leave. Michael didn't seem sure if the Attorney General had enough evidence to prosecute.

The rest of the day fairly rushed by. We went straight on to a meeting on the machinery of government. This was more than a slight charade, since I'd sent the Prime Minister a more advanced note only the day before through Stephen Sherbourne. When the meeting was over, I went to say a brief thank-you to Albert Frost,† who did an absolutely splendid job with Remploy, the factory group for the disabled.

The unemployment figures were being released on a Wednesday, a day earlier than usual because of the Easter weekend. There was always a press briefing in the department, which Adrian Moorey, our chief press officer, would usually take while I was locked up in Cabinet. This time, though, I could join them. I'm not sure how good it was, for it degenerated into a rather long, wrangling row with the journalist from *The Guardian*. But the fact is, the figures are marvellous.

Then I did all the rounds of the media – the whole lot – but the only thing of note was some professor who published a report issued by the unemployment unit, which said that

---

* In 1985, Ponting, was acquitted after a trial brought under the Official Secrets Act. He had been accused of leaking documents relating to the sinking of the Argentine cruiser *General Belgrano* during the Falklands War.

† Albert Frost CBE, 1914–2010. Originally a civil servant; director, British Airways, 1976–80; Marks & Spencer, 1976–87; British Leyland, 1977–80; British Steel, 1980–83; and chairman of Remploy, 1983–87.

unemployment in London was 50 per cent higher than the figures actually show.* I pooh-poohed this.

Since it was a holiday week, I had time to go to the Savile Club for lunch and afterwards to speak to the National Union. I cracked a few jokes and really had them going very well indeed. I then came back to the department in order to meet Jimmy Savile,† the president of the Hands Across Britain campaign. This is a movement, run by Molly Meacher,‡ which is planning to demonstrate on 3 May by getting 350,000 people to hold hands to show their concern about unemployment. Well, I'm not sure what good it will do. But I was very worried that it would take place in the week of the local elections, which rather rubbished their claim that they were non-political. Rather surprisingly, and rather naïvely, Molly had been to see me previously and had asked me to sign a ridiculous note saying I would press government for more resources for unemployment. I told her that if more resources were required – and I did not think they were – this was not the way to get them. When I had mentioned my concern about this to Norman Tebbit, he arranged for me to see Jimmy Savile.

When he came in Savile insisted on kissing every girl in the office – I think he kissed every girl he ever meets. There is a very shrewd brain behind that sort of very jazzy exterior. I agreed

---

* Because of regular changes to the method by which official unemployment figures were calculated, the government's critics frequently disputed any evidence of a declining tally.

† Jimmy Savile, 1926–2011. An English DJ and TV and radio personality. Following Savile's death, hundreds of sexual abuse allegations were made against him, leading police to conclude he had been one of Britain's most prolific predatory sex offenders.

‡ Molly Meacher (Baroness Meacher since 2006), 1940–. Worked for the Mental Health Foundation in the 1980s.

with him – after a very long chat, I could not persuade him to resign from being president – that he would give away 500 Action for Jobs leaflets at Stoke Mandeville hospital. Perhaps I'll ring him during his radio programme on the day.

Then I gave a long interview to *Woman's Own*, followed by a profile by Robert Taylor for *The Observer*. I seem to be the flavour of the day; it won't last long, because the past two days I've done more media than I think I've ever done.

Tim Bell popped in and brought with him the proofs of the manifesto. I think we're getting somewhere. He was certainly in good form. We realised that at that moment the meeting was going on with the Prime Minister and Maurice Saatchi. I said I would try to find out what happened, if I could. Peter Morrison came in for a drink and I introduced Peter to Tim – oddly enough, they have never actually met. There is no doubt that Peter's terribly worried about Norman's attitude. We spent half an hour discussing what the hell we do, how we try to smooth things so there are no explosions between Norman and Tim. We agreed that perhaps the best thing might be, during the campaign, to see if Norman will go on the road and maybe I'll mind the shop. I said we would keep in touch. I tried to ring Stephen to see how he was getting on, but we still couldn't get through.

I went home, started doing the boxes – getting more and more tired, incidentally – and then Stephen rang to say they'd had a three-and-a-quarter-hour meeting with the Prime Minister. He thought she was very fired up at the beginning but calmed down towards the end. He and Maurice Saatchi thought it was a satisfactory meeting. He left Norman with her having a drink.

It appeared that the Prime Minister had made up her mind that she must be in touch with Norman all the way through the campaign. So, it looks as if Norman is going to be in central office minding the shop after all. They seemed to be all right together. Tomorrow is the big day – we'll just have to see how well it goes.

Later in the evening, David Hart rang. I told him his paper had gone in to the Prime Minister and I thought it was very good. Then Peter rang just to find out if there was any news and I told him what there was. We agreed to meet in the morning.

Maundy Thursday, 16 April–Easter Sunday, 19 April

I drove myself in to No. 10 that morning, for Maundy Thursday was a traditional holiday for most people in the civil service and Norman Dodds, my driver, had the day off. It was a lovely, bright, sunny spring morning and I remember how tired I was, thinking how much I was looking forward to the weekend and slightly dreading the day ahead of us.

As ever, I arrived a minute or so late. We were meeting in the Cabinet room with Norman in the centre, flanked by Peter Morrison and myself, facing the Prime Minister with Stephen Sherbourne and Robin Harris on one side and a new girl, Christine Wall,* who was to take responsibility for television, on the other.

The day started off well. The Prime Minister opened the proceedings fairly briskly and said she hoped that, as we had a fairly short agenda, we could be finished by lunchtime. That, alas, was

---

* Christine Wall had previously worked with the Prime Minister's press secretary, Bernard Ingham.

not destined to happen. She was in a slightly hyped-up mood. Norman took the first paper, which dealt with general strategy and our tactics towards the SDP and the Liberals, which was to separate them. She heard his introduction without interruption, and I think in the main agreed the message. She refused to contemplate a hung parliament – even to talk about it would be defeatist. She said that we must present to the public the dangers of an inconclusive result and the dangers of a Lib–Lab pact. But above all else, moderation in itself was not a policy. We must present ourselves as a team, she concluded, at which point Norman referred to 'The Next Moves Forward' as a motto.

I saw it was the right time to introduce the draft manifesto, which I brought out and passed round the table. That led to a discussion of our motto. I thought aloud that perhaps 'Moving Forward' would be better. But as that had no takers, in the end we compromised on 'The Next *Moves* Forward', which will be the printed message, while the 'Next *Move* Forward' is the way we will perhaps express it in our speeches.

I did say during this time that I thought the one advantage we have is depth – that we have not just the Prime Minister and not just Norman but also a large number of ministers who are familiar faces, who are good on television and who should be used. This general point was agreed.

Eventually, we finished the first item on the agenda. Then we went on to the candidates' conference, which Norman took. First, he talked about the autumn conference, which he presented as an idea which he and I had come to independently. Well, I wonder about that but never mind. Then he reported that we had a possibility of booking the Friends Meeting House on Euston Road. He went on to say that he had discussed my other idea, which was to have a televisual candidates' conference, with his chief press officer. The balance of opinion was that the press would not like it. My own view at that time was that he wasn't thinking in the television age, but I was determined not to cross Norman that day, in order to keep relationships right for the future.

Then followed a fairly long discussion about the conference. We all realised that it was down to Cranley Onslow, as chairman of the 1922 Committee, to settle the details. In the end, after a fairly good debate, we decided that we should bring the date forward and launch the manifesto on the Tuesday, with the candidates' meeting in closed session, followed by the formal launching and press conference. That would give us the Wednesday to have our first press conference in central office, and the Thursday would be the PM's adoption meeting in Finchley. Then we discussed whether or not we were going to have a press conference on the Friday morning but decided that, on balance, we probably wouldn't.

What I did get was general approval for my format of the manifesto in separate books: an achievements book, to act as a record of our first eight years; the manifesto itself; and a third book, which would be a summary – a plain man's guide. All this gives one hell of a lot of work for me to do in very little time.

We then moved on to discuss the morning press conferences. We agreed the themes of each day, who would be there and who wouldn't. I will not appear, although I am going to be in some of the bigger ones towards the end. I suspect that when it comes to it there's going to be quite a bit more for me to do in the conferences, but it was quite clear that for now we had managed to bring forward a good sprinkling of what we should do. I've got Kenneth Clarke into one, and we have, I think, enough new faces and new names coming into the conferences.

We then moved on to advertising, starting with poster sites. Norman reported that he'd booked about 800 sites, and I told her that I was entering into a massive advertising campaign for my department 'by coincidence', I said with a twinkle, 'in May and June'. There would be 1,200 poster sites nationally. It so happened that Saatchis would have an option on these sites in the event of an election, because as the government of course we could no longer advertise. After discussing the location of all these sites, we moved on to an election newspaper and then leaflets. Finally, we went through the party election broadcasts and the way in which we would use the media.

We broke for lunch and then carried on for some time afterwards. The interesting thing about the whole session was that Norman was in a very good mood and so was Thatcher. Although she was tensed up at the beginning, she did relax. Obviously the three-and-a-half-hour meeting she and Norman had over a drink the night before must have worked wonders, because the atmosphere is certainly very much better. Occasionally, both of them would tease me about never having been elected. Afterwards, having a wash with Norman and Peter, I turned round to Norman and said that it was a lot of rubbish my never having been elected – why, I said, I was elected to a golf club committee in 1956! Alas, this is just about true – the only election I have ever fought!

There was one further incident – one of those 'I wish the floor would swallow me up' moments. When we were discussing the tour, Margaret realised – and Norman realised at the very same moment – that I had arranged for the last day of her tour to be back on the Isle of Wight, and for her to be photographed before that enormous Union Jack at Hovercraft – of course quite forgetting that Hovercraft was part of Westland!* So that certainly put paid to that idea.

Anyway, I came away that evening really quite content and delighted even to be held up in the holiday weekend traffic to go down to the country.

Peter rang me the following day. We both said how amazed we were at how well the meeting had gone. We agreed that we should get together soon, because throughout the meeting the Prime Minister asked for Peter to do a whole series of things, for Peter to be responsible for this and for Peter to be responsible for that – all this would appear in the minutes of the meeting – whereas she didn't ask me to do a single thing. Which was just as well, as I had asked her at an earlier meeting, whatever she did, not to ask me to do anything because that would only make Norman feel threatened.

---

* Westland's main activity was the manufacture of helicopters, but it had been struggling in early 1986, when a takeover bid by the US firm Sikorsky provoked an argument within the Cabinet. The Secretary of State for Defence, Michael Heseltine, resigned because he felt that he had been prevented from putting the case for a rival bid by a European consortium. The Secretary of State for Trade and Industry, Leon Brittan, was later forced to resign for having authorised the leak of confidential legal advice from the Solicitor General in a way calculated to undermine Heseltine. At one time it was widely felt that Mrs Thatcher herself might have to leave office.

It was a delightful weekend. My mother was down, and Bernard and Karen, my elder daughter and her husband. Judith, my younger daughter who was working in New York, had been back for the week, and she went back on Sunday to the States. Leslie, my late brother's eldest daughter, and her husband, Dennis, were down with little Sophie, and it was really very calm – I did hardly any work, slept a great deal and was very relaxed indeed.

I did, though, sit down for some time on the Sunday, and again on the Monday morning, to read the draft of the manifesto. I was more than appalled – it was discursive: quite well written but far, far, far too long.

So, in the afternoon, I rang the Prime Minister. After agreeing with her how well Thursday had gone, I said: 'Look, can I just give you one or two ideas for tomorrow?'

'Oh, let me get my notebook and pencil,' she said.

'No, no, it's not drafting details, Prime Minister,' I said. 'What I suggest is this: we have seven chapters if we limit ourselves to half an hour a chapter. So, let us just discuss the general shape, the balance and whether you think it should be reduced by a half, by a third or by a quarter or whatever. If we sit down to draft it at the next meeting, we will achieve absolutely nothing.'

She agreed, and then I said, 'Perhaps you might let me take over the production of the achievements booklet? There is no policy involved.'

'Oh, well,' she said, 'John MacGregor should be involved because of the Treasury.'

'Yes,' I said, 'of course I'll do it with John, more than happy to do that. Incidentally, I think John should be relieved from much

of his Cabinet committee work – there's nothing more important than the manifesto, and I know he has to spend a great deal
of time on the committees.' She agreed.

I then said, 'Well, we will agree more for the tour in the afternoon,' and went on that I thought things were going well – very
well, at the moment – and we've really got to be ready. The way
she agreed made me more and more sure that she's already made
up her mind, and she will go in June.

Easter Monday, 20 April

The next morning, I left at about 8 o'clock and drove across on a
nice sunny morning to Chequers, arriving, once again, a minute
or two late. Everybody was in the hall at Chequers having coffee
– Willie Whitelaw, Peter, of course, and Norman, John O'Sullivan who introduced himself to me as the new speech-writer,
Robin Harris, Brian Griffiths,* John MacGregor, Stephen Sherbourne and Michael Alison, Margaret's PPS. After a minute or
two and a quick cup of coffee, we went upstairs, and by quarter
to ten we were in session.

She started off at a tremendous rate of knots, saying that the
manifesto wouldn't do and that it wasn't enough to talk about
the past. We had to really give people the reason why we were
going to do this, why we had to succeed and why our policies
were really there. It's the reasons *why*, she kept on saying, that
we've really got to deal with. We spent quite a long time on the

---

* Brian Griffiths (Baron Griffiths of Fforestfach since 1991), 1941–. Director of Bank of England, 1983–85; head of Downing Street Policy Unit, 1985–90; director of Times Newspapers
since 1991.

introduction – in fact, the entire morning session, until perhaps five minutes to one. Eventually, we got through about three quarters of the manifesto. The whole time she'd been fairly firm, always saying *why?*

At one point, when we reached employment and jobs – my area – there had been quite a discussion as to where employment was going to go. She was very keen that it be part of trade and industry and all put together, which makes me wonder a little whether she has plans for the future, but that's another matter. Willie interceded and said he thought employment was so sensitive and so important that it should have a chapter by itself.

As a result of all the redrafting, a great deal of what we'd written would have to be shortened. I said: 'Look, Prime Minister, I'm afraid that, first, my section has got to be redone. But secondly, the rewrite doesn't allow for any of the structural or other changes.'

'Oh,' she said, 'no, no, no, you haven't got policy approval.' As there were a number of outsiders there, I didn't quite know what to say. But, of course, I'd already had her agreement, and that of Willie, that we had a place – unnamed as yet – in QL,* so our proposed changes could be in the Queen's Speech for the next session. The Prime Minister went on: 'You have to bring it forward as a policy matter to EA inside the next ten days.'

'Right,' said I.

As we went on, we were finding out more and more policy items that really had to go into the manifesto. She approved the principle that we were to have an achievement session, and I was

---

*   The Cabinet subcommittee which agrees the legislative proposals in the Queen's Speech.

to go ahead with John MacGregor or with Stephen – it wasn't too clear which – with the drafting. I was certainly given the task of redrafting my Enterprise and Jobs package. We broke for a quick drink at about five minutes to one.

We went into the Long Gallery. Denis was there, and we chatted quite cheerily – it was quite relaxed. Everybody appeared to be in a good mood, particularly Norman, who was very calm the entire morning and really taking things quite happily. Then we were joined by Christine Wall and Roger Boaden, who were there for the afternoon session.

I went down at lunchtime and tried to ring my office to give them instructions for the work that they were to do. At about ten past two, we went into session again – Roger Boaden, Christine Wall, me, Stephen Sherbourne, of course Norman, Peter Morrison and Michael Alison, and perhaps one or two others.

We began with a discussion as to how we were going to launch the manifesto. In the end we had it agreed that on Day Twenty-Three we would have a televisual launch, then a lunch break and then the normal candidates' conference. We would follow this on the next morning, Day Twenty-Two, with the press conference. Then on Day Twenty-One, down at Docklands we would show the battle bus for the first time and perhaps take in a visit to a youth training scheme (YTS).

We went all the way through the election. By about 4 o'clock, the Prime Minister started to get very fidgety about the timing of the election. But before that she had criticised some of the earlier places we are going to, saying, 'I must go to large factories, I must go to large factories.' I tried to point out to her that, in fact, some of these factories were dangerous for security – not so much physical security but because rent-a-mob could get there, which would not produce good television. She was very keen about David Alliance,* and I said I would organise things with him. In the end, although she was criticising a lot of things, when I look back we got a surprising amount approved.

We got back to about Day Two and Day One, and we eventually finished at about ten past four. The Prime Minister left for London, and the rest of us went down. I rang the office to try to clear what we had to do. Then I went back to London with Peter.

On the journey, Peter got out his notebook and started going through the various things we had to do. To my great joy, it appears that Peter is going to be very happy working with, and even for, me. No question now that everybody is in better heart. But I did discuss with Peter one or two areas where we were weak and fixed to come in and see him later in the week.

When I got back, I went into the office and saw John Turner, giving him instructions about drafting the paper to go to colleagues. He, in the meantime, had got on to Nigel Wicks, and we were discussing which colleagues were to be invited to our next meeting, since we were very keen to ensure that security would be very tight.

I carried on with other routine matters. It was really quite difficult trying to manage the department and dealing with central office, but I also had a chance of seeing Howell in order to instruct him about the printing of the manifesto.

---

* David Alliance (Baron Alliance of Manchester since 2004), 1932–. Chief executive, Coats Viyella, 1975–90; chairman, 1989–99.

When I came home, I had promised to take Lita out for a meal – she'd been in and cooking all over the long weekend – so we went out for an early Chinese. I returned for my boxes and then to rewrite my portion of the manifesto.

At about quarter past eleven, I had just got to the finishing touches when there was a sudden white flash and my computer cut out, started to reboot and then cut out again. I realised with a sinking heart that the machine had blown up just as it had done some months before – I suspect because the power supply was too weak. I was desperate. But then I remembered I had my portable laptop (the Zenith 181), so I got that out. Luckily, that had WordPerfect on it, so I sat down and started all over again. I went on and on and on and rewrote the entire thing, and at about quarter past one I had just about finished when I realised that I had never printed anything out from that machine. I went into another flat spin and it took me a further three quarters of an hour or more until I got some form of hard copy. I went to bed absolutely exhausted.

Wednesday 22 April

The following morning, I had to get up quite early for the *Today* programme. So, I only had about four hours' sleep, and right away all the benefits of that lovely long weekend seemed to be going. I went over to Broadcasting House and gave, for once, a rather good interview. I then had a Cabinet subcommittee meeting, and on the way I telephoned Margaret Bell* and asked her to see if she could do what she could to get the machine repaired.

---

* Margaret Bell had been my secretary for over twenty years before I came into government and acted as diary secretary in my private office.

It was a rather hectic morning, for after the subcommittee I was due at the Confederation of British Industry (CBI) to speak on our green paper at a conference on industrial relations. On the way, Margaret rang to tell me that she'd arranged for the engineer to go along to York Terrace West at 12 o'clock. I asked her to be there as well, as I was very nervous that, if anyone could read the files, there would have been a great deal about the manifesto and dates for the election.

I came out of the CBI – the speech went quite well, I thought, particularly as the subject was more of Ken Clarke's than mine – and popped home. Margaret was there and they had repaired the machine. I then had quite an enjoyable and productive lunch at the Savoy Grill with Robin Oakley,* who had written a very nice profile of me in *The Times* a few weeks back.

I thanked him for the article. 'Well,' he replied, 'it wasn't difficult, I couldn't find anybody to say anything nasty about you.'† It just goes to show, I suppose, that he doesn't know too many people! A rather amusing incident – when I came in, the waiting staff made a great fuss of me and showed me to Robin's table, which was near the back, but after a couple of minutes they returned and showed us to a better table in the front.

After lunch, I went back to central office to meet Howell, to discuss the arrangements about the manifesto. Then upstairs to Harvey Thomas, where he introduced me to a man called David

---

* Robin Oakley, 1941–. Journalist with the *Sunday Express*, 1970–79; *Daily Mail*, 1981–86; *The Times*, 1986–92; BBC, 1992–2000; CNN, 2000–08.
† That was to change, largely as a result of the next few weeks.

Wicks for my television training. Wicks certainly knew how to get around me – he wasn't very flattering about my interviews on television. At least he seems to think I'm doing all the things OK. I went through a few trial interviews, and there's no question that I certainly have improved over the past four or five years. Mind you, that would not be too difficult.

It wasn't too heavy a session, and we finished it fairly early. I spent a few minutes with Harvey Thomas going through his concerns. The battlewagon – not the bus but a converted podium from which the Prime Minister can speak on the campaign trail – had been designed but not yet ordered. I promised Harvey I would deal with it, but I got more than a slight fright when I realised we would only just have it in time if we ordered it immediately. Then there was some doubt as to what we'd agreed at our meeting with the Prime Minister last Thursday. Harvey had a message which he thought was wrong, that we would have the press conference first and then the launch afterwards. I promised to check up. I went downstairs, but the chairman was out and so was Michael Dobbs, so I left it and said I would give a call the next day.

Back at my office, Kenneth Baker came in for a drink and expressed some concern about the arrangements for the election. I told him that I thought we'd had some problems but they were now all being sorted out. I promised that we would keep in touch and see how things are going. We both agreed that we would in all probability be going back to our own departments after the election.

That evening, Lita and I were due to have dinner with Princess

Alexandra and Angus Ogilvy* – the Sieffs† were there and the
Gowries‡ and the Aldingtons.§ It was a very pleasant evening,
but it wasn't an early one, and so it was about midnight when
I returned to two big boxes. I then had to settle down to finish
off the manifesto – thank God the machine now worked – and I
finished it without any undue incident. I am not too displeased
with it.

Thursday 23 April

In the morning I had a late-ish start – nothing before Cabinet
at 10.30 – but I had to pack because was I due on the evening
Concorde to New York, where I had some long-standing speaking engagements. I messed around at home and only just made
Cabinet in time. We had a good Cabinet, and afterwards I gave
Stephen Sherbourne and John MacGregor a copy of the manifesto. I went on to a Cabinet subcommittee on local authority
finance before walking back with Norman to his office. Norman
was in a good mood and he told me of his plans to get the Conservative members of the National and Local Government Of-
ficers' Association to bring an injunction against their union for
running a political fund without authority.

---

* Princess Alexandra, 1936–. Cousin of the Queen. Sir Angus Ogilvy, 1928–2004. Princess Alexandra's husband was a very good friend of mine, working together in the Prince's Trust.
† Marcus Sieff (Baron Sieff of Brimpton after 1980), 1913–2001. A leading member of the
family that founded Marks & Spencer.
‡ Grey Ruthven, 2nd Earl Gowrie, 1939–. Held various posts for Conservative Party in House
of Lords; Minister for the Arts, 1983–85; director of Sotheby's, 1985–98.
§ Toby Low (Baron Aldington of Bispham since 1962), 1914–2000. Conservative MP, 1945–62;
junior minister, Ministry of Supply and Board of Trade; chairman of GEC and Sun Alliance.
He remained an influential figure in Conservative circles after taking a life peerage, and a
close friend of Edward Heath.

I told him a little of my plans for my department, which would be raised at the meeting next week. He promised to support me. I said, 'Oh, yes, I assume that I'm going back to my department after the election, and so I want to get it through.'

He replied with a smile: 'Oh, well, I *know* what I'm going to do after the election, and I'm very pleased about it.'

That's probably the reason why he's been so relaxed the past few days. I reckon that that Wednesday evening before Easter, when she had that marathon three-and-a-half-hour session with him, the Prime Minister must have told him what he was going to do after the election. It certainly pleased him and he's very relaxed about it.*

He said that he had been thinking about my role in the election. I am not to go out on tours, as I am not being elected myself. I have to be careful, he said, some people had been talking. We had a brief chat and I said, 'Look, Norman, you're far too valuable to sit round at central office.'

'You know she wants me to stay in contact.'

I said, 'Yes, Norman, but you're far too valuable to be wasted that way. Why don't Peter and I stay back and act at the centre, and I'll make sure that we are always in contact. When the Prime Minister comes through, I'll patch you through to her.'

I think he seemed quite keen on that. But I was left with a slight, perhaps unworthy, sneaking suspicion that he was just trying to cut down my role a bit. I made up my mind that I

---

* I was quite wrong. I was sure that Norman was going to the Home Office, where he would have done well, but he had told the Prime Minister that he wanted to stand down after the election to look after Margaret.

would take it up with the PM when I saw her on the following Tuesday.

Back to the office for a hurried bite. We had a whole series of meetings with Peter Morrison, who came in at 2.15 and ran through the proposed tour arrangements with me. I told him of my earlier conversation with Norman. Speculating about it, we both reckoned he'd got the Home Office. Peter went through a whole lot of detail, and I thought things were making reasonable progress.

Richard Branson[*] came in for a chat, and then Roger Boaden and Harvey Thomas came in for the first of a series of meetings to flesh out the details of the tour. It became apparent that I would have to settle one or two points with the Prime Minister, but we went through everything, and I told Roger that I had decided, having agreed this with Norman, to ignore her instructions about getting on to David Alliance, at least until I'd seen her on the following Tuesday.

I was slightly concerned when Harvey Thomas said that as far as he knew the battle bus had not been ordered. I promised to have a quick word with Peter, who told me that it had now been ordered.[†] He undertook to do one or two things about the manifesto, and I said I'd ring him either from the States or on my return.

During the previous forty-eight hours I'd been working overtime to get the green paper agreed to go in to Cabinet

---

[*]   Richard (since 2000 Sir Richard) Branson, 1950–. Entrepreneur; founded Virgin Records in 1972; set up Virgin Atlantic in 1984.
[†]   On the night before delivery, the bus was involved in an accident and had to be resprayed.

colleagues, and I was told on the way to the airport that a meeting had actually been fixed for 11.30 on the Tuesday of my return. I had even gone so far in that paper (and in the private note I had put to the Prime Minister) to say that my real target for unemployment for the next parliament was under 2 million. Well, I reckon if nothing else shakes them, that will.

The US visit did not start off auspiciously. The Concorde was kept sitting at the ramp for two hours before we moved. Nevertheless, I was picked up at Kennedy airport and taken to the hotel before going out with Lita, Judith and Howell to a very pleasant Japanese restaurant. Typical of me, I invited Howell, but when I got there I found I hadn't got my credit cards.

Friday 24–Monday 27 April

The day started off with the corporate forum breakfast, which went well, followed by a very interesting hour-and-a-half chat with the editorial board of *Forbes* magazine. Back to the hotel for a few minutes, then I went on to speak to the Council on Foreign Relations. Old friends were there to greet me – Hank,[*] Dan Rose etc. Even if I say so myself, it turned out to be a rather good occasion of mine – not quite important enough to warrant flying the Atlantic, I would have thought, but nevertheless it was an extremely splendid occasion. In the evening, we went out Westchester way to have dinner with Hank and family.

It was a very pleasant weekend in New York, but Monday brought a slightly disappointing press conference, followed by

---

[*] Hank Graff, 1921–2020. Professor at Columbia University and a friend of many years' standing.

a good departmental visit. Concorde back, which was actually more than enjoyable because I sat in the cockpit for the take-off and landing, which shows just what a little boy I really am. I was met at the airport with a whole pile of work – three boxes – which kept me going until very late at night.

Tuesday 28 April

The following morning – rather groggily, because I didn't get to bed until 3 a.m. and was up again at 6.30 – I went in to the Prime Minister. I can't say it was one of my better meetings. While I was away, Peter Morrison had come in with another set of dates for the manifesto. We talked round that. She was very exercised because that morning the Labour Party were producing something called 'The Real Conservative Manifesto', which looked very much like ours and made all sorts of outrageous promises. I thought it was a two-day wonder, but she got quite concerned about it and we discussed whether or not we should change the 'Next Moves Forward' motto.

I went through my agenda. We agreed that I would not contact David Alliance and that her visits would be to small industrial locations rather than large ones, unless down in the south. Afterwards I told her that things were very much better in central office and Norman Tebbit was much more relaxed.

My new programme was delayed for half an hour when Norman came to discuss the Labour Party's alternative manifesto. We then had some interminable meetings, first about the new urban development corporations (the new public/private bodies to redevelop the inner cities – the London Docklands

Development Corporation being the biggest), and then one to deal with the future of the Manpower Services Commission and all the other matters. Willie was there, but he didn't stay for the whole meeting, as were John MacGregor, Norman Tebbit, Norman Fowler and Kenneth Baker.

I said right at the outset, 'Prime Minister, my objective in the next parliament is to get unemployment down under 2 million.'

I don't think anybody's ever promised them that before. I produced a chart which showed that if we did that, we would be saving some £2.75 billion a year in reduction of benefits. We then had a slightly difficult conversation. John MacGregor is totally supportive, but he does feel, I think, that he's got to take the Treasury line and was objecting to the transfer of the Public Expenditure Survey from the Department of Health and Social Security (DHSS) to my department, which would be necessary to pay for my three guarantees.

We went through the guarantees. The first, to get all school leavers on the Youth Training Scheme, would be paid for by taking benefit away from under-eighteens, and that was agreed. The second, to ensure all unemployed people had between six and twelve months on the JTS, didn't require a PES transfer, and that was also agreed. The third, to guarantee a place on all programmes for those between eighteen and fifty, was not agreed. After some dickering, I agreed on a formula whereby we would move towards the provision of such a guarantee. That was fine with me, because that was the most I suspected we could do for some considerable time.

We then looked at the structure of the MSC. Right away,

I could see the Prime Minister was very nervous at the question of abolishing the commission. So, in one of my rare happy thoughts, I suggested that instead of abolishing it outright, we would say we would have plans to amend it in order to increase employer representation. This got the general agreement, and the more I thought about it the better it seemed.

I left the meeting and went back to the office to see Geoffrey Holland, Roger Dawe, Clive Tucker and, of course, my private secretary, John Turner. I explained to them that what I really visualised was an MSC with an amended constitution that would have 75 per cent employer representation. The remaining 25 per cent would be the unions and educational training interests. We wouldn't be looking for the employers to all be members from the CBI but from many other employer bodies. This was received with some relief.

I asked Geoffrey to stay back and on the spot asked him if he would become the first chairman of the new commission. He almost said yes, but then promised me that he would think about it for a day or so.

After lunch I had to speak to all the Restart teams. When I returned to central office, Peter Morrison was there with Stephen Sherbourne. Peter had taken over the running of the manifesto while I was away. We had a long meeting in which we went through all the bits and pieces, then Howell went off with Peter. I was snowed under with a series of other meetings. Howell came back a little later and said he was worried because everything was now being done through Peter's assistant. He could work with that, but there was no single person actually running things. He went on to say that Tim Bell had rung with an idea for making a video in which ministers would extoll the main virtues of their manifesto for three or four minutes each.

I rang Stephen Sherbourne and told him about Tim's plan. After a moment or two, he became quite taken with the idea. Then I went on about some worries I had about the manifesto. To my surprise, he too was very worried. We agreed between us that he would put a note in to the Prime Minister in her overnight box, and hopefully we would resolve the question of who does what.

The more I think that the election could well be called on Monday week, the more terrified I get at how much there still has to be done. But the only thing you can do is put your head down and go ploughing straight ahead. It now looks as if the Friday I was hoping to have off will be taken up with the Prime Minister to go through her tour. I have now agreed that tomorrow morning, I will meet with Harvey Thomas to go through the tour. I say tomorrow morning, but as I'm dictating this, I am looking at my watch – it's five to one again, and I'm exhausted. I'm going to bed.

Wednesday 29 April

I was tired last night and went into a deep sleep – I think dreamless – and was suddenly woken by the telephone at twenty past seven. It was Greville Janner on the way to Leicester. He told me that after my big write-ups of the weekend, one of his colleagues on the Labour front bench said to him: 'I didn't realise that David Young once voted Labour – it's a pity we let him go.' Well, it shows you can be popular somewhere.

I dashed into the office. It turned out to be one of those days which in years to come I will only remember with amazement. At 9 o'clock I was due at Queen Elizabeth II Conference Centre for a big NEDO conference, in which I made the opening keynote speech. Norman Willis* was there from the TUC. When I saw Norman, I was glad that, in the end, we had decided only to change the constitution of the MSC rather than abolishing it entirely. That will certainly be easier to deal with later.

From there over to the office, dealing with some immediate problems. It looks as if the civil service strike dispute is going to end. According to a note in the box last night, as many as 100,000 people could be without their benefit next week, so I had a quick meeting on that. I'm told the unemployment figures may or may not be affected – we'll just have to see. But I'll get the first sight on Thursday or Friday – a week early – so my fingers are crossed till then.

When I walked into the office there was a case of Mouton Cadet, together with a lovely note from Peter Morrison, saying he'd been presented with this case of wine by the Association of Demolition Contractors. He must have thought he owed me a case of wine, because he said he was happy to pay up his debts. He also said he was very happy to be working for me for real. I think he really does mean it.

Harvey Thomas and Roger Boaden came in with Howell, and we started to go through the tour once more. It is beginning to take shape. The Docklands arrangements are nearly there,

---

* Norman Willis, 1933–2014. General secretary of the TUC, 1984–93.

and I'm getting Christopher Benson* to come in on Friday morning for a few minutes. We had to firm up on the Prime Minister's meeting for 12 o'clock on Friday, which means my chance of going down to the country on Thursday night has gone. I have asked for a list for her, with a summary showing the number of factories, hotels, restaurants and other places she will visit. I asked them to provide the communication facilities for Norman Tebbit as well, so, if necessary, Norman could go out too. Peter or I could be in central office manning the communications desk. I've also been told that I will have to go through the achievements booklet with the Prime Minister on Monday evening.

We have to firm up the slogan for the campaign at some time, so I got through to Stephen Sherbourne, who told me in a slightly surprised voice that, quite out of character, the Prime Minister didn't do the box last night. She was now on her way to a meeting at Frimley; she had the papers to look at in the car and they'd telephone back. The message came later – the achievements package is going to be called 'Our First Eight Years' and the manifesto 'The Next Moves Forward'. Neither Harvey Thomas nor I nor anyone really liked the names. But at least the position is clarified. Stephen said that, as she's quite relaxed and thinks we're all working properly, he did not put the note into her about the 'demarcation disputes' with Peter.† I

---

* Christopher (since 1988 Sir Christopher) Benson, 1933–. Chairman of the Docklands Development Corporation, 1987; Boots, 1990–94; Sun Alliance, 1993–96; Costains, 1993–96; Housing Corporation, 1990–94.

† Initially, Peter objected to my role, but I came to an accommodation with him, and we worked happily together.

agreed with him that we would get on quite well as we are, and I'm sure we really will.

I dealt with the employment page of the manifesto. Having got all my new programmes agreed at my meeting with John MacGregor, I had to have a quick sight at the first draft of the manifesto. I got Clive and Roger to take it away with Howell, and they came back with very satisfactory amendments. The letter from the Prime Minister has come in and everybody in the department was absolutely delighted with what we have been promised, namely the financial allocations for future programmes.

I then had to go downstairs to speak to the department's benevolent fund, of all things. In the meantime, a request had come in for one or two interviews. I did *The World at One* with Robin Day, and then Independent Radio News (IRN), all about my speech in the morning. I had a long debate in the afternoon to prepare for, on the industrial relations green paper. But before that, there was a question in the House on shareholding, which led me into a lovely tub-thumping bit. Obviously, the election is in the air, even in the Lords. And then the industrial relations debate, which involved sitting for six long hours without a break in the chamber, making my speech, paying attention to all the contributions, making notes, then winding up. There weren't many people in the House, but our people seemed to be pleased with it. It was just an occasion to get over, and then back home.

Lita was now back from the United States, and I stopped to buy some sandwiches on the way home because, quite rightly, it was far too late for her to start cooking. Back to the boxes!

After all the departmental work was finished, I had to rewrite two pages of my manifesto commitment and then look at the achievements package. Now it is already Thursday, just gone midnight. Once again I'm more than tired; once again it's another day. The only slightly frightening thought is that it's one day nearer, and the day of decision is probably going to be Monday week. Still, we've got a lot of work to do before then, and I'll worry about it later.

Thursday 30 April

I had an appointment to meet Norman for breakfast at Granby's and arrived only a minute late. I sat there waiting for about ten or twelve minutes until Norman turned up – in fact, I almost began to wonder if he knew the appointment was on. He was in a good mood. But I've noticed Norman has become very quiet – he has been speaking in a very muted way recently; I'm not sure he always did. But he started off once again with an attack on Tim Bell – repeated all the poison about Tim that led to the Saatchis refusing to work with him. He then said that Tim was putting it about that he was working for me. 'Well, Norman,' I said, 'he is working for me on the manifesto – it's his people doing all the artwork.'

We then passed on to other things. Norman told me how he went to dinner with Nick Lloyd.* Well, I'm going next week, so I suppose Lloyd must be having a series of weekly dinners

---

* Nicholas (since 1990 Sir Nicholas) Lloyd, 1942–. Editor, *News of the World*, 1984–85; *Daily Express*, 1986–95.

with his chairman, David Stevens.* During the evening, the conversation came round to a very good article about Bryan Gould† in the *Express*. Norman said that, in his view, the race for succession in the Labour Party had already started between John Smith‡ and Gould.§ David Stevens had slightly told off Nick Lloyd for publishing a rather rosy article about Gould, and Norman had told him it was absolutely right to encourage dissension afterwards. I think this is a slightly odd priority, but whatever.

Norman was very concerned about security, with good reason. He went on in some detail about how he thought that the IRA might really start to do something in the first half of the campaign – he didn't think they would bother in the second half, because that would only lead to a big wave of sympathy, which would help us. He certainly saw the PM as a real target. I suggested to him that perhaps the sensible thing to do would be to change the tour round for the last few days. I told him I would organise something.

As we walked out of Granby's I said, 'By the way, Norman, I did speak to her last week. You know she wants you to sit by the phone ready to talk to her at a moment's notice? Well, I told her that would be a terrible waste and fixed that if you want to go

---

* David Stephens (Baron Stephens of Ludgate since 1987), 1936–. Chairman, Express Newspapers, 1985–99.

† Bryan Gould, 1939–. Diplomat, journalist and academic; Labour MP 1974–79 and 1983–94; frontbench opposition spokesman, 1983–92; shadow Secretary of State for Trade and Industry, 1987–89; vice-chancellor of Waikato University in his native New Zealand, 1994–2004.

‡ John Smith, 1938–94. Labour MP, 1970–94; Secretary of State for Trade, 1978–79; shadow Secretary of State for Employment, 1983–84; Trade and Industry, 1984–87; leader of Labour Party, 1992–94.

§ He was right, for Smith beat Gould after the election.

out, either Peter or I will be there to make sure that we can link things up.'

Our relationship is still good, and Norman is still very relaxed. Over breakfast he said that I would be very surprised at what he was going to do after the election, but he was very happy about it. He slightly teased me – he said, 'Who knows, perhaps you will be Leader of the Lords?'

'What, with all the geriatrics?' said I. Then I kept quiet, just in case that rumour was true. But I think more and more that he's going to be Leader of the Commons.

Back to the office for the weekly prayer meeting,* which produced nothing more than the usual concerns about central office. After it broke up, Howell came in and we went through the draft achievements book. There was a very long, hand-written note from Stephen, in which he suggested that Peter and I should sort out our arrangements between ourselves, rather than get the Prime Minister involved. At the moment, she was very happy and relaxed that all was going well.

I immediately rang Stephen and agreed. I also told him that my part of the manifesto was ready, and we should meet. I would bring Howell with me when I came over for Cabinet, and Howell could take my manifesto part on to Brian Griffiths after our meeting. I invited Howell home for dinner that evening, in order to get all the editing completed on the achievements book.

By then it was getting late for Cabinet, so I got Dodds to drop us at the bottom of the steps, so we could enter Downing

---

* A meeting of a department's ministers and senior officials, to provide the team with an over-view of progress on a range of issues relating to departmental business.

Street through the gate. As we came through the gate, I could see some television cameras. 'Right,' I said to Howell, 'you watch, you're going to be on television now. Walk next to me.' We walked together and I pulled my old trick – as we came near the cameras, I nodded to them, said good morning, smiled broadly and walked on. Howell later told me that he'd been on the *One O'Clock News* with me. So the trick that I had worked out for myself really does continue to work.

We went into No. 10 and I was in time, for everybody was milling around outside the Cabinet room waiting for the start. I took Howell through to Stephen's room and left them at it. In Cabinet, before we came to parliamentary business, the Prime Minister said how very fed up she was with the way that all the papers were writing about the date of the election. Every paper that day had been remarkably consistent, as they all had 11 June. I suspect it came out of John Biffen's* lobby meeting, for in one paper they mentioned 'senior ministers' before going on to talk about John.

She gave us all a lecture, saying, 'There is no point in closing options off, we really shouldn't talk,' while looking fiercely at a rather hapless John. I sat back and caught Norman's eye at the other end of the table. We grinned at each other as he pointed at John, reminding me that one of the topics over breakfast had been how we thought the leak had come from John.

Later I raised the civil service strike, which was rumbling on,

---

* John Biffen (Baron Biffen of Tanat after 1997), 1930–2007. Conservative MP, 1961–97; chief secretary to the Treasury, 1979–81; Secretary of State for Trade, 1981–82; Lord President of the Council, 1982–83; Leader of the House of Commons, 1982–87; Lord Privy Seal, 1983–87.

and pointed out that up to 100,000 people could be without their benefit in the forthcoming week. Nigel suddenly popped up and said he was unhappy with some media coverage we'd had, although he didn't suggest how to improve matters.

As we were walking out of Cabinet, Willie Whitelaw invited Lita and I to stay at Dorneywood with him the following weekend, which will be the big Chequers decision weekend.

Then followed a Cabinet subcommittee to clear further policy items for the manifesto. I then dashed back to the office at about 1 o'clock. There was some trouble stirring with the chief secretary because I still had to clear my three guarantees before they could be in the manifesto. Throughout Cabinet, messages were being delivered to me from my office, and I was scribbling notes to John MacGregor. Afterwards I spoke to John, suggesting that we meet. So far nothing has been fixed up.

I did a television interview about the strike, which went reasonably well, and then on to the House for a quick lunch and then Front Bench.* I did not stay on afterwards but went back to the department for some more meetings about our guarantees. I then went into a presentation by Gallup, joined by Brian Griffiths, Norman Blackstone† and all our people. They were showing many video tapes of discussion groups, talking about the black economy. It was amazing to see many unemployed people freely admitting they were in the black economy while collecting benefit.

---

* The weekly meeting of Conservative frontbenchers in the Lords, when strategy and tactics are discussed.
† Norman Blackstone was part of the No. 10 Policy Unit and did really valuable work around the country.

Later, the minister of the Chinese embassy came in to give me my formal invitation to visit his country. I had been invited by the training minister, and they also wanted to invite my tourism minister. I pointed out that I was responsible for that subject too, and I might very well cover tourism during my visit.

Nick (Bryan Nicholson) came in after that to cover what would happen should the TUC walk out of our programmes during the election. After the departmental meeting, I saw him privately and told him of my plans for the MSC. I think he was quite pleased. I also told him that his knighthood was in the list for June, for which he thanked me very much. I said no, he did a very good job and I wanted to make sure that when he left us to go to the post office he'd go there with his K.

I did some box work and then went home. Howell was waiting for me and we had dinner, just Howell, Lita and me. After dinner, Howell and I went upstairs to my study, turned on my machine, used the disc Margaret Bell had prepared and, happily, this time all the technology worked. I printed the manifesto and the achievements book out item by item and got it sorted into the right order. By 11 or 11.15 it was all done. I think it's beginning to take good shape.

Then Howell left, and I had to go back to my boxes. Once again, it was about 1 o'clock before I finished – at least, I thought, tomorrow is Friday, and Friday shouldn't be too difficult a day.

Friday 1–Saturday 2 May

Early in the morning, Peter Morrison rang and invited me to lunch, but I declined as we were going down to the country.

Afterwards, I arranged with Lita that we would stay up in town after all, so I rang Peter's home number to let him know of the change. To my great surprise, he wasn't at home but in the office. Normally I am the early starter, not Peter. I rang him in the office, and we fixed to have lunch together after the Prime Minister's meeting.

As I arrived, Paul Dworkin and Ann Wheatcroft, the employment department's statisticians, were waiting for me outside my office. They were normally the most gloomy of couples, and it was said that Tom King,* during his time, had refused even to meet with Paul. My heart sank; I suspect I paled. 'Oh God,' I thought.

'Come on in, come on in,' I said with my thoughts racing away – the figures are going to be bad, the figures are going to be bad.

I followed them in. Then Paul said, 'Secretary of State, I think that you had better sit down.'

As he said that, I had a sudden rush and knew that the figures were going to be marvellous – under 3 million, I thought.

I sat down. Paul smiled – the first time I had ever seen him smile – and said, 'I shouldn't have done that to you.' Then they told me the headline total was 40,000 down, seasonally adjusted 20,000 down. The seasonal adjustments had been recalculated so that this would be the tenth consecutive month unemployment would have fallen. The total looks like it could be

---

* Tom King (Baron King of Bridgwater since 2001), 1933–. Conservative MP, 1970–2001; Secretary of State for the Environment, 1983; for Transport, 1983; for Employment, 1983–85; for Northern Ireland, 1985–89; and for Defence, 1989–92.

3,019,000 – slightly higher than it would otherwise be because of the strike.

So much for that problem! I swore everyone to secrecy and then cancelled the ensuing meeting dealing with the figures, because this is two weeks before the results are announced, and I don't want anyone to know.

My first appointment proper was with Christopher Benson, the chairman of Docklands, to clear what we would do there for the tour. He was tickled pink with the whole idea, but I told him that he should keep it to himself. He proposed that she go down the river by boat. I went along with the suggestion, but I know her attitude already and I think it extremely unlikely.

Howell popped in on his way to the printers to settle one or two outstanding matters. At 11 o'clock, I saw the Sunday lobby. *The Observer*'s Robert Taylor was there. He had given me a really good profile the week before. The Sunday lobby were a very cheery lot, always looking for a spectacular story. We got on very well. I was talking about 'Hands Across Britain', which was due the following Sunday, and also about local authorities not cooperating. I went on a bit about lack of literacy and numeracy amongst the long-term unemployed, which I think will probably be the story they pick up. The only thing which was a bit awkward was about the Church. I did say that some of the bishops had sounded unreal in recent debates in the Lords. But it went well.

Later on, when I finished with the lobby, I went over to No. 10. The lobby journalists were still outside and one of them asked me as I got out of the car: 'Was that on the record or off the record?' I said, airily, 'Oh, all on the record.' Then I said, but please, just one thing – the bishops and the Church, that's off the record. 'Oh, yes, yes.' I don't think they were interested in that. They seemed very pleased and off they went. I suspect we will have quite a bit of a story.

I went in to see the Prime Minister, who appeared fairly relaxed. It was a small meeting with Christine Wall, Peter Morrison, of course, Stephen Sherbourne, Roger Boaden and myself. Peter told us about some amazingly good council by-election results that had just come in. I took out a scrap of paper and wrote a note that said, 'Prime Minister, from the very early flash results, next month's figures are going to be all right.' I passed it to her, she unfolded the note, looked at it, folded it and just passed it straight back to me. She didn't even twitch. I suspect that it must be a great relief to her.

I started off with the tour and she was quite happy with the first two days. She disagreed right away with going by the river barge, but she liked the idea of testing the battle bus in Docklands. Then we went through and agreed the very first day – the Friday – as Farmhouse Biscuits day, the famous small vs big factory visit which we'd had so much trouble with at Chequers.* She liked the whole thing. In fact, it was an amazing meeting, lasting the best part of an hour. With one or two small exceptions, she was very happy with the whole tour. We had to make contingency plans about what would happen if she went to Venice, to the Council of Ministers meetings, and the effects

---

* This meeting, at a biscuit factory in Lancashire, was not, in the end, very successful in grabbing media attention at the start of the campaign.

that would have on two of the days. But I think, with one or two very small allowances, the entire tour has been approved.

I went off with Peter to White's and we had a jolly good, slightly liquid lunch. We both felt very relaxed and in a very good mood. The manifesto – at least the achievements book – was now with the printers and the tour was virtually agreed. Over lunch, Peter and I went through our roles for the campaign. He suggested that my job should be – apart from the press conferences and television – to be responsible for contact with the editors and journalists and television people. I would be very happy with that, so I suggested that we should see the Prime Minister early next week to confirm the details.

Back at the office all seemed to be quiet, so I packed up a box and came home. At half past five the phone went. It was the office, and they wanted me to go and record something for *Today*. Evidently Molly Meacher had got wind that I had briefed the Sunday lobby attacking – so it was said – 'Hands Across Britain'. I was rather reluctant to do anything, because it would only elevate the whole matter. Eventually they managed to persuade the *Today* programme to drop it by revealing exactly what I had said to the lobby.

Dinner at Karen's and Bernard's and then down to the country. On Saturday, David Hart rang for a general chat, in the course of which he asked me what the slogans of the campaign were. I didn't have the faintest idea, and I've asked him to get a note and put it in to Thatcher. He also offered to read through the alternative manifesto, which will be coming up on the Sunday. I think that would be more than useful.

Howell rang to really make my long weekend. We are now going to meet at York Terrace* at 10.30 on Sunday morning for an IRN interview at 11.15, followed by *This Week, Next Week*, when I will be taking on Bryan Gould and John Prescott.† In many ways the campaign is already starting. Still, I will get back to the country after that.

Monday 4 May

Today is a holiday, so I spent it in the country. Peter rang at about 9.15 a.m. and a) said that he was in the office working, and b) made one or two comments about the achievements part of the manifesto. Obviously he was making the point that he was there working while I was idling in the country. I pointed out to him where I'd been the day before, and we just had a joke about it. I came up to London this evening.

Tuesday 5 May

Life started off in earnest. At 7.15, Howell came round with Norman Dodds, and we went off to LBC, where I did an interview about the civil service strike. I made a point of asking the civil service to spare the long-term unemployed.

After that on to an editorial breakfast at TV-am. The whole crowd were there. It went on a bit, and people obviously thought I had something to do with the central conduct of the campaign. They produced polls which showed some amazing figures – not

---

* My home in London.
† John Prescott, 1938–. Labour MP for Kingston upon Hull East, 1970–2010; shadow Secretary of State for Energy, 1987–88; Transport, 1988–93; Employment, 1993–94; Deputy Prime Minister, 1997–2007.

only we were 44/45 per cent, Labour 30 per cent and the Alliance about 25 per cent, but even in the local government polls we were 40, Labour were 30 and the Alliance were about 28 or 29. We appear to be a very, very long way ahead.

Left for the office at 9.15 for a fairly tedious meeting about programme development, which would be very important in my old world but now so much had changed was of no great moment. I kept Geoffrey Holland and Roger Dawe back and agreed the wording of our part of the manifesto. They were quite happy with it, and Geoffrey looked as if he'd accept the chairmanship of the new modified commission. I saw Howell for a moment or two and then off to No. 10.

I met Norman inside the door. He came over to me with a broad grin and said, 'Ah, David, I see we've been fighting again.'

'Good lord, Norman,' I said, 'you've been reading all the wrong papers,' and he burst out laughing and went off. Well, as long as we can keep the relationship on this basis, I don't think we really do have any particular problems.

Thatcher was in tremendous form, criticising the work that had been done so far and having a go at a great deal of Nigel's section – Part One. I was just sitting back letting them get on with it. I did intervene once. Part of the draft said that when threatened we had gone in to protect the Falklands, and I said, 'No, no, what we want to protect is the people of the Falklands, not the Falklands – it's about people, not property.'

'Oh no,' she said and gave me a terribly fierce look, 'Georgia, South Georgia was about property – we're about protecting property *and* people,' and that was an end to that.

Later we came to my chapter, employment and jobs, which had been put together with Trade and Industry. My whole world suddenly started to unravel because out of the blue they produced a brand-new paper – one that I'd just not seen before. What made it rather worse was that, before long, it became quite clear that the Prime Minister herself had redrafted the whole section the evening before, so naturally she was very much wedded to it.

There wasn't too much wrong with it, for she had put it, I must confess, in much better shape and rather more tersely than I had written it. I did try to point out, rather gingerly, that at the Chequers meeting I had been asked to pad it out, but no one paid much attention.

Then we came to the third of my guarantees. This was the great bone of contention with the Treasury: whether we could give a guarantee of work (my choice) or use the words 'work towards a guarantee' (the Treasury's choice) for all those unemployed between eighteen and fifty for more than two years. This only meant that they could have a place on either the new community programme or a job club or an enterprise allowance. But the Prime Minister had rephrased it so that the third guarantee appeared merely to give a place on the Restart programme, which is a six-month interview.

I protested, probably too strongly, and once or twice intervened, saying, 'I'm sorry, but if you really want to have my great prize of unemployment coming down to 2 million, then I really do need to have this guarantee.'* To no avail. In the end the

---

* I was quite wrong – unemployment came steadily down well beneath 2 million in 1989.

Prime Minister agreed on a fairly soggy form of words which said that after the third guarantee – applying particularly to the Restart interview – we could say that it is our aim within the lifetime of the government to move towards a position in which we could make various offerings to all those under fifty etc. etc. At that point, realising that this was not a winnable battle, I decided to keep quiet.

After this, we moved on to the Home Office, and I got into a dust-up with Douglas Hurd.* They had come up with the idea of a broadcasting review board, which would look at all programmes. I said I thought that this would be a source of strength to the BBC and would help them keep their people under control. The Home Secretary disagreed with me publicly, which, I suspect, shows that it's probably not a bad thing to do.

The meeting dragged on interminably until about 1 o'clock. I left the Prime Minister sitting with Nigel Lawson, who was saying that the dollar has been under a tremendous strain – 'You know, on Friday we supported the pound as much as we could and now...' – and I left them to it.

As we walked out of the building, I told Douglas Hurd that I didn't mean to interfere with his area, and he was quite under-standing about it.

When I came out of No. 10, instead of going to the Savile Club, I turned round and went back to the office and asked them for a little lunch. Looking up the charts, I noticed that

---

* Douglas Hurd (Baron Hurd of Westwell since 1997), 1930–. Entered the government in 1979; Home Secretary, 1985–89.

interest rates had dropped to 9 per cent on Interbank on my screen, but the pound had still climbed up to 1.69. It does look to me that there is considerable scope for cuts in interest rates.

That morning, on the way to my Gough Street interview with IRN, Howell had shown me the first manifesto mock-up. Although I was quite pleased with it, there was a statement at the end which we couldn't possibly show to the Prime Minister. I'm afraid she has such a detailed mind that unless every last thing is accurate, we won't be able to get any of it past her. I arranged for Roger and the others to come in at 2 o'clock.

It was already about twenty past one, so I rang Stephen Sherbourne and told him that tomorrow we would have got the 'First Eight Years' booklet into a better shape for the Prime Minister to see. We fixed a provisional appointment at 3.15 tomorrow, when Peter Morrison and I would bring Margaret not only the draft of the accomplishments booklet but also a note detailing the jobs of various people at central office.

Then I had meetings with Roger Dawe and all my other officials about the new form of wording in the manifesto, and we agreed some guarantees which could be extended. In the early afternoon, I had a meeting fixed with John MacGregor, Nick Ridley* and other colleagues. We discussed the way the Scottish

---

* Nicholas Ridley (Baron Ridley of Liddesdale after 1992), 1929–93. Conservative MP, 1959–92; junior minister in the 1970–74 Heath government, sacked in 1972; Minister of State, Foreign Office, 1979–81; financial secretary to the Treasury, 1981–83; Secretary of State for Transport, 1983–86; Environment, 1986–89; Trade, 1989–90; resigned after ill-judged remarks about Germany.

Rating Bill (or community charge)* would work. I think it's moderately all right, but it turned out to be a long discussion. Eventually, we got to the point where we said that if you exclude one or two categories of the disabled or the difficult cases in our society from having to pay the new charge, you've really got to exclude the whole lot. Anyway, the meeting on rates didn't finish until I think after 4.

I went back to the department to have another series of meetings, including a discussion about the Public Expenditure Survey round. This was fairly boring, except that just looking down the list, I hit upon the great wheeze of perhaps doing something to get rid of the Job Release Scheme, which would give us some £70 or £80 million a year to spend. That made everybody enormously happy, and I said, 'Well, whatever you do, keep all your calculations yourself, agree them with me and I will take them to the Treasury, and let's see if we can get some benefit from all the work we're actually going to give up.' So it was quite a satisfactory meeting.

I then went on to meet Peter Lane, the National Union chairman, at Boodles for a drink. Peter's problem was simple: he didn't quite know what to do during the election campaign. I told him that there were two great areas on which he could perhaps concentrate. First of all, I said, there are our marginal seats.

---

* This measure, passed by the Commons in December 1986, abolished domestic rates as a means of raising local government revenue in Scotland. The replacement of the system by the new 'community charge' meant everyone liable to the tax in a given area would pay the same regardless of income and sparked off a widespread campaign of civil disobedience in Scotland, where feelings were particularly strong because it was felt that the country was being used as a 'guinea pig' before the tax was applied to England and Wales. The poll tax fiasco is richly documented in David Butler, Andrew Adonis and Tony Travis, *Failure in British Government: The Politics of the Poll Tax* (Oxford: Oxford University Press, 1994).

He should concentrate not on the whole list of 140 or 150 critical seats but on those where the Alliance is likely to make a break-through – that could be a very useful and valuable area. Then I discussed the prospect of him setting up some sort of network, in which he can get feedback on the reaction to television and speeches and everything else that we do from our people out in the field, so we can have our finger on the pulse throughout the campaign. He seemed very enthralled by both prospects and off he went.

Later, I went home and worked on the box for an hour, then went off to the Swiss Cottage Hotel to meet with Lita.

Wednesday 6 May

I woke this morning with some difficulty. I'd had an extremely good dinner at Nick Lloyd's the night before – there were all sorts of people there, including Michael Dobbs and Howell. In any event, when I painfully got myself sensible, I realised that I was due to have breakfast with Jeffrey Archer* at the Savoy. For once I got there about a minute or two after eight and actually before him. He was in very good form, and we chatted about all sorts of inconsequentials. I told him that the Prime Minister was very delighted with what he'd been doing, and this cheered him up immensely. He told me that his case was about to come to court and that the *News of the World* were on the point of admitting he couldn't possibly have been with any girl. Poor

---

* Jeffrey Archer (Baron Archer of Weston-super-Mare since 1992), 1940–. Conservative MP, 1969–74; deputy chairman of Conservative Party, 1985–86; prolific author and indefatigable source of controversy. For his difficulties with the *News of the World* (and the *Daily Star*), see Michael Crick, *Jeffrey Archer: Stranger than Fiction* (London: Fourth Estate, 1999 edition).

Jeffrey. What he fails to understand is that his difficulty is not whether he went with this girl, but really because he paid somebody £12,000 in cash for an alibi. Anyway, he told me he was going to campaign in forty-two constituencies in the twenty-one days of the campaign, and there is no doubt he's very ambitious and works hard.

I was very grateful to him – at least, I hope I'm grateful – for allowing me to put £3,000 into his new play.* On the way to the car, I said, 'By the way, Jeffrey, there's a very odd story I've heard from one or two sources from the media that I'm going to be chairman of the party.'

'Oh, well, let me explain,' he said. 'I was in the House last week and three ministers – two ministers of state and one parliamentary secretary' – he offered to give me the names but I wasn't interested – 'came up to me and told me that Lord Young had gone into central office this side of the election but that he'd come out the other side as chairman of the party and would sort the whole thing out to get the organisation right.' He added that they thought he would be my deputy chairman. Evidently, I would be chairman of the party *and* carry on my Secretary of State job. Well, I just don't see that for one moment, and I suspect more than anything else it's wishful thinking on the part of Jeffrey.

I went off to No. 10 for a meeting of EF, the subcommittee on local finance. I had a brief chat with John MacGregor, who said he'd looked at the new wording of my manifesto section at

---

* *Beyond Reasonable Doubt*, performed at the Queen's Theatre in London the same year. I passed my financial interest in the play to my daughters, who eventually made a small profit.

3 o'clock that morning and eventually got too tired to work it all out, but he would return to it later that day. We went into the meeting, which went on for two hours and twenty-five minutes. I think we got a lot of things done, including rent decontrol and a number of other matters. I was sitting next to John Patten,* and at one point, he turned round and said: 'David, I do hope we're going to have a video for the manifesto,' then told me some work he'd been doing with videos. This jogged my mind, since I'd forgotten all about it – the Prime Minister had turned the idea down a week or so ago. I resolved to do something about it. I came out at 11.25 and decided to go back to the department. I sent a message to Peter Morrison saying I would come over to central office at noon.

I saw John Turner, who had a number of routine matters which I still have to deal with in the department. Then I saw Howell, who told me he was waiting for the final proof of the 'Our First Eight Years' achievements booklet. I told him of my conversation with John Patten, and that I was going to try to clear it to see if we should have the video after all. I was going over to speak to Peter to see what we could do – in the meantime, could he have words with Tim Bell to start to clear the ground?

Peter was in splendid form. He'd just had to go dashing off to Chiswick or somewhere because the Prime Minister couldn't attend some function and he was standing in for her. We agreed

---

* John Patten (Baron Patten of Wincanton since 1997), 1945–. Lecturer, 1969–79; councillor in Oxford, 1973–76; Conservative MP, 1979–97; junior minister, 1985–92; Secretary of State for Education, 1992–94.

that we were going to see the Prime Minister later on and went through a list. We agreed between us that I would go ahead and deal with the media over the adoption conference. I told Peter of the idea of the video, and he was very pleased, although he suggested that I clear it with Norman.

After Peter went off, I saw Roger Boaden and fixed that if he was in the building after Cabinet, I would meet him and Nick Edwards to see if we could agree the Welsh day of the Prime Minister's tour. Then I saw Michael Dobbs, who was in very good form. I told him about the video. Michael said he would take it up with the chairman and let me know. I also asked him to clear Tim's position and said, as a compromise, that if Norman was still uncomfortable we could say that Tim is working for me.

Anyway, I then went off for lunch at the Ritz with Simon Heffer of the *Daily Telegraph*, which was very pleasant. Came back to the House and had a splendid up and downer – a question on unemployment where I was on moderately good form. I think it went quite well. Then I came out, and there was Howell waiting for me with the first draft. There are still one or two things to be done to it. We went off to a meeting at No. 10 – I should explain that I'd had a message just before lunch that a private notice question had come up in the House on the scandal that was going on about MI5 investigating Harold Wilson.[*] The Prime Minister had to go off to the House to answer the

---

[*] This saga, brought to public notice by the publication of Peter Wright's *Spycatcher* (London: Doubleday, 1987), is discussed by Stephen Dorril and Robin Ramsay in *Smear! Wilson and the Secret State* (London: Fourth Estate, 1991).

question, and so we had all fixed to meet at Stephen Sherbourne's office in No. 10.

Peter Morrison, Stephen, Howell and I went through and agreed the final form of the achievements book. We agreed that on the following day, Howell would take the final proof and agree it with Robin Harris over at central office before it went off for publication.

Michael Dobbs rang through to say that Norman had been in favour of the video, so I fixed with Stephen that we would just go ahead and do it without telling the Prime Minister. I would just take it as part of my manifesto arrangements. Then I went upstairs for a long chat with Brian Griffiths. We agreed all the wording of my part of the manifesto, which I think is all right, though I'm still a bit worried about the third guarantee.

The President of Mozambique was there on a state visit, and I got slightly isolated in Brian's office till I found the old way back, going through the garden room of the basement. I came out of the Cabinet Office to rush back to the department, where we had a quick meeting on the future structure of the MSC, after all the changes. Then a very relaxed Keith Joseph was waiting to see me. We talked about a number of matters, including some policy issues for after the election. He told me he hadn't made up his mind quite definitely, but if he was approached, he would like to consider going into the Lords. He also asked me to be a witness at his wedding, which I thought was really marvellous and told him nothing would give me greater pleasure.*

---

* In fact, Joseph did not marry Yolanda Sheriff, his second wife, until August 1990.

After Keith left, I gave an interview on the civil service strike, which I expect to get worse in the next few days. Tim Bell arrived. Howell just popped in for a second, as he was getting very busy finalising all the matters with the printer. I think it's given him rather a lot of work to do. I should say that earlier on, when I discussed this with Michael Dobbs, he'd suggested that we get Antony Jay,* from Video Arts, involved. I'd also mentioned this to Howell. Well, speaking to Tim, it was immediately apparent that a) Tim had got this message, and b) he'd spoken to Antony and was fixing to see him tomorrow afternoon, when he would get all the details going. We discussed the form the video would take, and the more we discussed it the better it got. I finally agreed with Tim that he would see Antony and we would meet on Friday afternoon to start to flesh out the whole thing.

Tim was quite kind about my performance on *This Week, Next Week* last Sunday, and he's very keen about the work we've been doing. He very much liked the JTS advertising, and the more I think about it the more the past year has been a marvellous dream. I really am beginning to think that we can turn unemployment into an election-winning issue.

Anyway, we settled the video. It looks as if now my role is more clear-cut for the campaign itself. The polls and everything appear to be going on quite well. I'm beginning to see there is some light at the end of the tunnel, but there is one hell of a lot more work to be done. I suppose the frightening thing is that

---

* Antony (after 1988 Sir Antony) Jay, 1930–2016. Worked for BBC; co-author (with Jonathan Lynn) of highly successful BBC comedies *Yes, Minister* and *Yes, Prime Minister*. Mrs Thatcher was a great fan of these programmes.

the following weekend is the decision, and a week or so – eight or nine days – after that, all the early arrangements have to be in place. Oh well!

Thursday 7 May

I was woken at about quarter past seven by David Hart, who rang concerned about whether the Prime Minister had looked at his slogan. He was very keen that we should be using 'Britain's on the Move Again', which I actually thought was very much better. I said I would go and raise it with everyone after Cabinet. I had hardly put the phone down from him when Paul Twyman rang. He was concerned that sufficient work wasn't being done at central office about all the backing briefs – poor Paul, he's really looking for a job to do... I don't think I've got one for him. He's a bit of a fish out of water there, but still, we'll just have to see how we go.

I then went into the office, and the first thing we had was prayers. Robert wasn't there, but I remembered that he was going up for the local elections and everybody, as you can imagine, was in a very cheery mood. John Lee[*] was very complimentary about my appearance on *This Week, Next Week* – in fact, he told me that I looked much better in the suit I had worn then than the one I was now wearing, which was light blue. It was less formal. This led us into a very amusing conversation about personal appearance, in which we suggested new clothes and a diet for Ken Clarke. I don't think he paid the slightest bit of attention to us.

---

[*] John Lee (Baron Lee of Trafford since 2006), 1942–. Conservative MP, 1979–92; junior minister, Department of Employment, 1986–89.

I also told them all about the plans we had for producing a video, and that seemed to go down very well. Over to No. 10 at 9.30, where there was a meeting on the effects of agriculture, which I quite liked because I managed to repulse the plans of both Agriculture and the Greens for sending out a circular, which would have slowed down the development of agricultural land. John Patten was there. 'Well, David, what about the video?' he asked.

I said, 'It's on.' He looked very pleased and not a little surprised.

That meeting finished, and there was a gap for a chat before Cabinet. I had a quick word with John Wakeham* – I said, 'John, I know that you're organising the appearances on television during the campaign. I hope to be doing quite a bit with the media – perhaps you and I should have a word together on Monday?' He agreed, quite happily, I thought. We then went back into Cabinet, which was really quite a cheery occasion. I reported on the civil service strike, which was beginning to go a little bit more severe. It looks as if as many as 100,000 people could have their payments late this week. Cabinet finished, and we had a few minutes before the next meeting, which gave me the chance to have a word with the Prime Minister. I said, 'Prime Minister, would you please see Peter Morrison, who's got some things to agree with you about the press conferences?' She said she would.

---

* John Wakeham (Baron Wakeham of Maldon since 1992), 1932–. Conservative MP, 1974–92; Chief Whip, 1983–87; Lord Privy Seal, 1987–88; Leader of the House of Commons, 1987–89; Lord President of the Council, 1988–89; Secretary of State for Energy, 1989–92; Leader of the House of Lords, 1992–94. John was seriously injured in the 1984 Brighton bombing, which killed his first wife.

I went outside and saw Norman, so I told him about the manifesto video. He was a little bit startled at first, then seemed to relax. I mentioned about the radio and television and at first he said, 'Well, we've got to be very careful about this. We've got to make sure the same messages get across.'

So I said, 'Norman, don't be silly, I'm only there just to make sure you can be contacted when you're out,' and this seemed to make him happier. But I have little doubt at all that I'm going to have some difficulties with Norman, and probably quite rightly. Possibly I'm trying to push my way in in ways perhaps I shouldn't. However, I think it's quite important.

I also caught hold of John MacGregor, and we fixed that we would meet later on today to agree the wording of the manifesto.

We then went back into a rather long EA and came out just before lunch. I sat down with Nick Edwards and Roger Boaden, and we agreed more details of the Prime Minister's tour in Wales. Nick had some good ideas about where she should go.

I dashed back to the office for a few minutes to see Howell and to find out how things were getting on. Everything has now gone in for the achievements booklet, so let's hope that will be all right. I then went to an industrial fund lunch in the House. It was only a small lunch for a dozen people, and to my surprise I knew half of them.

I went back to the office and saw Roger. We agreed what I could actually concede on the manifesto and got a message that I was to see the chief secretary at 7.35.

Peter and Roger Boaden then came round and we went through the tour again. Peter told me that he'd arranged to see the Prime Minister the following morning. As I was due to go up north, I said, 'Go ahead and see her by yourself.' We started going through the tour business – I think everything was more or less fixed. We have some problems, though, because there is a Whit Monday Bank Holiday, and many of the items that we had planned for her to do, which we thought would be all right on a Bank Holiday, now turn out to be difficult. So, we're now considering going to Alton Towers.

Before that got very far, I got hauled out to do two television interviews about the civil service strike. One was on the green opposite the Commons. When I did my piece the first time, a passing ambulance succeeded in making sure that it was all drowned out.

Then back to No. 10 for another two hours of policy meetings, including the changes we were making to housing and, of course, the Inner London Education Authority.* I think these will be quite interesting items in the manifesto.

I called in to see Stephen, who is very worried about the video and says I should see the Prime Minister about it. I agreed with him that when I came back from Middlesbrough, I would see her. I then just had a few minutes to go back to the department to finish off the box, which is happily now getting less and less, and then over to the House to see John MacGregor and Brian Griffiths. We actually managed to agree the wording for the

---

* This was duly abolished after the election.

manifesto. I also agreed with John about the PES transfers and about the spend. So, it looks as if now I'm all set and we're ready to go.

I had little time to do anything after that, and I was due to meet David and Susan Wolfson for dinner. Just as I was going over, I got a message to ring Howell at home. He told me he'd had a very good meeting with Antony Jay and we fixed up for 4.30 on Friday.

After a very good dinner with David and Susan, I decided at the last minute to go back to central office, for this was the day of the local authority elections, and I'd told Peter I might call in.

When I got near the building, all the television lights were bathing the front of the place. I went in for a moment to the television room and then up to Peter's office, where I sat next to him. A whole crowd was there: Michael Dobbs, Nick Edwards, Nick Ridley and John Patten, and all the flock from central office. I was immediately given another large Scotch, and we carried on gradually getting more and more elated. I ended up doing television interviews, radio and TV-am until 2 o'clock in the morning. I retired home very happy indeed, because it looked as if we were doing far better in the local government elections than anybody had ever dreamed.

Friday 8 May

I woke up with a very sore head – I'd obviously celebrated too much the night before – and slowly and painfully came awake. John Turner was waiting for me downstairs, and we went off to fly to Middlesbrough for the day. When we got to the raised portion of the M4, we could see right away that something was up – the traffic was entirely at a standstill. So, we cut off down the A4 and that was almost as bad. By ten to nine it was quite clear we weren't going to make the flight. This was slightly embarrassing because I was going to see the two bishops – the Bishops of Whitby and Middlesbrough – and I'd already had to cancel a visit in January because of snow.

However, we eventually reached the airport, and to my surprise we were just a couple of minutes after nine. They rushed us up to the plane, which had actually left the gate but had stopped, and they opened the door. It was a DC9 with a ladder on board, which came down so we were able to get on. It took us some time to get back to take-off position. When we landed, I said to the captain, 'Thank you very much for enabling us to catch the plane' – 'And thank you very much', said someone behind, 'for making us all so late.' So, I suppose that it cost us a hundred votes, which is a very expensive way to fly.

Thankfully, we had a very good visit to Middlesbrough. The bishops weren't asking for very much really, and I was able to keep them quite satisfied. On the way back, I went to see John Hall,* who had just bought a great Londonderry place. I took him aside and told him we were probably going to visit the MetroCentre in Gateshead during the Prime Minister's tour. This really bucked him up enormously. Driving away, I suddenly thought I would check to see what he was down for in the

---

* John (since 1991 Sir John) Hall, 1933–. Chairman of Cameron Hall Developments, 1973–93; chairman of Newcastle United, 1992–97; director of the Bank of England, 1996–98; developer of the MetroCentre.

honours list, to make sure he was properly rewarded at the right time.

We flew back to London, arriving before 2 o'clock for the drive back to the office. I saw Roger Daw and reported to him on a deal I was able to do with the chief secretary. Norman Blackwell came round with Howell. They had rewritten the manifesto, so we went through checking all the wording.

At 4.30, Tim Bell came along with Antony Jay, the director of the film, and the first draft of the script. Well, I must say that the first draft was very good indeed, and I'm getting keener and keener on the whole thing. I only hope that the Prime Minister goes for it. Tim held back and told me that she had invited him to Chequers at 6.30 on Saturday evening. The problem will be keeping the visit secret. We discussed all the slogans that he and David Hart had come up with. I also asked him to raise the whole idea of the video with her. I think he will do such a very good job at selling it, and I gave him a couple of spare copies of the scripts. I also asked him to discuss with her exactly what I would be doing over that period, in particular the media work.

We had another look at the achievements booklet, and the more I look at it the better it now appears to be. I think it's going to be a fabulous little production.

I went home for dinner. The whole family were there for Friday night. I was feeling very tired indeed, but I had a commitment that evening to go and do *Newsnight*. Howell came round to pick me up at ten to ten. I had a wash and a change, then off we went. There had been some high jinks during the day, as Bryan Gould couldn't appear on the programme. We had a succession of different names from the Labour side before we ended up with John Prescott, which pleased me immensely. I made up my mind that I would keep as quiet and sweet and reasonable as possible.

On the way up, Howell said to me: 'I must tell you a marvellous story.' He said that after prayers yesterday, Colin Moynihan,* who is Kenneth Clarke's PPS, came up to him and said: 'You must tell me, is there any way in which David can renounce his peerage?'

'Course not,' said Howell, 'it takes an Act of Parliament.'

'Ah, if it's an Act it possibly can be done. Then we've got to persuade him to renounce it and come and join our House.'

'Why?' asked Howell, knowing full well.

'Well,' he said, 'after she goes, he will be acceptable to all of her people and he will also be acceptable to all the other side.'

So there I was being sounded out for Prime Minister! I was told afterwards that the *Evening News* had been running the same sort of line recently. I've got to be very careful about this because it's totally impossible, and certainly if it ever were to appear probable, or even remotely possible, it would compromise my working relationship with her for ever.

Newsnight went very well – I'm now getting more and more relaxed on the television, and I think it's coming through very well indeed. I suppose by the time the whole campaign is over I might be quite polished.

---

* Colin Moynihan (Baron Moynihan of Leeds since 1997), 1955–. Conservative MP, 1983–92; Minister for Sport, 1987–90.

Saturday 9 May

I slept late after the exertions of the night before and got up and messed around for most of the morning. David Hart rang through to discuss slogans. I suggested that he call the Prime Minister and mention them to her. Apart from that it was a quiet and fairly peaceful sort of day. Late in the afternoon we packed up, dropped Tiffany* over at Karen and Bernard's, and drove down to Willie Whitelaw's. It was a gorgeous summer's day, and when we got to Dorneywood it was still very warm, although it was about 6.30 in the evening. I'd been slightly worried – more than slightly, I had been worrying all day about her meeting with Tim and the effect on Norman – because in the morning I had made up my mind I was going to ring the Prime Minister but didn't get round to it because they delivered a new video tape recorder and there one or two other domestic distractions. By the time we got to Dorneywood it was too late to ring her, because Tim Bell was due to see her at half past six.

Willie and Celia were sitting in the garden. Willie had been speaking up in Droitwich and had taken off his jacket and tie. We had a drink in the sunshine. Willie was quite relaxed, and Celia is really a marvellous person. We chatted about general political things – chit chat about who does what. After a while, we went up to have a wash and get ready for dinner, for the Hurds had arrived together with Kenneth and Mary Baker.

It was a very enjoyable, slightly liquid dinner, in which everything came round to political matters. Afterwards we

---

* Our miniature long-haired dachshund.

adjourned into their study. At one point in the conversation, talking about the Prime Minister, Douglas Hurd turned round to me and said: 'David, you really must keep the Prime Minister calm during the election – she'll listen to you.' We were talking in general about political dispositions, and I suddenly realised for the first time that almost unknown to myself I'd become part of the charmed circle. I actually was very much in. Kenneth let slip during the evening that he'd been invited to do *Question Time* as one of the three special editions they would be having during the campaign, and I wondered slightly about that – how many people would be going off on their own and booking their own television, even though John Wakeham was supposed to be coordinating it.

Willie was full of reminiscence about earlier elections – after all, this is his eleventh election; he fought his first campaign (the first two or three, I think, were unsuccessful)* in 1950. So, he really does go back a very long way.

As we all broke up to go, I took Kenneth aside and told him to ring me on Sunday evening, and I would let him know how things were going. And so, we went off slightly unsteadily to bed. I slept through – rather heavily – to about ten to nine the following morning.

We came down for breakfast – all the papers were there, all full of this meeting which was to take place at No. 10. Some papers went very heavily for 4 June – I think personally just to get some variety. The *Express* in particular went for 4 June, but

---

* Whitelaw lost his first two election battles in East Dunbartonshire in 1950 and 1951.

most went for the 11th. Two or three said we would be having steak for lunch, which slightly surprised Willie and I because as far as I recall the Prime Minister never has steak for lunch. One thing which amused me particularly was an article by Robert Taylor in *The Observer*, which talked about the Strategy Group: me, Willie, Douglas Hurd, Nigel Lawson, Norman Tebbit, John Wakeham, Geoffrey Howe and, of course, Margaret. Evidently, according to the press, we are known as the 'Seven Dwarfs', which Willie thought was very funny.

We discussed personalities. Willie said that he thought Paul Channon[*] would probably lose, and certainly it looks that way from the local election results. If he did, Willie would suggest he came to the Lords and try to get him the Minister of State's job in the Foreign Office, which actually I think Paul would be very good at. He also thought that there was a chance that George Younger[†] might not come through. I think Willie saw him very much as being the next Leader of the Lords, which certainly doesn't upset me, because Willie knows already that's a job I'm not the slightest bit interested in.

We spent a pleasant morning sitting reading all the papers and comparing the stories. Peregrine Worsthorne's leader in the *Sunday Telegraph* was particularly favourable. At about 11.30, we set off for Chequers. I went with Willie, his driver and his security man in his government Daimler Jaguar. Then Lita went off

---

[*] Paul Channon (Baron Kelvedon after 1997), 1935–2007. Conservative MP, 1959–97; Minister for Trade, 1983–86; Secretary of State for Trade and Industry, 1986–87; Secretary of State for Transport, 1987–89.

[†] George Younger (Viscount Younger of Leckie after 1992), 1931–2003. Distinguished military record; Conservative MP, 1964–92; Secretary of State for Scotland, 1979–86; Defence, 1986–89; chairman, Royal Bank of Scotland, 1992–2001.

with Celia. We got quite close to Chequers by about noon. We were obviously half an hour early, so we took a side turning and went on a long detour right up over the hills and back again. This was very amusing because we got thoroughly lost and ended up only a hundred yards from where we'd set off. We came out right behind one of the look-out scouts with a walkie-talkie, who was there to warn of our arrival. We went past the main gates of Chequers, which no one ever uses. There were two cameramen there, and when we came to the main entrance there was quite a big crowd of photographers, who took pictures. I don't know what sort of picture they could have taken as we swept past.

John Wakeham got there ahead of us, and Norman arrived shortly afterwards. Then Nigel arrived and Geoffrey and Douglas, so we were all set.

We started off with drinks in the downstairs room, and the Prime Minister started to talk through dates. The first date we really went through was 4 June. The real drawback was not so much the fact that it was a Jewish holiday, rather that we wouldn't have been able to get the business through in the House. But we did have a fairly long discussion about that. Then we had a far longer discussion about 11 June. The Prime Minister knew the unemployment figures were out on the Thursday, six days after the Retail Price Index figures. We had a clear idea for unemployment and a vague-ish sensible sort of guess for the Recognition of Prior Learning. Then the only other figure to come out would be the balance of payments figures, which it was impossible to even guess at.

Next, we considered 18 June. There were some arguments

about letting the campaign go too long. I said, 'Look, Prime Minister, there are three good reasons: one is there will be more City fraud cases – Saunders* has just been arrested, and that will rebound on us whatever, even though it's no fault of ours. The second lot of unemployment figures are due on the 18th, and I can't be sure what they'll be because the civil service dispute will actually make it worse.' There was another reason too, which just now escapes me.

We went round the table and she concluded quite firmly that it would have to be 11 June. We went on to discuss some administrative arrangements and particular roles that people would be doing, but certainly the political issue in the choice of a date for the election now seemed to be absolutely clear.

At about quarter past one, we went in for lunch. I sat between Nigel and Douglas, and contrary to all the stories in the papers we weren't having steak – we actually had turkey. Denis Thatcher joined us. It was his birthday, and I clean forgot to wish him happy birthday, but never mind. DT can't actually eat steak; he has to have it in a stew because of his teeth, so I now know I can never expect to ever have steak there. It was a cheery lunch and everybody was very relaxed. At about ten past two, we went into the hall to have coffee. Keith Britto was there, the party's chief statistician who studies all the polling data. Over coffee I saw my chance and went up to the Prime Minister and said: 'Did you have a good meeting with Tim?'

---

* Ernest Saunders, 1935–, was the chairman of Guinness, who, with three other businessmen, was charged with insider trading while the company fought to take over Distillers. The case eventually reached the European Court of Human Rights, which found in favour of the defendants.

She looked startled and said, 'Ssshhh!' She didn't want Norman to hear. Evidently it was a very good meeting with Tim, and I found out she was now keen on the idea of the video. So, my big worry was over, and I told her it was going to be my task, my own selected task, to deal with the media and the newspapers and everyone else over the period of the campaign. She was very happy and very relaxed with that.

On the way upstairs Norman said: 'David, I see from the papers that you're now the favourite to follow her and you're prepared to renounce your peerage and fight a by-election.'

'What a lot of rubbish!' I said. I think it was that story in the *Evening News* the week before – obviously Norman was only half joking with me, so I've got to be very careful about that sort of thing.

In the meeting downstairs things were still quite relaxed. Margaret wanted to go into all the details of the campaign. And it was quite clear that she'd agreed the list of those who were going to be at the press conferences, that she was going to go out during the day and that Norman would go out to make speeches elsewhere. It was agreed that I'd be at central office and that I would also work along with John Wakeham on the television, but John would be in charge of those going on the box. Willie was in charge of matters of policy. That part went very well. But she was concerned about the party election broadcasts, and I think she was getting the impression that things weren't far enough advanced – there's still a great deal of tension between her and Norman.

Once we'd cleared all the administrative details, the Prime

Minister said, 'Let's go and look at the figures.' We went up-stairs and Keith Britto joined us. Norman gave a first-rate résumé of all the polls, including our private polls and the effect of the local government elections. He said that they'd looked at the local government election results for 1983 and seen the shift between them and the general election of that year. They'd taken this year's local government election results – unfortunately there were no elections in London or Scotland, and he couldn't get the figures from the '83 Welsh results – but nevertheless, they'd calculated what the result would be in the general elec-tion itself. Depending on the poll you used, there was a broad range of possible results. There was one at only eight seats clear majority, which was just taking the straight local government results, up to some which went as high as 126. Norman summed up that, in his own view, at the moment we were looking at about a nineteen-seat majority.

We discussed that round and round for about three quarters of an hour and in the end, she said, 'Right, I've got as much as I need now, I shall sleep on it.' Then we discussed the arrange-ments we were going to have for tomorrow when there would be a Cabinet.

As we were breaking up, I told Douglas and Nigel and Geoffrey that they might be required for making the video on Thursday. I told them I would ring through to their offices. Then Willie and I were driven away together. The photographers were still patiently waiting outside, and I said to Willie in the car that it had gone very well. He said it went remarkably well. I think we are all very happy and content.

We went back to Dorneywood, arriving back before Lita and Celia. Willie and I went for a walk in the garden. He explained to me exactly how Dorneywood operates, which is a bit bizarre. Evidently, he pays for all the food and drink himself. The government merely provides the house, and, I suppose, the household staff. We went through the garden and he showed me how the National Trust had been looking after it. After about three quarters of an hour, Lita and Celia came back, and then we went in for a chat and a drink. Later we watched the news, which was very amusing – the BBC mentioned us but didn't have pictures, while ITV had a fairly spectacular shot. It said: 'Now comes the Lordly car, the car with the two Lords.' They managed to freeze-frame a picture and highlight it, and there was Willie and there was I sitting in the car. All the programmes were speculating on 11 June and taking it as a pretty foregone conclusion but saying that the Prime Minister would decide tomorrow.

Over dinner, Willie became quite expansive. He told us the story of what happened with Ted Heath and how he, Willie, went into the leadership contest; how Margaret stood against Ted and what tremendous courage she had. She went to Ted at the beginning to tell him that she was going to run. She actually beat Ted in the first round, and then Willie, Jim Prior and Geoffrey Howe went in. Willie then pulled out, and told us how he'd been loyal to her. He said that he didn't come from the same natural constituency – he was not the same side of the party – but noted how well they had worked together in all those years although actually they were very dissimilar people. He was very entertaining, and it was very relaxed. We sat down and had a brief chat before looking at *Mastermind* and one or two other things on the television. At about quarter past nine, we drove back to London.

I had a box to do – all these interminable boxes! Then Kenneth Baker rang, as arranged, and I hinted to him that everything was fine – I'd told him we would get together during the week. I think he was quite relaxed, and he discussed with me briefly some graphs and charts, which he is going to ask Tim Bell to do tomorrow. And then a little after that Howell rang, full of beans, absolutely full of beans. Evidently Tim Bell had had a fantastic meeting – oh, I'd forgotten to say that when I spoke to Margaret in the hall after lunch, she told me she kept Tim waiting until twenty to eight yesterday evening, but it had gone very well. Howell confirmed to me that it had been a fantastic meeting. Tim and Virginia were there till just after midnight, and he really sold her the idea of the videos. So, I arranged to see Howell in the office early the following day. A little after that, Peter Morrison rang and I told him everything was set. He had one or two things to talk to me about, and he would come into the office at quarter to nine on Monday morning. In fact, he asked me to see if I had the time free. I looked at my diary, and to my total amazement the only appointment I had the entire day was a lunchtime one with Alistair McAlpine,[*] and that I'm going to keep, even though there's probably a Strategy Group lunch at No. 10. I'll just have to bow out of that.

---

[*] Alistair McAlpine (Baron McAlpine of West Green after 1984), 1942–2014. Director, Sir Robert McAlpine & Sons, 1963–95; treasurer of Conservative Party, 1975–90; deputy chairman, 1979–83.

Tomorrow's going to be a busy day, since we've got Cabinet at 11 o'clock in all probability. And then we're started.

Monday 11 May

Peter Morrison had said he would come in to see me at 8.45, and I got to the office a few minutes late. Peter was in with Michael Quinlan. We started to go through all the arrangements. Peter said he wanted the manifesto printed on Monday night and I said no, the Tuesday or Wednesday. We went through the details and chatted a little bit about the weekend. I told him what a very good job Norman Tebbit did with his presentation. I enquired at the office and John Turner told me that, in fact, no Cabinet had yet been called. But I told Peter I was almost absolutely certain the election was going to be on 11 June, and everything about her seemed to indicate that.

He left after a while to go to a meeting with Norman. After he had gone, I used the time to make one or two phone calls. I phoned Alistair McAlpine and he very happily – I think with a sigh of relief – called off our lunch. I asked him for his home address, and he gave it to me straight away so we could shoot the video there.

Well, a few minutes later I heard that a Cabinet meeting had been booked for 11 o'clock, so everything was on. Then I found that I'd been invited in for lunch with the Strategy Group. So, I think I'm probably now a fully paid-up member. I saw Roger and made one or two detailed arrangements over the next few days. I also got a number of private things done and organised with Margaret Bell.

Anyway, off to Cabinet. There was an enormous crowd of photographers outside, taking pictures all over the place. The Prime Minister was in a very calm mood. She said she had met with a few colleagues over the weekend, and after considering all the implications she'd concluded that the time was now right for us to go for an election on 11 June. She was going now partly because of all the pressure in the media but more, much more, because we had almost completed this year's work, and we had a very exciting, imaginative and radical manifesto. We had a great deal to do, and we should now call the election and get on with it. Also, there were things on the international scene which really needed the stability of knowing who the next government was going to be.

We went through all the business. Then she asked me to report on what figures would come up during an election campaign, and I told my colleagues the unemployment figures would be released on Thursday. I couldn't give the numbers then, but I think I smiled. On the Friday would be the cost of living, and that looked all right. Paul Channon reported on the trade data. And then we came to Commons business – she turned to the Chief Whip, John Wakeham, but in fact Wakeham said that John Biffen had all the information. Biffen was sitting there looking very depressed indeed – in fact, over the past few weeks he'd been looking more and more depressed. He read out the business in Parliament in such a flat voice, you would think he was reading the last rites. Actually, my PPS, Robert Atkins, told me about a month ago that he had come across Biffen sitting, looking very disconsolate in the House, and Biffen had more or less said to him that he thought he was coming to the end of his time in government. There is no question that ever since he made that foolish appearance on television last year, saying that we needed a more balanced ticket and disavowing Thatcher, the skids have been under him.*

Anyway, we went through all the business in Parliament. There was a certain amount of dickering about what should be taken now and what should be left for after the election. The Prime Minister told us that a complete copy of the manifesto was outside. We should read it very carefully but we shouldn't ring through any alterations; we should come along to Cabinet tomorrow, where we were meeting at 9.30, and we should be prepared to settle the whole document.

She then asked us to leave and look confident but not to give a clue about the date or timing of the election because that was not going to be announced until 2 o'clock, when she was going off to the see the Queen.

As the Cabinet room emptied, I walked over to her side of the table and sat down next to her, although I noticed Tom King was still fiddling with some papers. I said, 'Prime Minister, it just occurred to me – everything is going very well, but there are one or two things. We should have a meeting, and you should see Peter about the video tape of you – the one that's going to be used for the warm-up.' She promised to have a meeting and that was fixed. I said, 'By the way, Prime Minister, I had the

---

* Biffen had also been described as a 'semi-detached' member of the Cabinet by the Prime Minister's chief press officer, Bernard Ingham.

thought that while you are about, perhaps I can take a couple of meetings for you in Finchley.'

'Oh, would you really?' she said, and her eyes lit up.

I said, 'Whatever you want me to do, just fix with your agent and I'll do whatever you like.' And then we started chatting about one or two things until Charles Powell* came over and said, 'Now, excuse us, the Northern Ireland Secretary would like to see the Prime Minister.'

'Oh well,' I joked. 'Listen, you can't talk about government; this is politics.'

'Oh no,' he said, 'what he wants to talk about is very much the heart of the campaign – the safety and security of all the people on the campaign.' I suddenly realised, feeling a little bit sick, that obviously it was about the IRA and all that, so I left rather hurriedly and went out. I picked up my copy of the manifesto and walked out with Willie and all the others.

Again, there was an enormous crowd shouting over, 'Can you give us the date of the election?' We just waved cheerily and went back to the department. I spoke to my private secretary, John Turner, and gave him the manifesto – it was quite improper, I suppose – and asked him if he could see Roger Dawe and just make sure that the wording hadn't changed. I saw Howell, who was going on fixing up appointments for the video. We had run into a snag because there was now going to be a Cabinet on the Thursday morning, which left us short of time. We discussed whether we could make the video early in

---

* Charles Powell (Baron Powell of Bayswater since 2000), 1941–. Diplomatic service, 1963–81; private secretary to Prime Minister, 1983–91.

the morning. Eventually, we concluded that we would have to go back to doing it on the Wednesday, which would be quite difficult. Then John Lee came in for a moment. I had a nice chat with him. He was obviously going to go up to his constituency – I think he will have quite a bit of work to do, but I said, 'Look, John, I'm going to be about central office. If there are any problems let me know.' And a few minutes later David Trippier* came in. He said how much he enjoyed working with me and how sorry he'd be because I told him I thought he would be going off to do something else. He certainly deserves a promotion – I think he'd rather like to be back working with me. I'll just have to think about that over the next few weeks. A few minutes after he left, it was time to return to No. 10. Again, the photographers were outside, so I gave another cheery wave before I went in. I think they are probably getting a bit fed up of seeing me.

Willie, Norman and John Wakeham were waiting inside. Margaret was still at the Palace. Willie said he thought, as Deputy Prime Minister, he would take executive authority and we could go up and help ourselves to a drink. So, we all went upstairs and started off with a drink. She came in a few minutes later and said, 'Yes, Her Majesty has consented that an election be called.' The announcement was going to go out at 2 o'clock. We had a drink and were quite cheerful and chatting – it was a big crowd, not just the Strategy Group. John Sullivan was there, and Brian Griffiths and Stephen Sherbourne – in fact, the whole

---

* David (since 1992 Sir David) Trippier, 1946–. Conservative MP, 1979–92; various junior ministerial posts, including Department of Employment, 1985–87.

team responsible for writing the manifesto. It was a relaxed sort of lunch – not too much serious business being discussed. She nagged away a couple of times – probably quite rightly – about the party election broadcasts but otherwise was fairly relaxed. I knew that Norman had to go off to a private meeting with her, but straight after lunch, I went with Peter and Norman into her study – there were some details to be settled, which took about five or ten minutes. Stephen Sherbourne was also there. Then, rather tactfully, I got out with Peter to leave Norman with her, which I think he was quite grateful for, and I went back to the department.

When I got there, it transpired that Howell would have to resign almost immediately, as he was a special adviser and not a career civil servant, and the moment the Prime Minister called the election, all these political appointments came to an end. Also, I was much more limited in the use of the government car than Norman Dodds had led me to believe, and I discussed briefly where Margaret Bell would go.

What I am very concerned about is that on Thursday we are due to announce the unemployment figures, and evidently the department couldn't hold a press conference about them. So, we discussed very briefly how that would be handled, and Michael Quinlan said he would go and check to be absolutely sure.

I had one or two phone calls again, just clearing up personal matters, and then I decided I would walk over to central office. It wasn't a bad afternoon for a walk. When I arrived, there were cameramen outside. I just went in as bold as brass. They didn't see me, I suspect, and I went up to the first floor. Peter had just slipped over to the House for a few minutes, and I sat down and spoke to Michael Dobbs – things seemed to be going quite well. Alistair McAlpine said he wanted a word, so I popped in and he talked about Tim Bell and how very valuable he is – but occasionally he goes off the handle. I told him I thought it would be best if I dealt with Tim, and then I could pass on any messages from Tim to the Prime Minister. Alistair seemed to think this was quite good, and we chatted about one or two things. He's invited me to go in at 6 o'clock most evenings for drinks with the contributors to the party, so I shall go along and do my little bit.

Then I went back and went through one or two details with Peter Morrison, who again was in a good mood and was delightful to work with. Norman came in, and I asked if he could have a few minutes. We wandered off and sat down, and there was a cutting I hadn't seen before – an article in *The Times* of that day, which had a remarkably good drawing, I thought, of me, Willie, Norman, John Wakeham and the Prime Minister. The article described our strategy meeting at No. 10 – actually at Chequers the day before – really remarkably accurately, which is quite funny really. Norman wondered how on earth they'd got it. I think he was quite worried about leaks until he saw that the description of what he had said at the meeting was actually totally inaccurate. Then I think he relaxed and realised it was just fiction.

I went through the video with him, and we agreed amongst other things that we would drop Douglas Hurd and put in Nick Ridley – not because Nick Ridley is very good on television but because of the importance of the housing element of the manifesto. Antony Jay called, and we took it together. It was only really to rehearse Norman's points, so I left Norman to get on with it. I was just chatting with Michael Dobbs and Peter when Norman came in. He said he'd been chatting with Alistair. He proceeded really to slag Tim off for a few minutes, making all sorts of inferences. He concluded that 'perhaps the best way to contain him would be if Tim went and worked through David, provided that he doesn't put it out that he's working for David, because David's got the entire charge of the campaign or the advertising or whatever'. So I reassured him, and I thought I would have to warn Tim about that point. At least Tim's position is now a little bit clearer.

When I went downstairs, the television people were there. Norman Dodds had seen me and warned me about this. They said they were terribly sorry – they looked quite disconsolate really – but could I give them an interview? 'Of course,' I said. I joked away with them a bit, and evidently they had been sitting there all afternoon and got nothing. So, I did a sort of interview which I don't think was ever used anywhere. But it seemed to make them happy – at least they could go back with something.

I walked back to the department and thought I'd speak to Tim. I told him I had cleared things with Norman, so that was all right. Then I settled down to some work on the boxes. While I was working, Howell came bustling in to say central office had been on and would I do the *Seven O'Clock News*? Norman was going to do it, but he was caught up in a meeting. I would be on with John Smith and John Pardoe,* the chairman of the Alliance campaign. Anyway, I agreed. I did a bit more box work and told Howell he should carry on with his work. Then I went over to the studio and both Johns were there. Actually, we're all quite friend-ly and they were very civilised. We did the interview, and I think it was all right – those two tended to argue with each other, and I tried to stay a bit above it. And then, walking back to the hos-pitality suite, John Pardoe told me the reason why he was chair-ing the Alliance campaign was that he was the only chap with whom the two Davids† got on well, which I thought was quite amusing.

When I got back there was a message: could I call central office? They asked me if I could do what I thought was *Newsnight*, as Norman was tied up and couldn't do it. I fixed that they would ring me at 8.30 to let me know. When I got home, Howell rang to confirm it was on. Tim rang and was very flattering about the earlier appearance on television. One or two other friends rang. I called my mother to say I would be on television at 9.30 and looked at my watch: it was ten past nine. I suddenly thought, 'Crikey, I can't get there that quickly.' I had primed up the video tape recorder for *Newsnight* and went dashing down just as Norman Dodds rang up – he'd been there since ten to but hadn't bothered. So I got in a frightful tizz and we went charging off to *Newsnight* – got there just in time, only to find out it was in fact

---

*   John Pardoe, 1934–. Liberal MP, 1966–79.
†   David Owen and David Steel, the joint leaders of the SDP–Liberal Alliance.

a 9.35 special programme as an extension of the news – it was on BBC 1 not 2, and I was on with Roy Hattersley* and Roy Jenkins.†

I thought it went all right – rather good, in fact. I went back to the hospitality suite. Michael Grade‡ was there as well as David Attenborough§ and all the people in the programme. Hattersley is a bit strange with me – Roy Jenkins is very nice, but he looked very old and in fact during the programme he lost his microphone and got carried away on all sorts of points. In hindsight, I don't think I made too much sense. Eventually I came back feeling really rather shagged and thinking 'My God, this is the very first day!' I'd been invited to do TV-am breakfast television for the following morning. So tomorrow I will have done the *Seven O'Clock News*, the *Nine O'Clock News* and *Breakfast Time* – and the campaign hasn't even started!

Tuesday 12 May

I got up slightly groggily and went down at 7.30. Howell was already in the car waiting for me. We went over to TV-am. In fact, we got there in very good time, because we weren't on until

---

* Roy Hattersley (Baron Hattersley of Sparkbrook since 1997), 1932–. Labour MP, 1964–97; Minister of State, Foreign Office, 1974–76; Secretary of State for Prices and Consumer Protection, 1976–79; shadow Chancellor of the Exchequer, 1983–87; deputy leader of Labour Party, 1983–92; shadow Home Secretary, 1987–92; award-winning journalist and prolific author.

† Roy Jenkins (Baron Jenkins of Hillhead after 1987), 1920–2003. Labour MP, 1950–77; SDP MP, 1982–87; Home Secretary, 1965–67 and 1974–76; Chancellor of the Exchequer, 1967–70; president of the European Commission, 1977–81; leader of the SDP, 1982–83; Chancellor of Oxford University, 1987–2003.

‡ Michael Grade (Baron Grade of Yarmouth since 2011), 1943–. At this time director of programmes for the BBC; chief executive, Channel 4, 1988–97.

§ David (since 1985 Sir David) Attenborough, 1926–. Joined the BBC in 1952; distinguished broadcaster and naturalist.

ten past eight. Bryan Gould was on with me, as well as David Alton,* whom I didn't know very well. Gould is quite a cheery chap – we sat there talking a bit, and TV-am is really now quite a friendly sort of place. We did our bit, which was a ten-minute or so chat – nothing very serious, kept quite light – I think for breakfast television serious politics is probably rather out. Anne Diamond was the interviewer and I really thought she had quite a good way about her.

Anyway, I went and managed to get a haircut and still got to No. 10 by 9.30, in time for a special Cabinet to deal with the manifesto, which I'd been reading all the way through. From my own particular viewpoint, there were only two things that had to be done. Firstly, the industrial relations chapter referred to the green paper as if it was a *fait accompli*, as if we were going to accept all the recommendations. Secondly, there was one word, describing young people on YTSs, that was incorrect.

We went slowly and painfully, chapter by chapter. The Prime Minister was in fine form. Geoffrey Howe was in a slightly sour-ish mood, I thought, and was chipping in all over the place but not really getting his own way. We had a tremendous to-do when we came to Nick Ridley's section, particularly on the treatment of resident landlords under the new community charge. The more we discussed Ridley's proposals the more I began to realise they weren't worked out very clearly, and I just hope that they won't let us down during the campaign itself – I

---

* David Alton (Baron Alton of Liverpool since 1997), 1951–. Liberal/Liberal Democrat MP, 1979–97; Liberal Chief Whip, 1985–87.

suppose there's time to get it put right afterwards.* Anyway, at about quarter to eleven or so we were interrupted because the whole time the band was rehearsing for Trooping the Colour outside. We had some coffee and then eventually came to the first of my parts, which was industrial relations. Kenneth Clarke was next to me and was also ready to butt in. I said: 'Prime Minister, we have consulted widely – the date for closing was four days ago. We've seen the TUC and others – what we really want to do is to amend the manifesto to say we've issued a green paper; we received the consultations; and we propose to legislate in the next parliament.'

I was really not too happy with what we are proposing to do on IR. I thought Ken had gone a bit over the top actually in one part, where we had proposed that where a member of a union decides he doesn't want to strike but votes in a properly conducted ballot and the majority of members decide they will strike, he shouldn't be penalised by members of the union for breaking the strike. That seemed to me to be not quite fair and gave us some small problems.

The Prime Minister gave me a right old look and said, 'No, I don't think we can have that at all.'

'No,' said Norman, 'of course we can't.'

'Well,' I said, 'we haven't had time for proper consultations.'

'Well, tough,' said Norman, 'this is what a manifesto is about.' All my colleagues seemed to be firmly of that view, and I suppose we've just had the quickest policy agreement you can have

---

* These expectations proved over-optimistic, and the community charge (or poll tax) helped to bring Mrs Thatcher down in 1990.

on any subject. The entire green paper proposals are now going into the manifesto unchanged.

'Well – I think this might give me a slight problem when it comes to my relationships with the TUC later,' I said, 'but I suppose they will have many other reasons to be slightly annoyed with me.'

We carried on through the rest of the manifesto. I got my other alteration, on young people and unemployment, agreed quite easily. I must confess that towards the end my attention wandered just a little. We only finished at about ten minutes to one, and on the way out I had a quick word with Kenneth Baker. We said we would get together and tried once more to arrange a meeting with John Wakeham, but I think he's as busy as I am.

On the way out, I realised that it was too late to go back to the office, so I went straight to the Savoy Grill, where I was meeting David English for lunch.* When I went in, who was sitting at the next table but Jeffrey Archer and Leon Brittan. We had a cheery hello, and Jeffrey mumbled to me very quickly that he thought I was doing well. In fact, I'd had one or two comments from colleagues – including one rather nice one from Willie – on my performance the night before on *Panorama*. I then had a good chat with David English, who is very homeside and supportive. He gave me his telephone numbers. I suggested to him that since the Labour manifesto was promising to be very light and sketchy, it would be worthwhile getting someone to do some work looking at all the Labour proposals of the past

---

*	David (after 1982 Sir David) English, 1931–98. Editor of the *Daily Mail*, 1971–92; chairman of Associated Newspapers, 1992–98.

year and then writing an article on 'the manifesto that never was'.

I had to leave at about ten past two to hurry back to the House because I was on for Questions, where dear Lord Hatch of Lusby* was asking a question on Restart. When I got into the House I received quite a few good-luck wishes from our people. We had a jolly little ding-dong – not one of my best, but quite a good jostle, which everybody really appreciated. There is no doubt that the political temperature is really rising.

I got out of the House at about ten past three and went back to the department. My appointment with the Prime Minister had been brought forward to 4 o'clock. So, I saw Howell to work out exactly how the manifesto was going. I must say he's working very hard and looking quite tired. And then I had a meeting to look at the unemployment figures. It now transpires that, because of the new rules now the election has been called, the department won't even have a press conference to issue the figures, and any statement I issue has to come out of central office. Well, the figures are good, and we are certainly going to make a fuss of it, but I still thought the rules were slightly odd.

At 4 o'clock, I went over to No. 10 and discussed the tour with Roger Boaden, Peter Morrison and Christine Wall. The Prime Minister is actually in quite a relaxed mood. We were there for an hour and a quarter, and believe it or not we've agreed the last few days and the tour looks like it's being set in concrete, which I think is absolutely smashing. As I was leaving, at about twenty

---

* John Hatch (Baron Hatch of Lusby after 1978), 1917–92. His main expertise was on Africa.

past five, Brian Griffiths had a chat with me about the bishops of all things. We talked about setting up a seminar the other side of the election, in which we'll get a number of the bishops and perhaps even the Chief Rabbi to come and talk about economic and political issues.

I went back to the office. While I was there, Peter Morrison rang through to say a friend of his who owned a big airship had offered to put it at our disposal for the campaign – what did we think about it? So, I told him that I would get back to him. I called in Howell and we thought we'd go and ask Tim Bell. Howell came back a few minutes later and said, 'Why don't we paint it up and get it to follow the Prime Minister on the tour?'

'What a marvellous idea,' I said. So, I rang back Peter, who said he thought it was a good idea too, so we'll have to see what happens.

Shortly after that, John Carvel* came in for an on-the-record discussion, and he produced a tape recorder. 'Did I mind if we actually had it on?' I said no, I was perfectly happy. He asked about my role in central office and said: 'It doesn't appear that you've got an actual position.'

'No,' I said, quite cheerily.

'Well, who reports to you?' he asked.

'No one,' said I, 'I'm just there to help out.'

Then he said, 'But I understood that Tim Bell reported to you?'

---

* *Guardian* journalist since 1973; at time of the election, chief political correspondent, 1985–89.

'Oh no, no, no,' I said, 'nothing in that way.'

And so we carried on. I thought I'd sort of killed that story, but on the way he out he said to me, 'Look, I'm terribly sorry but I've already written something; it'll be in the paper tomorrow, but I will endeavour to change it over the next week or two.'

'Well,' I thought to myself, 'that's not so good, is it; it's going to give us a bit more trouble.'

Anyway, I cleared up some odd papers in the office and took home what was left in my box. I had an article to write, and during the course of the evening I received two or three phone calls – one in particular which went backwards and forwards from central office. Evidently Michael Grade of the BBC had been trying to contact me, and I found out afterwards he was put on to me by Brian Griffiths. I was reluctant to give him my number, and I think he was reluctant to give me his, so we fixed that we'd call in the morning.

I messed around, did a few things, got my address book out and went to bed too late.

Wednesday 13 May

I got into the office rather early – prayers were at 9.30, but I was in just after nine to find that Robert Atkins and Colin Moynihan were both there. Colin had a very real problem: the true cost of the community charge was starting to rear its very ugly head in his constituency. I found out to my horror that a list of the costs in all the boroughs – the difference between the community charge and the present tax rating system – had been issued in answer to a PMQ six or eight weeks ago, and there was a frightful fuss going on, which got me quite worried. Then Michael Grade phoned, and I discovered that it was to do with a Radio 1 programme in which he wanted the Prime Minister to appear in the last day or two of the campaign. I said to leave it with me; I would do what I could.

Gradually my ministerial colleagues arrived. They were all in a fairly good mood, although this rates thing certainly got them going. It does look unfortunate – I'm going to save a lot of money on my own house, but there are an awful lot of people who may well have to pay more than they can afford.

Norman Willis came on the phone. I'd had a message that he wanted to speak to me, and I wondered what on earth it was about. But in fact it was only that he wanted Ken Graham* to be a governor of the BBC, and I said I would certainly back that.

After winding up prayers, I then spent a moment or two more on the unemployment figures before dashing off to No. 10, where there was a meeting of ELF, the local authority finance committee. We were talking about the present position on the two-year transition period for the community charge rates, during which we will have to pay out another £385 million in order to ensure that people on supplementary benefit and others in the end don't pay any of the costs themselves. And I think in one fell swoop all the savings of the supplementary benefit reviews have gone. I'm more determined than ever that after the

---

* Kenneth Graham CBE, 1922–2005. Commissioner, Manpower Services Commission, 1974–87; deputy general secretary, TUC, 1985–87.

election I shall ask the Prime Minister to put someone like Parkinson* in charge of that policy.

ELF didn't finish until about ten to twelve, and I had originally fixed to see John Wakeham afterwards. In the meeting, incidentally, I'd passed a note over to Norman explaining what had happened at the John Carvel meeting the night before, because Norman was so very sensitive about the position of Tim Bell. When we came out it was too late really for a meeting with John Wakeham, so instead we walked together towards No. 12. Then I peeled off to Alistair McAlpine's house to film the manifesto video. When I got there, Howell, Tim Bell and Antony Jay were there with the producer and the director. I filmed my bit. It took quite a long time even though it was only to film fifty-five or fifty-six seconds. I think it went all right, but we'll just have to see what it looks like when it's all finished.

Then I went off again to Simply Nico for lunch with David Hughes and Jill Hartley of the *Sunday Times*. I must say, they make a fuss of me every time I walk into Simply Nico – perhaps I'm the first minister to go there, but every time the chef makes a fuss. When I had sat down, the waiting staff came over and offered us something off-menu, which I thought was rather nice. It was a friendly sort of lunch. I left at 2.30 to make the party election broadcast at the Saatchis' place in Lower Regent Street.

I'd received the script when I was working at home the night

---

* Cecil Parkinson (Baron Parkinson of Carnforth after 1992), 1931–2016. Conservative MP, 1970–92; chairman of Conservative Party, 1981–83 and 1997–98; Secretary of State for Trade and Industry, 1983; for Energy, 1987–89; for Transport, 1989–90. As it turned out, Ridley stayed in charge of presenting the poll tax until 1989.

before. It was a good script, I thought, but it had three politicians in it, and as the chairman hadn't decided who would do which part, we'd all shoot all three bits and then he'd choose which ones to use. Well, I recorded all my three bits. It was quite hard going, taking about an hour and a quarter. I think I did it all right. I'll just have to see if any of my contributions are going to be used or not. It was rather bizarre, because they are going to get Geoffrey Howe and Nigel Lawson there, and I'm sure they will be upset if their bits won't be used. I know I will be!

Afterwards I rushed back to the department for a while because there were a number of matters to settle. Roger and some of the others wanted a steer on what we were going to do with young people and also some other policy matters, so they could get on with work during the election. I must say they are all taking it as a pretty foregone conclusion that we're going to win the election. Well, I'm glad someone's got confidence. John Turner came in and said, 'Would you like some good news now?'

I said, 'I'm always ready for good news.' It turns out we've heard from the embassy that Bill Brock, the American Secretary for Labor, is proposing to hold a meeting in Aspen, Colorado, sometime in September. He's going to invite ministers from a number of countries, and I will be invited together with Lita and a private secretary. I've always wanted to go to Aspen. I reckon that's going to be a super meeting and a bit of a fun trip, so it really has given me something to look forward to.*

I saw Howell and he proudly brought in to me 'Our First

---

* I presume that my successor, Norman Fowler, enjoyed the trip after the election.

Eight Years'. We've done it in about eight days, and he's done it in the main. It seems quite remarkable to me, and it looks very good indeed. He also showed me the packaging for the video, which I had decided on the day before. It's going to look like part of a matched set with the manifesto. It looks very good too, and I'm very pleased with it.

At 5 o'clock, Michael Phillips* came in with Anne Green.† Margaret Bell sat in as well. We went through the dinner next week, which I'm beginning to dread. I've got to write my speech over the weekend. It's for the Stuart Young Foundation,‡ and we've got 182 people coming.

Having dealt with Michael Phillips and Anne Green, I packed up and went over to central office. A bit earlier, I'd spoken on the phone to Peter Morrison, who told me that the first of the strategy meetings was fixed up. I went in and had a chat with Peter. Norman was delayed a bit – he was evidently making his part of our video. When he came in, he asked Peter and me for our opinions on the party election broadcasts. Between us we decided on what the second, third and fourth broadcasts would be. The last is – as Norman described it – a 'Hosanna!' broadcast, which the Prime Minister will star in. The first of them is the one I'd helped to make that day. I don't think I'm going to be in it after all, but I'm not awfully bothered.

We started the strategy meeting, which Norman took. It lasted about forty-five minutes. We discussed what were going

---

* A very old friend of mine and one-time partner of my late brother, Stuart.
† Stuart's old secretary.
‡ A foundation for educational purposes, set up in Stuart's memory.

to be the issues for the next two or three days and how we would get on over the weekend. Norman is going up to Scotland, and then we're going to have a dummy-run on Friday morning of the first of the press conferences. Alas, I am going up to Scunthorpe with Basil Feldman and Phil Harris.[*]

After the strategy meeting, I went back to the office. Brian Griffiths wanted to get hold of me. He suggested that when it came to launching the manifesto, perhaps he should have words with John Cole[†] or one or two other people in the media, so he could explain it in more detail. I thought that was a very good idea, so I got hold of John, our press officer. The more I thought about it, I thought we could develop this further. John and I worked out a way we could do in-depth briefing on the manifesto, and I resolved to take this up with Norman.

I wandered back and Norman was there doing his constituency post, so I said I would see him a little later on when he had finished. Just then, the phone went for me. It was Norman Blackwell, who was very worried that something wrong had slipped into the IR part of the manifesto. I couldn't get hold of Brian Griffiths, who had left, and Howell had also gone. So, I went up to the fifth floor to see Robin Harris. To my great relief, Robin told me that it had all been sorted out. The right words were off to the printers, and in fact it wasn't too late anyway, because the button was going to be pushed on the printing at 10 o'clock tomorrow morning.

---

[*] Philip Harris (Baron Harris of Peckham since 1996), 1942–. A very successful businessman in the carpet business, who also built up a large academy schools network, the Harris Federation.

[†] John Cole, 1927–2013. Journalist at *The Guardian*, 1956–75; *The Observer*, 1975–81; political editor of the BBC, 1981–92.

I went down to see Roger Boaden to deal with one or two matters on the tour. One matter I'd forgotten – at 10 o'clock in the morning, I'd spoken to Christine Wall about the message I'd had from Michael Grade about the Prime Minister appearing on Radio 1 and left it with her. I must remember to chase her up tomorrow. I'd told Roger about using the airship, and he was very keen on the idea.* Then Norman became free, and he approved the idea of more in-depth briefing on the Monday. I must say that my relationship with Norman is steadily improving, really.

Anyway, then I came back home – this is about the third evening I've come home; I'm getting quite used to the idea. I took Peter Makeham's draft article, and I think I've turned in a reasonably good piece for the *FT* on Friday. I finished, or at least part-finished, my box. The election is four weeks tomorrow.

Thursday 14 May

I woke up feeling tired, as usual. I went into the office a little bit late. Peter Orminston, one of my employment department officials, rang me in the car, fretting a little about the statement on the unemployment figures. When I got to the office, I gave them to him. I also handed over the article I'd completed last night to give to John so it can be checked for facts, and I saw Howell for a moment, trying to clear one or two small matters.

I went over to Cabinet, which was at 10 o'clock. It was fairly

---

* According to Rod Tyler (*Campaign*, p. 141), the idea was to adorn the airship with the Tory logo on one side and to hang the message 'Maggie's Coming' in flashing lights underneath whenever the Prime Minister was approaching a town. Regrettably, this stratagem was never put into practice.

light-hearted. Geoffrey reported on a revolution in Fiji and one or two other matters. We finished home affairs, and I reported on the unemployment figures. I said we should concentrate on the figure that shows 177,000 down since last year, because that equates to the headline unemployment figure of 3,020,000. I should of course recount that on Monday the department said it couldn't issue the press statement, so it had to go through central office. Howell had drafted it and I handed it out. Towards the end of Cabinet, the office sent over the statement. One or two of my colleagues – I think with a certain amount of concealed glee, because I suspect at the end of the day, I've got too many things right – pointed out that in the statement unemployment was 200,000 down, and that this was the headline figure. So I said as it was only about twelve minutes past eleven, it wasn't too late; I would get the statement stopped. The Prime Minister said that she wanted to talk about some political matters, but she'd excuse me. I was in such a tizz about getting this wrong, and feeling so sick about it, that I went out, rang through to the office and in no uncertain measure got them to get it right. Then I came back in as she was reaching the end. She wanted to thank everybody for the work they had done; she wanted to thank Robert Armstrong and all the civil servants; she wanted to wish everybody luck; and she looked forward to meeting us all in six weeks' time. This caused general amusement before we went off.

I went outside with Norman. The usual photographers were there, asking me what I thought about the polls, which have been showing very well. My car wasn't there, and I was getting slightly hot under the collar. But it did turn up eventually, with

Howell, and we went off back to the department in plenty of time. I did the first radio interview, then went off with Howell to Norman Shaw North* to do the television.

I did ITN, and John Prescott came in after me. My bit was all right, but Howell said that Prescott had been using 'stagnant pools'. Now, in a debate in the Lords and on one or two other occasions, I'd used the expression that as unemployment went down we would leave some 'stagnant pools' – inner cities, sometimes the suburbs in the north or the south – and they were a much more intractable problem. I was very pleased Howell had given me that tip-off, because when I did the next interview, I got the conversation round, repeated the 'stagnant pools' line and explained it in full.

I then went and had a three-cornered *World at One* conversation, in which Prescott repeated that line. I suddenly realised he was using it because it was part of a Labour Party briefing. The interview was a general run round the mill, and they were going on complaining that I was fiddling the figures as ever. I'm not sure many people actually believe that.

Later on that day, Howell told me that Prescott was speaking to him while I was in doing the interview. Prescott had asked if Howell was a civil servant. 'Oh no,' said Howell, 'I'm an apparatchik.' Whereupon Prescott went off at enormous length that Labour couldn't get any poster sites because the department, or the Central Office of Information, had given all the poster sites to Saatchi & Saatchi. He was really going on about it. Well,

---

* Building off Whitehall which housed the offices of many backbench MPs.

that was very amusing indeed, because, as I'd mentioned to the Prime Minister at Chequers, some two or three months before-hand I'd decided with malice aforethought that we were going to have a poster campaign in May and June, and I fixed up with Michael Dobbs that we would book all the sites. We then let Saatchis know where they were, so they could take a first option agreement with the poster companies. In the event that an election was called, which would stop the government using the sites, Saatchis would have first option on them. I'd gone out and booked 1,200 sites up and down the country. Little did John Prescott know he was complaining to the presiding genius of the whole affair, because Howell was the very chap who had or-ganised it in the beginning!

The interview seemed to go all right. I went back to the de-partment, still hopping mad about the way the unemployment statement had gone. I had complained that the civil servants had decided the moment the election was called they couldn't even issue the press releases, which meant we were going through the ridiculous situation whereby we had to get them printed and distributed from central office, even though they contained financially sensitive information. So, we'd have to send the headed notepaper from central office to the department and get it duplicated there. I complained that this was all nonsense. In Cabinet, half a dozen other colleagues had also complained about the same ruling, saying that they'd not known it before.

I felt better after complaining, even if there was noth-ing I could do about it. Then I went off to Admiralty House, where I was hosting a lunch for Jar Shay, who was originally a vice-minister of the Chinese Ministry of Overseas Foreign Trade. He had retired and now become the head of CCIPT, which was their overseas chamber of trade. It was pouring with rain, and I was told he was sitting in the car waiting for me because he had arrived early. I came in and met quite a few friends there, who had been with me on China trips. When Shay came in, he gave me such a warm, effusive welcome, kissing me on both cheeks with a bear-hug. I suddenly realised that I was a very old friend indeed in China. We had a very good lunch. Shay sat on my right, the ambassador on my left. I managed to tell them that my interest was in tourism, and the ambassador picked this up. They are going to do something about it for my forthcoming trip. When we came to do the speeches, I'd given Shay quite a nice print – an engraving of Trafalgar Square. He gave me a marvellous painting, which he said was done by an eighty-year-old woman – a bird picture on silk that really was beautiful.

Anyway, we finished at about 3 o'clock. I went back to the department, and there I found amongst other things that Howell was in the process of writing his letter of resignation. Under the rules, he would have to resign as soon as the election was called. I then went over to central office because I was getting more and more worried about where Margaret Bell and I were going to be accommodated in central office. My arrangement with Peter was that I was going to use the Prime Minister's room. I went in and found that it was set up with about thirty or forty seats for the morning prime ministerial conference. But there was someone in there with a computer and a printer, and

I gathered they were going to stay there. I suddenly realised that this was no good. I went back to Peter and said, 'Come on, Peter, I'm going to throw a ministerial wobbly – come and show me where my room is.' His assistant, Duncan, took me out across the landing into a corridor and we walked down, past where I knew John Wakeham was going to be and past the entrance to the Prime Minister's rooms. Further down, we opened another door and walked through. Duncan turned round and said, 'It's not as far as it looks,' at which point we both burst out laughing. I got shown into a little indoor cubicle with a bit of glass that looked onto another office. I said, 'Come off it, Peter, we've got to do something about it.'

In the end, we've decided that Howell and I will share the office that was being used by the women's vice-president, Emma Nicholson,* and Sally Oppenheim-Barnes† will use a cubicle nearby. So that seemed to be OK.

I hung round a little bit, and then I had to go back to the department office for 5 o'clock, where I was giving an interview to the *Jewish Chronicle*. I thought the interview would be very much about me as a person, instead of which it was mostly about politics. I'm always slightly worried about the *Jewish Chronicle*, since it has treated poor Stuart and myself not very well over the years. Hyam Cornick, the interviewer, said he knew Stuart

---

* Emma Nicholson (Baroness Nicholson of Winterbourne since 1997), 1941–. Conservative MP, 1987–95; Liberal Democrat MP, 1995–97; vice-chair of Conservative Party, 1983–87; Liberal Democrat MEP, 1999–2009.

† Sally Oppenheim-Barnes (Baroness Oppenheim of Gloucester since 1989), 1928–. Conservative MP, 1970–87; shadow Cabinet, 1975–79; junior minister, Department of Transport, 1979–82. She was taking an active role in the central campaign because she had decided to step down from her seat.

from the old Board of Deputies days. We'll just have to see, but I must say I have quite a few forebodings about how it will come out.

I then did some work and got rid of some letters in the box before going over to the House. There was a reception for the University of London. Lord Flowers* was there, and I think he was quite glad to see me. I then went down to speak at a meeting of the 66 Club. I must say they gave me a marvellous welcome; people were so friendly. I got slightly carried away – tired and emotional, I think – in speaking. I really got worked up on the moral fervour bit. But there is such warmth now with people that you can see the effect of the coming election. It was a good evening.

I arrived home, and as I walked in Lita said, 'Oh, you're going to be in trouble, this is going to run against you.'

I said, 'What's "this"?'

'Well, "stagnant pools",' she said. Apparently, David Blunkett had been using it a couple of times on *Question Time*. I went to bed rather depressed, thinking that perhaps I had made a mistake which would run during the election.

Friday 15–Saturday 16 May

Norman Dodds was waiting for me downstairs at half past seven. We had a long-standing commitment to fly up to Scunthorpe to open a factory. I'd cut the day down by half, but I decided still to keep it. We went to Leavesden airport and flew

---

* Brian Flowers (Baron Flowers of Queen's Gate after 1979), 1924–2010. A physicist, academician and public servant.

up in a rather nice aircraft. All the papers I'd seen seemed to be perfectly OK in dealing with the unemployment figures, and nothing I'd seen made me think my fears of the previous night had any justification. Phil Harris was waiting to meet us when we arrived at Scunthorpe, and we went off to his carpet factory. It had a marvellous atmosphere, I must say. There were up to 600 employees – they started with thirty three or four years ago. I went off to a technical college and was reminded that I'd been there three or four years ago as well. I saw my first JTS trainees at work – doing bricklaying, of all things – and I thought it was very well done. It was a very good morning. There was some television and a bit of radio before we came back.

On the way back, Phil Harris was in the plane together with the others. There had been a £100 bet as to whether I would be in business in two years. My friend Harry Solomons said he and Phil Harris would get together – they'd buy GUS and I'd be chairman of the lot. Phil Harris turned round and said, 'No, he won't; you see, after the election he'll be chairman of the party.' Well, that really did make me think.

It had been a miserable day apart from what I was doing – it had been raining hard. We landed at 1.15. Norman Dodds was there. I called in at the department to change into dry clothes, and then I went in to Howell, who had finished his letter of resignation. Then we went off to a place called Rushes to look at how the manifesto video was coming on.

Howell had got *Channel 4 News* to come down and film me watching the whole thing being put together. When we got there, they were waiting for us and I went in and saw some of the film. They were going to send the completed video – which is looking better and better – over to me this evening. We had to be quite careful to make sure Channel 4 didn't see parts dealing with the confidential side of the manifesto, so they took care and we filmed it. It was rather funny: Tim was keeping out of the way, although I suspect in the end they brought him into the picture. The manifesto film has made Norman the hero, but I think Channel 4 and maybe Telethon News will use some of today's filming.

After that I went back to central office. I bought myself a silk tie – I thought the least I should do is have a Conservative Party tie – and probably shall buy another one soon. Then I went back to the department and Rod Tyler came in. I gave him an interview about what's been happening.

Then I went for a Friday family night. I'm feeling more and more tired as the end of the week goes on. We drove down to the country, where I am now dictating this. On Saturday, I had a quiet day. David Hart telephoned and we had a long chat. He is in touch with the Prime Minister and is seeing her on Monday at 11 o'clock after my meeting, so that should take us somewhere. She's using quite a few of his ideas. Then Howell phoned to say the film was delayed but it's coming. He was off to central office. During the afternoon I received a 150-page briefing on the manifesto. A quiet weekend to prepare for the gathering storm!

Sunday 17–Monday 18 May

If today was the first day of the campaign proper, then I hate to think how long it will actually last. I'd had a fairly indolent weekend. I'd been quite quiet down in the country, looking at one or two things but not really getting down to it. On Sunday morning, I rang through to the Prime Minister, who was at Chequers, to say that the manifesto was now in print – that Howell had worked over the weekend and read it from the proofs, and that it looked very good. The video was there, too. I offered to come round and show it to her on Sunday evening, when she came back from Chequers. She said she had one or two things she had to do that evening and it wouldn't quite be possible. So I said, 'No matter, I'm coming round to see you Monday morning.' And so we left it.

When I came back from the country, Howell was waiting for me with the video in the porter's lodge. I played it and it looked fantastic all the way through to the end. It was really very well photographed. So, on Monday morning I got up and went into central office, arriving a minute or two late for one of Norman's management meetings, which I'd forgotten about. Norman was in a reasonable mood. At least Sally Oppenheim-Barnes was even later than me. When it came to discussing the arrangements for the manifesto conference, I was quite careful. Norman got agitated about whether or not the manifesto video would be used. I said that I haven't made any decision, and he said something like, 'Well, you know, I'm the chap who makes all the decisions about the manifesto.'

I said, 'Absolutely, Norman, I'm just preparing this. You have a look at it and see what you think of it when it's ready.' It was a warning light to me that things weren't quite so straightforward.

I was sitting next to Peter Morrison at the time, and we just looked at each other.

At about twenty-five past ten, Peter and I went over to No. 10. John Wakeham was there, and Stephen Sherbourne. The only video recorder in the whole of No. 10 happened to be in Bernard Ingham's quarters – the office in the front. It was rather odd to think that in the whole of No. 10 there is no video tape recorder. While we were waiting for the Prime Minister, I decided we would go down ahead and set the whole thing up. When she came in I put on the tape. At the end she said, 'Marvellous! It's so fantastic – we should use it as a party election broadcast.' Then she added, 'Well, on the other hand, it only shows me overseas. The manifesto is mine, but it all appears to be Norman. It is *my* manifesto,' she said, 'I was the one who created it, I drove it through. Yes, David, you did your bit about presenting it properly. But it's *my* manifesto!' She worked herself up in a rather embarrassing way. I must confess that neither Stephen nor John Wakeham, whom I spoke to afterwards, nor Peter had ever seen her like that. But she was convinced that the whole thing was wrong – it denigrated her efforts. Really for the first time ever I thought she appeared very emotional – I don't say that dismissively, but that was how she appeared. This went on for more than a few minutes and it got quite difficult.

Eventually I said, 'Don't worry, Prime Minister, I will put it right – leave it with me.' I said to Peter: 'I'll take your car and send it back afterwards.' I got into the car and I really felt as if the whole world had come to an end. All this effort has gone into this video, which I thought was tremendous. But not only did she not like it – she felt somehow that I'd let her down. I was very, very conscious of this, so I rang Howell and said: 'Just hold on for me, there are problems.' When I got back I went straight in and got Howell out of Margaret Bell's room. After I'd explained the position, we rang up the producers and told them to come straight over. Meanwhile, I said to Howell: 'Let's not show this film to anybody.' The producers came over and we told them what the problem was. With some comings and goings, we arranged to get Alistair McAlpine's house again, because we couldn't use No. 10. We booked it for either 2.30 or 5 o'clock.

While we were making all these arrangements, Peter came back. He grinned at me broadly and I had a joke with him. But I was still feeling terribly anxious. I said, 'Whatever happens, we must make this so we can still keep the original timetable.' Peter told me she was talking about maybe releasing the film on Wednesday or Thursday, but I was determined to keep to the original arrangement, since the only time it would have any impact would be on the day of the manifesto launch.

Over to Downing Street for lunch, and the Prime Minister was still giving an interview. There was quite a small lunch party. To my slight surprise, David Hart was there, having joined her speech-writing team. There was also Stephen Sherbourne, John O'Sullivan and Brian Griffiths. The lunch went quite well. Towards the end we were talking about the themes. I was trying to draw her out on giving power to the people or choice to the people. Then, at the end of lunch, a message came in for me from Howell, saying that the chairman had been pushing him to see the video and could I please ring him. It was getting quite difficult to stall it, so I passed the message to the Prime Minister, saying that we should talk about it just for a moment. We went off to her study with Stephen. I said, 'Look, Prime Minister, we've got all the filming arranged again, but I'm afraid I'll have to tell Norman. Perhaps I should say that you appreciated the video so much you wanted to play your part in it.' She was really quite difficult about upsetting Norman in any way about it. Stephen and I talked about it, and I said, 'Don't worry, I'll get John Wakeham involved and we will sort something out – just put it out of your mind.'

We went downstairs to Stephen's room, and I suggested that we should ring Wakeham. We spoke to John, and as luck would have it, he was over at central office. I explained the problem and said, 'Look, John, you and I will have to go and see the chairman and say that you advise me that, having looked at it, we should change the video.' I went out the front door and then came back and said to Stephen: 'I'm a bit worried – I mean, I haven't got authority to change the film, have I?'

He said, 'Well, who's making the video in the first place?'

I said, 'I suppose I am.'

I went back to central office with a sinking heart. I saw Howell upstairs. He told me that the chairman was rather unpleasant to him about releasing the video. So I said, 'It's all right, I'll show it to him.' I was told that John Wakeham was with Peter, so I went in to Peter and I said, 'Now, look, we've got to organise this right. There is only one way we can deal with it: John, you've got to tell Norman that the Prime Minister hasn't seen it, that you and I and Peter were sitting there waiting for her to come, we had a run-through and as soon as you saw the film finish, you said to me, "David, what was that Liberal Party broadcast? They said that she's happy to go to Moscow, but she never goes to Middlesbrough – all that about her going overseas and nothing about this country. We've got to do something about it." So I agreed with you that we shouldn't show it to her, and that we've got to re-do it.'

'OK,' he said, 'we'll do that.'

So we went in to Norman. George Younger was with him. I said, 'Norman, I've got the video to show you. It's not quite right, it needs some things to be done to it.'

'Oh, yes,' he said, 'OK, I'll come and have a look at it,' and he was as relaxed as anything. He said, 'Let's go upstairs.' So as we were going up, I told Norman that John and I had looked at it and John had pointed out the problems.

'I realised he was dead right, and I want to show it to you and see if you agree with him.' As we went up another floor, I said it was all about 'Moscow and not Middlesbrough'. Anyway, we went upstairs to his chief press officer's room and showed the video through. As luck would have it, they loved it. But thankfully Norman said, 'I quite see what you mean about the end.' Then I went down to see Howell and said, 'Thank God, we got away with it,' and I gave John Wakeham a broad wink – we had Norman's approval to change the video.

By then it was time to start seeing the editors. David English from the *Mail* came in. I started talking to him, and then by arrangement Brian Griffiths came to join me. He was enormously enthusiastic about the manifesto. We went through all the points, and we were running way over time. It was quite difficult to get rid of David, and when Norman called in to say hello and began having a chat with him, I pushed off.

I went off with Brian, and first we went all the way down to the *Financial Times*, where we got a fairly cool-ish welcome – not nearly as enthusiastic as David English. Then we went on to the *Express*, where Nick Lloyd and Paul Potts gave us a much warmer and more enthusiastic welcome. At the *Telegraph*, Max Hastings[*] was on the phone – of all things to Conrad Black.[†] I shouted out, 'Give Conrad my good regards.' He wanted to speak to me, so we had a nice chat and I fixed to meet with him. I think the psychology was right – it certainly seemed to make Max, who's quite friendly already, even more receptive.

We had a chat, and I fixed I would get the article I was writing to him in a few days' time. When I went through the manifesto, he took notes and looked very interested. I think we'll get a moderately good response out of it. When we came out, I dropped Brian Griffiths back and then I went back to the office. *The Times* was there, and I finished that interview. And that was hours of interviews about the manifesto, but the general reception seemed to make it all worthwhile.

---

[*] Max (since 2002 Sir Max) Hastings, 1945–. Distinguished war reporter; editor, *Daily Telegraph*, 1986–95; *Evening Standard*, 1996–2002.

[†] Conrad Black (Baron Black of Crossharbour since 2001), 1944–. Canadian-born proprietor of the *Telegraph* from 1987 and *The Spectator* from 1990, until he was jailed on fraud charges in 2007.

Howell popped his head round the door to say the re-filming had gone like a dream – the Prime Minister had been in fantastic form. It was a bit quicker this time because they did it on tape and not on film.

Anyway, I spent a minute or two chatting with Peter and looked round the office. Jonathan Hill* came in to tell me that the long-term unemployed figures were very good and they were proposing to issue them the next day. I got them to sit on it until we'd had our press conference, which would be Wednesday the following week. Then I said, 'Come on, Howell, I'm not going home for dinner, I'll take you out for a meal.' We went to an Italian restaurant and Tim Bell came in to join us. It was quite a jolly sort of meal.

Then, at about 10 o'clock, we went back to Rushes, where we saw the whole manifesto film. I was absolutely delighted with what I saw. When I'd seen the ending, I rang the Prime Minister at No. 10 and told her I thought it was a thousand times better. 'Oh,' she said, 'it can't really be a thousand times better.'

I said, 'Prime Minister, it really is; you give it a lift.' I asked her if she wanted to see it and she said no – if I was happy, she'd be happy with it too. So I went back, saw it through again and left at about midnight with a VHS copy. Now I'm all set for tomorrow – I'm leaving at just after seven to do breakfast television, and there will be enough broadcast copies and everything else to get the whole thing going in the morning.

---

* Jonathan Hill CBE (Baron Hill of Oareford since 2010), 1960–. Conservative Research Department, 1985–86; special adviser to Kenneth Clarke, 1986–89; political secretary to John Major, 1992–94.

Tuesday 19 May

An early start. Howell picked me up with Norman Dodds at 7.15, and we arrived at central office at about 7.30. I was due to do an interview for breakfast-time television. I arrived at the BBC studio and they had a canteen going, so I had started to have breakfast when the BBC people came dashing in. I wanted to be on early, so they took me in and wired me up in the press room, where we were going to have the launch a little later on. I did the interview, which was fairly innocuous stuff – they kept on asking me what was going to be in the manifesto and I kept on dodging the questions but occasionally just teasing a little bit. I went back to central office and had a coffee before going up to see Alistair. Alistair always seems to be in very early and is an avid watcher of breakfast television. John Prescott had been on the other channel and was very put down by a businessman from the Midlands, who kept on asking for his plans for employment. Every time Prescott went on, the businessman said, 'That's absolute nonsense – that's not going to help me at all.' I realised for the first time that non-politicians have a considerable advantage, and I began to think of ways in which we could put out suitable non-politicians.

At 8.30, we had the first of the chairman's briefing meetings. Norman sits at the head of the table, Peter sits next to him and I sit next to Peter – those seem to be established positions. It's not the most inspiring of meetings, partly because Norman's not a tremendously good chairman. I should say that before the meeting started, I showed Alistair the new video. John Wakeham was there too and when he saw it he gave me a wink and a broad grin and said, 'It's very good now.' Then I got Howell to wind it back just to the ending, and we brought Norman in to see it. He didn't say very much, but he didn't seem to take against it.

So, then we had the meeting. I reported on all the editors I'd seen the night before, the general reaction and the bits of the manifesto that seemed exciting and the bits that didn't.

The meeting broke up at about quarter past nine, and we all had a couple of minutes' break waiting for the Prime Minister to come. It was quite a crush in the Prime Minister's room, and this time we had seven or eight Cabinet colleagues sitting around the table. The meeting went quite well; everybody was in very relaxed mood. There was a lovely incident about a newspaper report that Labour were proposing to set up a Ministry for Women. The Prime Minister said that she'd had this question in the House and she'd said, having looked at the Honourable Gentlemen sitting opposite, 'I think it's about time we had a Ministry for Men.' This brought the room down. About five minutes later, we were reporting on the press. Both Kinnock and David Owen had photographs on the front pages kissing babies. She said, 'That's all the more reason there should be a Ministry for Men!' So it was all very good natured.

The polls look as if we are keeping constant, and Labour are rising slowly at the expense of the Alliance. That's probably as good a situation as we can hope for. The PM went through all the policy matters, and then we decided to break. We were due to go down for the 11 o'clock manifesto launch. Harvey Thomas came in and said he'd agreed that the immense crowd of photographers should have a free run for the first three or four minutes, then they would withdraw and we could go into the conference.

Well, we all filed down, waiting for Norman who would bring the Prime Minister in at the end. I have never seen such a crush. They seemed to be piled four or five high and you couldn't see anything of the rest of the room. When the Prime Minister and Norman came in, there was a real battery of flashes. After three or four minutes, Norman asked everybody to have some mercy on the Prime Minister, who was being blinded by all this.

Eventually the press conference started. She made her statement, then they asked three or four colleagues to say a few words. Then she went into questions, which went on and on and on. She asked me to respond to a question on the inner cities, and at the very end I managed to get something out on unemployment. But it was quite obvious that there was nothing very much of interest on employment or unemployment, and it looked like I had been totally successful in neutralising the issue. We'll see.

It ended at about twelve. I was just going out through the crush when the journalist Adam Raphael got hold of me. I did an interview for *Newsnight* which went across the whole manifesto. He did ask a question about unemployment – the old statement that we didn't deserve to be re-elected unless we had got unemployment down under 3 million, allegedly made by Norman Tebbit, seems to be running a bit. Then I had to dash off to the Institute of Directors (IoD), for their policy and executive committee lunch.

I was worried the whole time by the prospect of speaking at the Stuart Young Foundation dinner, which was due tonight at the Savoy, but I kept on being overtaken by events. Anyway, Howell and I went off to the IoD. I suppose I was on a high anyway after the press conference, but it was inspiring to be with such supportive people. They asked me to speak, and I waxed lyrical about the manifesto, which got a tremendously good response – no question I was with friends and all on the same side. I suppose I had a glass or two at the lunch, and I certainly came away in a very good mood.

Afterwards, at 3 o'clock, Charlie Leadbeater of the *Financial Times* came in. He's evidently writing some sort of profile on me. He looks very unlike a *Financial Times*-type journalist, and the interview was more than a little hostile. At about half past three, Margaret Bell put her head round the door – I had to go to ITN and do an interview for the news. Leadbeater obviously hadn't finished, and so we fixed that we would carry on another time. So, we went down to ITN. On the way down I picked up the *Standard* and saw a slightly unflattering reference to the employment policy in the leader article. I agreed with Howell that we would start to see the leader writers and all the industrial correspondents to get our policies over.

On the rush down to ITN there was a slight incident. I opened the door of the car and nearly knocked down a motorcyclist – happily only nearly. But I got there OK and did a fairly straightforward interview with ITN – nothing very taxing. I hope they use it.* Then back after that to the central office,

---

*   I never found out.

where I tried to get a few minutes' peace and quiet to collect my thoughts – rather unsuccessfully – for the dinner that evening.

At twenty past five, I went over to No. 10, where we were due to meet the Prime Minister to finish arranging the tours. When we got there, she still had speech-writers with her, talking over what she would say at the manifesto conference. We all gave a few ideas, and she's obviously looking for new themes. I suddenly began to realise that if she wasn't careful, if she kept on having new themes, she would run out of faces before the first week of the campaign. She's in a very relaxed frame of mind, and all the arrangements for the tour seem to be going very well.

At about half past six I had to pull out to go off to the dinner, and I rushed back to the department to change. Well... the dinner's not really part of these notes, but it couldn't have gone better. Arnold Goodman* spoke very well. I made up my speech over the dinner table in the end. I spoke as well about Stuart as I could do, but it was very painful. The fund now has over £400,000, so I think we are going to make it into a very good memorial for Stuart.

I came back afterwards and found that the new video tape recorder had worked. I played back some of the news. To my great disappointment, I saw that *Channel 4 News* had not used the footage they shot of us making the video film. I'm not awfully happy with the coverage we've been getting so far. Went to bed quite tired.

---

* Arnold Goodman (Baron Goodman of the City of Westminster after 1965), 1913–95. Lawyer and businessman with special expertise in charities.

Wednesday 20 May

Another early start. Howell came and picked me up with Norman Dodds at about half past seven, and we went over to TV-am at Camden Lock. I always like going in there. They are a cheery lot, and it was a straightforward interview which I thought went quite well; they handed me questions on a plate. Then I went back to central office, where Ian Greer* was due to come in.

Now, Ian is a PR chap, and they have been discussing intermittently for the past eighteen months that he should get a group of businessmen together who could do the right sort of thing (i.e. speak in support of the government). But such is the chaos of the organisation at central office that absolutely nothing had come of it. When I came in at about half past eight, Paul Twyman was there to see me, and he had been working on the scheme. I heard all about it, then told Paul that I would fix that we will work together on it. I popped over to see Peter Morrison to get the necessary clearance, and then I saw Ian Greer. He brought in his chap who is working on the project, and he told me that they were getting in a number of industrialists to make the case for the government. We also discussed the possibility of getting letters or press releases in the local press before the Prime Minister's tour so she could refer to them. I suddenly had the idea that what we really needed was a round-robin letter, signed by fifty manufacturing chiefs supporting the

---

* Ian Greer, 1933–2015. At Conservative central office, 1956–57; chairman, Ian Greer Associates, 1982–96. A central figure in the 'cash for questions' allegations against Conservative MPs in the 1990s.

government's policy on manufacturing and condemning John Smith's. I thought that would be a good thing to mention when I go to see *The Times* tomorrow evening.

Afterwards, I went to see Alistair for a chat. I saw John Wakeham on the television first, and he wasn't looking awfully happy. Alistair said he could give one or two names to help with my letter. Then we all left at 11.15-sharp to be over at Central Hall Westminster for the candidates' conference.

We all got there early, assembled, had some coffee, and then we all went into the room. Harvey Thomas told us to give a wave and a smile when we went in, and I certainly did. He was dead right – it looked very good on television. It's a lousy hall, the Central Hall; the acoustics aren't very good. I think there were two rows of Cabinet colleagues. I was on the back row. In the front would be the Prime Minister and the 1922 Committee – an archaic sort of institution, but there you are, that's the party for you. Cranley Onslow came in and said a few words, and they read the minutes of the last meeting, which said absolutely nothing. But it was quite cheery and a good atmosphere. All the television and press cameras were there. Then Norman came in and dealt with some nuts and bolts before the Prime Minister came and I must say wowed them – she spoke for about twenty-five minutes. I'm sure it will be reasonably good television.

We finished at about 12.30, and on my way down I was collared by the ITN people, who told me that the other side had been making the running on unemployment that day. I was just about to give an interview when I got dragged away and we all assembled for some bizarre reason to have a Cabinet photograph

– I couldn't really think why, because we'd had the official Cabinet photograph only a week or two before. But there you are, that's what happened. We hung around for a while and had the photograph taken. We were about to break off for drinks when I went off and gave the interview. I saw that Malcolm Bruce* had issued a press release and was going on about the cost of advertising, which is all rather nonsense. Hattersley had also been saying something. I've been invited to go on the box for *Weekend World* against Hattersley and I think Roy Jenkins. We'll take that one up.

After I gave that interview, I got dragged away by the BBC for another. It was so noisy in the hall that they pushed open some doors and went into a part of the building where there was a bookshop. While I gave the interview, there were people rushing past. As soon as it finished some furious chap came up and said that the BBC shouldn't be there and had no right to be and this, that and the other. I beat a hasty retreat and went back to where all my colleagues were. At least I could have a drink.

We had a fairly cheerful lunch, although there wasn't very much to eat. I went round and circulated with all the candidates. At 1.30, we showed the video, which went down very well indeed. Then the Prime Minister asked four of the group – Nick Ridley, Douglas Hurd and I think Norman Fowler and Kenneth Baker – to say a few words. It went on and on. About halfway through I slipped her a note saying no need to say anything about unemployment. She signalled to me that we should leave

---

* Malcolm Bruce, 1944–. Liberal, then Liberal Democrat MP, 1983–2015; Alliance spokesman on employment, 1987.

it for the question time. I should mention that when we came up on the platform there was one chair short. Douglas Hurd was sitting on the back row by himself, even though he'd been asked to speak and I hadn't. I quickly changed places with him and sat in the back row all the way through.

Then we had about an hour of questions, and out of about forty-five or fifty questions, not one had been anywhere near employment or unemployment – it's clearly not an issue. Eventually she said, 'I've got time for two more questions now, one of them must be about unemployment.' When somebody asked a question I said my bit, but it's quite clear that it is not an issue at all. And this, I suppose, is my real ambition – to make it a non-issue.

In the morning before the 11.15 meeting, David Hart had rung to say that he was getting very concerned about coordination. I suggested to Stephen Sherbourne that perhaps I could see the Prime Minister. It was fixed that I would call in to see her, say from 2.45 to 3.30, just to have a private chat about the way the campaign was going. I really wanted to get some better coordination going between the newspaper advertising, the television and the party politicals and all the rest. In fact, on Monday or Tuesday of this week we had used an advert that I thought should have been saved for the last day: 'You don't throw away eight years in three seconds' – something like that.

We finished all the questions about quarter to three, so I just dashed back to the department to pick up my papers, then went over to No. 10. I found her in quite a relaxed frame of mind, sitting in Stephen's room with Michael Alison and talking about how the candidates' conference had gone so well. Then Stephen and I went upstairs, and we sat down. Incidentally, I found out that after I left, David Wolfson* had told the Prime Minister that the tour is far better than last time's. So at least she's quite happy – I think she's relaxed about almost everything I'm doing with her at the moment, having got over the slight awkwardness over the video.

In our meeting, I told her that I was concerned about the coordination of things and I suggested that she might get two or three people together to handle this. She decided that she would hold two or three people back every other day after her morning meetings. We discussed the conduct of the campaign. She had been told that Kinnock was coming up and actually getting the best of the media coverage. But I said to her, 'Look, Prime Minister, we agreed that the strategy was that we would run a short campaign. You are not really going out until Thursday – tomorrow. Friday's the first of the tours – we start then; it's much better this way.' She agreed it was better. Then I managed to raise the question of her last day. I'd heard that if we weren't careful, because of her planned trip to Venice she couldn't do the last of the Robin Day election calls,† which would go by default to Kinnock. I told her that Michael Grade had rung me early in the campaign, and I thought I could do something with him. We discussed a slightly complicated procedure which would allow her to manage both. On the way out I saw Christine Wall.

---

* David Wolfson (Baron Wolfson of Sunningdale after 1991), 1935–2021. Director, Great Universal Stores, 1973–78, 1993–2000; chief of staff, political office, 10 Downing Street, 1979–85.

† Robin Day ran the most listened-to political call-in programme, and he would have the leaders on in the last three days before the vote.

We had a chat about the Radio 1 plan, and I told her I would go and speak to Michael Grade.

I went back to the department, then to central office at 4 o'clock. I saw Charles Rice from the *Standard* and, I think, managed to get not only our point of view over but to fix with him that on the day of the jobs press conference we would leak quite a bit of the stuff. So, they would come out with good headlines that morning.

Then I rang Michael Grade and after a long conversation I finally suggested that perhaps he could bring the Robin Day programme forward to 8.30, which would give the Prime Minister time to do everything. I thought that would be marvellous, and he promised to come back to me.

Charlie Leadbetter came in and finished another 45-minute interview. I think it's the most exhaustive interview I've had. He was fairly hostile, so I'm not really looking forward to what's going to come out of it.

Then Howell came in saying we've got another slight problem. That evening I was due to go and have dinner with Alan Campbell* at the Benchers' entrance of the Inner Temple – a black-tie dinner. Evidently, the unemployment thing had been running all day, and I'd been asked to do a short three-minute bit on the *Nine O'Clock News*. No question, that should take priority. Eventually, with a couple of phone calls to Campbell, I arranged that I would slip out of dinner halfway through. He quite understood. So, I went back to the department to change

---

* Alan Campbell (Baron Campbell of Alloway after 1981), 1917–2013. A distinguished lawyer.

again. It seemed very quiet and peaceful. I've had absolutely no time to look at any departmental work. I suppose I'll have to do it at some time. Anyway, it was good to see the old team.

I haven't noted that this morning, after I'd seen Ian Greer and Alistair McAlpine, I'd come back to the office and Howell had said: 'There is a letter you must read.' In came a four-page letter from Geoffrey Holland, in which he turned down the idea of becoming chairman of the new MSC and went on about all the reasons why he couldn't do it. This really was a bolt from the blue, coming at a time when my mind was on all sorts of other things. I thought about it for a while and then decided I should just put it away. I asked my PS John to let Roger Dawe have a copy himself, and we discussed it very briefly. I think the feeling of all of us is that Geoffrey is still negotiating, and we can certainly deal with that later.

Then I went off to the Bencher dinner. I met a few people I knew quite well – Max Hastings was there – and I was received very nicely. It would have been a lovely evening, but of course I had to leave promptly at quarter past eight, just as soon as I had the main course. I slipped off, met Norman Dodds and dashed over to White City, getting there in plenty of time. I changed and waited around. Kenneth Baker came in with Giles Radice* and others – they were obviously doing a debate. I went on and did my bit, which I thought went well, and came home at about half past nine. Ironically, it seems I'm getting many more earlier nights than before the campaign started. I switched on the

---

* Giles Radice (Baron Radice of Chester-le-Street since 2001), 1936–. Labour MP, 1973–2001; shadow Secretary of State for Education, 1983–87.

television and saw the end of Kenneth Baker's bit – it all seemed to be going moderately well. Tomorrow, it's exactly three weeks to go.

Thursday 21 May

This was the first of the mornings without the early press call or chairman's briefing, so it was a fairly relaxed start and I left at about quarter past ten. On the previous day rows had been building up because the Labour Party had put an advert in the *Mirror* which said: "'If unemployment isn't under 3 million by the time of the next election I don't deserve to be re-elected" – Norman Tebbit.' Norman had issued a challenge for them to prove that he'd used those precise words. Before I left, I got a phone call from Howell saying there was a story that somewhere in the depths of Transport House they had found a tape of Brian Hayes's programme, on which Norman had appeared back in 1983. We had the radio on driving into central office, and at about 10.30 Brian Hayes kept on saying, 'In a few minutes we'll have the tape.' When he played it, though, it said something rather different. Hayes said, 'Well, let's play it again.' Then he said, 'Ah, well, that's conclusive. Norman Tebbit didn't say it and that should be an end to the matter.'

Even so, when it came to 11 o'clock there was quite a bit of hoo-ha. The Prime Minister was there, and we started the strategy meeting. I must confess to having a slightly uneasy feeling. Although there was some dispute as to whether Norman or Kinnock had won their £500 alleged bet on the level of unemployment, the result had been to put the subject somewhere on the agenda. We have fallen just very slightly in the polls, Labour are continuing to climb and the Alliance have fallen away. There is an undercurrent of feeling – although nobody said anything – that somehow the campaign isn't going quite as well as it should be.

We covered the usual routine matters within the meeting, and it ended fairly inconclusively. My main impression is that none of these meetings is ever a 'you do this and you do that' type of affair, which I suppose it should be. But, on the other hand, it is called a 'strategy' meeting!

I went back to my office and asked Paul Twyman to come down. I asked him how he was getting on with the round-robin letter I dreamed up at the meeting with Ian Greer yesterday – getting all the industrialists to sign. He showed me a list of fifty-odd names and the letter, which was rather wordy. I wasn't awfully keen on it, but we left it at that.

I discussed with John Desborough* and Norman the idea of issuing a press release which would come in very much on Norman's side in the row about the 3 million unemployed. But perhaps it might look as if I was having to come to Norman's rescue, so I agreed that we should just leave it, though I did draft a press release which subsequently just disappeared – sank out of sight. Then I went to a lunch engagement I'd decided to keep. I was the guest of honour of the Society of British Gas Industries lunch at the Café Royal. It was quite a cheerful sort of thing, although there were not many people there I knew. I made a

---

* John Desborough, 1929–2013. Former chief political correspondent at the *Mirror*, Conservative spin doctor from 1986.

fairly robust sort of speech. It was a very homeside audience – no doubt at all about support at that particular place.

I came back and Howell and I got talking. Although I was rather happy after lunch, I still had this rather uneasy sinking feeling, and I was getting more and more worried. It wasn't helped when David Hart rang earlier; Howell told me Tim had also rung, and they were both very much concerned about co-ordination. The Labour campaign had got off to a much better start and was much better organised. I had one or two conversations, then I said to Howell, 'Why don't we fix lunch with Tim tomorrow?', which he said he would go and do.

Later on in the afternoon, at half past five, Grania Forbes of the *News of the World* came in for an interview, which turned out to be fairly long, all about Margaret Thatcher. She was asking me all sorts of personal information about her, which I was actually quite unable to answer. The interesting thing is that I realise now, despite how close I'd been to the Prime Minister over the past three years in a working relationship, it really is just that – a working relationship.

Just a little before the Grania Forbes meeting, I'd asked Paul Twyman to come down and said I'd been thinking again about the letters. I wasn't content with the long timescale he was thinking about. What we should do is have a punchy three-paragraph letter dealing with unemployment, with a dozen leading names in there, and get that in *The Times* for the following Wednesday morning, when we were due to have our jobs package press conference. I would speak to Rupert Murdoch that evening. We discussed the form of the letter and Paul went off to redraft it.

I then went into the next strategy meeting, which started at six. I could only spend a few minutes, as I had to go with Howell down to Wapping. I'd been invited there a long time before by Rupert Murdoch. The story really goes back to the early days of the News International dispute.* In January, I think – January or February of '86 – Kenneth Clarke had let slip to the lobby that Murdoch was 'not an immediately likeable figure'. The press comment was that as a government we were slightly distancing ourselves from Rupert. So, I immediately asked him to come in for a drink and said, 'Look, anything you want, just let me know, we are totally behind you.' I didn't have to do very much, but I did offer a great deal of support. I'd met him once again with Bruce Matthews, sometimes described as Murdoch's Cromwell, at a *Newsnight* recording. I said to Bruce: 'Just let me know if there is anything you need.' Evidently I'd gone down very well with Rupert. When the strike ended, I rang up and suggested that to celebrate I might go down to the Docklands and have a look round. The message came back, please could I wait until Rupert was in the country, as he wanted to show me around himself. It had taken all this time to fix the appointment.

When we got there at exactly quarter to seven, there was Rupert waiting for us – just by himself. He took Howell and me around. First, we went all round the floor of the *Sunday Times*, and I met quite a few of the editorial staff. Then on to the *News of the World*, then *The Times* and finally, of course, *The Sun*. It

---

* A bitter industrial dispute after Murdoch moved his newspapers to specially built premises in London's Docklands resulted in a drastic reduction in union influence over the production of his newspapers. The mass protests reached a peak in January 1987, the first anniversary of the move, but petered out shortly afterwards.

really was fascinating to go all the way through. I went down and was shown all over the printing floor. I actually pressed the button to get *The Sun*'s print-run started. Afterwards, we went back to Rupert's flat. Woodrow Wyatt* was there and the editor of *The Sun*, Kelvin MacKenzie.†

Before we went up to the flat, I told Rupert about the letter I was writing. He said, 'You've got to do it.' We had a very good dinner. T. E. Utley‡ was there. At one time he started talking about a leader he did for *The Times* during the war, when von Stauffenberg tried to kill Hitler. It is amazing to go back all that length of time and still be writing. The other people there were mainly Rupert's editors – like Frank Johnson, who is now, I think, the political editor of *The Times*,§ and Geoff Bell, who I think edits *The Times*'s business pages. On the way down, I got hold of Kelvin and agreed with him that I would let him know when the letter was going to go. It was a really very cheery evening – it didn't end till quarter to midnight – and if for that reason alone, I actually felt very much better.¶

Friday 22 May

I was a little fragile getting up in the morning and left for

---

* Woodrow Wyatt, 1918–97. A very well-connected politician and later chairman of the Tote.
† Kelvin MacKenzie, 1946–. Editor of *The Sun*, 1981–94.
‡ T. E. (Peter) Utley, 1921–88. A blind journalist with *The Times*, *The Observer* and *The Spectator*.
§ Frank Johnson, 1943–2006. Associate editor of *The Times*, 1987–88; editor of *The Spectator*, 1995–99; sketch-writer for the *Daily Telegraph*, 2000–06.
¶ *The Sun* certainly played its part in helping the Conservatives to victory. Amongst its contributions to the democratic process was an article in which a medium claimed to have received a supportive message for Labour from Stalin. Other notable visitors from the spirit world included Henry VIII, who plumped for Mrs Thatcher. Evidently Kelvin MacKenzie was confident that his readers would be ignorant of the fact that this blood-soaked monarch had actually been Britain's nearest parallel to Stalin.

central office at about 7.15. This was the first of the days when we had the chairman's briefing meeting before the Prime Minister was briefed herself. It started off on time at 7.45. We went through the polls, which looked marginally better – certainly no real change. No doubt about it, Kinnock had a very good day yesterday. The Prime Minister got a certain amount of coverage, the *Telegraph*, and others had said that Norman had won the battle over the '3 million' figure. But otherwise, I don't think we are doing awfully well, and there was again an undercurrent of unease. Earlier in the week, John Wakeham had done appallingly badly on a breakfast *Election Call* programme, and there was a certain amount of worry about how we were doing on television. But we had a reasonable briefing meeting, which lasted twenty to twenty-five minutes.

The Prime Minister came early, and we all went in for her briefing meeting. It was a Defence day. Geoffrey Howe was there, and George Younger. Before it started there was a bit of a kerfuffle. John Stanley* had arrived uninvited – I don't know why, but he walked into the room and sat himself down, so they had to find him a chair.

The Prime Minister was in good form throughout the meeting. Then we went into the press conference, which started at 9.30. It was very well attended. George Younger was tremendous – in very good form: incisive, biting, really managed to put every critical journalist down. Then we went on to the community charge, and the Prime Minister gave some very long answers.

---

* John (since 1988 Sir John) Stanley, 1942–. Conservative MP, 1974–2015; held several junior ministerial posts. Minister of State for Armed Forces in Ministry of Defence, 1983–87.

But that seemed to go all right. A question came up on education, and I thought the Prime Minister started to get herself into some hot water about whether there would be any selection procedure or charges for state schools. She kept on saying it would all be left to the governors. I realised immediately that it was an area we just hadn't thought through. All these proposals had come in from Kenneth Baker very late in the last week or so before we decided to call the election, and they were only agreed in two or three policy meetings.

Anyway, we went on to one or two other matters. Somebody asked a question for the Job Training Scheme, so she called for me and I came up and sat next to her on the platform in George's position. I gave a fairly forthright response. Then it got back to education again. I don't think it's gone very well, and I'm sure education will come out as the story when it should have been defence.

We went upstairs again, and the Prime Minister was in Norman's room. I went in as well, and I started to say something about a statement, which should say that we should make no charge for basic education. It was agreed that we would put out a statement, and Norman and I worked on this while the Prime Minister went off and got the train down to Gatwick. We checked it with her on the telephone when she was on the train, then tried to get hold of Kenneth Baker. There was a mad panic to do so – he was just about to go and do Jimmy Young.* We got hold of him in time and agreed the statement with him.

---

* Jimmy (after 2002 Sir Jimmy) Young, 1921–2016. Host of BBC Radio 2's *Jimmy Young Programme*, 1973–2002. One of Mrs Thatcher's favourite broadcasters.

I thought that, with a bit of luck, we had managed to contain it. Then we went on to a fairly short strategy meeting, which was really about the problems we had on education and keeping the press conferences right.

I was running very late with getting my statements done, and I was being briefed by Jonathan Hill, Norman and Howell, as I am due to do *Weekend World* on Sunday. While I was doing that in Alistair's room, we got a message – would I give an interview for the news? I went down to do it just before I went off to lunch. Evidently, Prof. Layard had made some sort of statement using my figures. So I went downstairs and said, 'It's absolute rubbish and nonsense.'

I then went off to Mark's Club to have lunch with Tim and Howell. I agreed with Tim that we have really got to get the coordination right. I suggested to him that he ring the Prime Minister when she returns in the evening, and perhaps we can work something out. While I was sitting at lunch, someone passed a note across which really criticised us for not using the television right. This chap said he'd twice been a candidate. I just passed it over to Tim and said: 'Show it to her; it's good evidence.'

We came back and Don Macintyre, labour correspondent for *The Times*, had come in to see me. He asked me for a fairly general-purpose interview, and I pointed out some of the things nobody else had pointed out up to then, notably the fairly revolutionary nature of our manifesto pledges. I think he may write something up for this Sunday.

Keith Britto popped his head round the door to tell me of

a *Sunday Times* poll which looked rather good news – in fact all the polls are keeping up very well. But during the course of the afternoon, it was quite evident that the education story was running and running. We had a terrible two and a half hours in which we just couldn't get hold of Kenneth Baker. He has a portable phone but obviously hadn't switched it on. We just wanted to make sure there was no question of conflict between him and the Prime Minister. We were in touch with the Prime Minister fairly frequently on the bus, but we just couldn't get Kenneth. In the nick of time, by using all the new technologies, we got the two together and she made a statement. I hope very much that the story has now been killed and we've confirmed irrevocably that we do not charge for education in state schools, even in the ones that have moved out of the Local Education Authority.

Robert Atkins rang me and was rather nervous about the way the campaign is going. I was inclined to dismiss his pessimism, because I was feeling better and better about things myself. I went home eventually at about seven, for dinner just with Karen and Bernard. Then David Hart rang me and re-emphasised his considerable worry about what was happening, and particularly about the lack of coordination. I thought this was getting a bit tedious, but I said that I agreed with him. Then candidate John Wheeler rang to complain that he couldn't get any manifestos in his constituency. Lita had told me this story when I came home – evidently, they just didn't have enough of them. David Wolfson rang and told me he was probably going to go out with the Prime Minister most of next week. He fixed to come and have dinner on Saturday night. At quarter to midnight the Prime Minister rang and said that she'd had two disturbing phone calls – one from Tim and one from Carol Thatcher. Carol thought we were about to lose the election and she was also very concerned about coordination. It was one of those occasions when the line is bad, and I could hardly hear her. But I got too far into the conversation to tell her this, so it was all rather unsatisfactory. After I had put the phone down from the Prime Minister, Lita suggested I should invite her back for dinner. So I rang No. 10. She was on the phone to Stephen Sherbourne, so I said, 'Well, call me back.' Then I thought about it again and cancelled it.

I went to bed feeling more than a little sick about the way the campaign is going. The Prime Minister is obviously very concerned about things, especially about coordination and the way we had been made to appear inefficient because of the handling of the education dispute. She told me Carol had been out with a lot of her friends, who had said we are about to lose the election the way things are going. She also said *The Times* is going to headline the disagreement about education policy. I'd said I would go and see her with Tim the next day.

One other matter I'd forgotten was when Norman came back to central office at about 6.30 in the early evening and I'd had all this problem getting hold of Kenneth, he agreed that only he or I had to be about the place at all times to make sure that we knew what was happening. And so, I'm re-doing my schedule to make sure it agrees with his. At least he's accepted me in this back-up role, which is a good step forward.

Saturday 23 May

This morning I woke up still feeling sick about the way the election is going. I got all the papers, which had headlined the disagreement on schools, although some were of course more virulent than others. There were a number of stories suggesting that the campaign was getting muddled and some stories about the 'lost week'. So, I rang the Prime Minister and said I was very concerned about the way the education story was going – we should get a statement put out. She agreed, and I said I would get something done during the day and call her in the coach. In any event, I'd see her at the end of the day, because we really had to do something about our coordination.

When I got to central office, there was a great big crowd as the Prime Minister was there. When I came in, I was told, 'Could you go upstairs? The Prime Minister is looking for you.' She was there with Norman. As we saw her off on the coach, she called me and said, 'Oh, do give me a call and let me know how the day goes.' We had a very brief chat, but she suddenly said that they were late and let's go. I think she is quite worried.

We then went into the briefing meeting with Nigel Lawson and John MacGregor, chief secretary to the Treasury, before the next press conference. Norman said that if anything came up on education, we should say we'd agreed that Kenneth Baker was going to make a speech that would set it all out, but actually he would merely make a very short statement and not take any questions. One of the things I'd suggested to the Prime Minister this morning was that we are going to shorten the press conferences, because they are dragging on too long. Norman had told me he wanted to act as chairman in them. This press conference actually went remarkably well. Indeed, at the end of it there was just one question on the periphery of education, which was: 'Do you think you've got off to a bad start in the campaign?'

When it was all over, I went back and saw Paul Twyman, who had redrafted the round-robin letter to make sure it was a fairly punchy three paragraphs. I sent him all the industrialists' names, and with a bit of luck we will get it done for Wednesday. Norman was around – I saw him on one or two things but there was nothing very much going on. Tim Bell rang, and I told him we were meeting together later on. He told me Carol was going to ring and he'd have a chat with her. So we left it and I took Howell out to lunch at an Italian restaurant – Mimo's. We came back, and I settled down to do a bit of paperwork in the office.

I'd had a chat with Norman just before lunch. I'd wandered into Shirley Oxenbury's* office, and Norman was there with his assistant, talking about television coordination. I jumped in at this. He said, 'Come next door,' and he volunteered the information to me that John Wakeham wasn't doing his job properly – coordination had been poor, and he had given a rather bad interview and lost everyone's confidence. He'd been pushed back to his constituency; the whole thing wasn't being handled and he, Norman, would have to take it on. I rehearsed with him one or two of the coordination matters I was going to suggest to the Prime Minister later on, which he seemed to accept quite well. I thought that was another good step forward.

---

* Norman's secretary.

After lunch, I was back in the office working again when Tim rang to tell me some of the things that had happened. So did David Hart, who evidently agrees thoroughly that there has been poor television coordination and not enough exposure of the PM, and he says the only way we are going to go ahead is for me to be made the campaign coordinator. We will just have to see.

Keith Britto popped in. The *Daily Telegraph* poll is rather good: we are still about forty-two to Labour's thirty-four. I'm getting some more briefing, which will help me for *Weekend World*, which I've got to do tomorrow.

I messed around for a while trying to continue with this slightly tedious article for the *Telegraph*. I was on my way through to Norman's office when I saw Steve Robin,* and I said I would like to have a chat with him. I went upstairs and spent a few minutes looking at his great big board, which showed all the bookings that had been made for television over the campaign. I was rather appalled at what I saw – there seemed to be an enormous amount of Nigel and quite a lot of other people who were worthy and valued colleagues but not necessarily the best on the box. Then he said, 'Let me show you the rest of what we're doing,' and he took me into the television monitoring place, where there were four televisions going. They were recording everything that took place all day long.

I had a sudden idea and said: 'Look, can we make tapes up at the end of the day?' He said that he could. I said, 'Right, what

---

* Steven Robin was part of the team working with John Wakeham, responsible for allocating ministers to particular television appearances.

we've got to do is get someone along here at midnight each night, and during the night they have got to put it all on one tape.' I said we should have two or three copies – I can have one and Norman can have one, but the Prime Minister's got to have one which will show all the political bits of all the news programmes of the day before.

Steve said, 'There's no problem, we can certainly get it done.'

So I said, 'All right, let's go and do it.'

On the way down with Steve Robin, I came across Tony Garner, one of the central office team, and told him what I wanted. He said he knew someone who could fix it up. I said what we actually need is a technician and what we've got to do is to get someone who is hopeful for a candidacy, who can come along each night and make sure we've got all the right bits. That was agreed.

Steve told me one other thing that gave me a great deal of concern. It was only on the Friday – when the campaign had already been going for quite a while – that he eventually got hold of the list that showed him the daily press conferences. There was no way in which he could plan the appearances on television without having that. Well, I asked him to let me have a list of what he had.

By then it was already twenty-five past six. I rang through to Stephen Sherbourne and said I would be a bit late. I drove round to Tim, who was waiting for me at the corner of the road. I picked him up and we went into what otherwise was a very quiet No. 10. The porter downstairs showed me into the lift and took me up to the flat. On the way in there, I said to Tim: 'Do you know, Tim, in all the years, this is the very first time I have ever been to the flat upstairs.' Tim looked amazed at the thought that someone who was reputedly a close colleague had not been there.

We went in. The Prime Minister was there with Carol and Denis. We sat down and had drinks. The Prime Minister said, 'Well?'

We said, 'Well, it's not been a good week for us, Kinnock had a marvellous programme.'*

'Well,' she said, 'it's hardly worth bothering. Let's give up; it's the end.' She was playing that sort of role in which everything was overdone.

'Nonsense, Prime Minister,' we said. 'There's everything to go for, we've just got to get our act in order.' And we started talking about what we could do. I said that what we've got to do is organise television. She said John Wakeham was a total disaster, and she really went on – I'm afraid she said he can never even be a minister again.

'Oh, nonsense,' I heard myself saying, 'of course he can, Prime Minister. He's been a whip for four years, it's the first time he's made a slip-up.' But certainly the impression I get is that John is out. Denis kept on encouraging her to listen to us. Eventually I said, 'Prime Minister, look, this is what we will do – this must be the strategy.' She asked Stephen Sherbourne to take notes. I said, 'Prime Minister, what we've got to do is simply this: you've got to release Norman the Assassin. He's got to go

---

* This refers to the famous broadcast, directed by Hugh Hudson of *Chariots of Fire* fame, which showcased Kinnock's tough stand against militants within his party. It was judged to be so successful that Labour strategists showed it on two occasions.

for Kinnock – we've really got to destroy this nonsensical image that Kinnock has made of all of us. And then you've got to go not against Kinnock but against the Labour Party, and show what their hidden manifesto is.'

I went on: 'What we've then got to do is to change the party politicals – we've got to show Kinnock making the speech about how he's got rid of all the militants, and then show Bernie Grant and Ken Livingstone* – all the others, one after the other, and then perhaps go on to the hidden manifesto.'

The next thing is that we've really got to fix who we have to do television. I said I can't do it on my own – I must do it with Norman because he's the chairman.

Tim chipped in: 'What you've got to do is have responsible people – like David, like the Home Secretary, like Douglas Hurd. And then you've got to have the combative people – Kenneth Baker and Kenneth Clarke – Geoffrey Howe would be one of the quiet people.' We went down a list of about four, five, six people and said we've got to concentrate on those and only those. She accepted this, and we talked a bit more. By now it was 8 or 8.15. I had asked David and Susan Wolfson home for dinner and Carol was very kind about it and said, 'I'll ring Susan.' The Prime Minister she said she would speak to Norman – not that evening but the following day – and she would agree that the next week we had to go out and really attack Labour.

'Prime Minister,' I said, 'if we do this; if you unleash Norman;

---

* Convenient left-wing bogeymen for the Conservatives. Bernie Grant, 1944–2000, was a Labour MP, 1987–2000. Ken Livingstone, 1945–, was leader of Greater London Council, 1981–86; Labour MP, 1987–2001; and the first elected Mayor of London, 2000–08.

if you go and make the speech you are going to make; if we get the party-political broadcasts; if we really go and attack them – I promise you that by the end of next week the whole position will be very different.'

I think gradually she was looking more relaxed. I slipped away with Stephen, leaving Tim with her. I went back home feeling that perhaps things would change more than a little.

Sunday 24 May

I got up fairly early, but only because I was due to do the *Weekend World* broadcast. After a while the papers came, and I read them. There was nothing very much, except that all the polls looked very comfortable – the Mori poll in the *Telegraph* was giving us the best part of a 100-seat advantage, and the other polls were looking very good indeed. I rang Howell early on. He said he had seen Tim the night before and that everything had gone very well. I rang Tim, who had stayed at No. 10 until about 10.15 or 10.30 and most of the time he'd been discussing who would write the speeches for the Prime Minister.

Howell came round at about half past ten. Keith Britto rang through to give me the latest poll because one of the weekend polls didn't look very good. Then we went off to the London Weekend Television studios. I was to appear in this programme with Roy Hattersley and Malcolm Bruce. The papers a day or two earlier had also been full of the case David Steel had settled, where apparently he had been paid £100,000 in damages out of court for allegations that he had a mistress. When I got to the studio, Bruce was already there.

We went on to *Weekend World*, which must have been the bore of the year because it was so very, very awful. It was all about unemployment. When it was all over, we had a quick drink. Then Howell and I went off to meet Lita, Bernard and Karen at Rossetti's. I released Howell for the rest of the day and had a walk before going back to central office at about five-thirty/quarter to six.

When I was in the restaurant having lunch, Stephen Sherbourne's secretary had rung essentially confirming that the Prime Minister had had a very amicable meeting with Norman, and that they had decided to do all the changes we had agreed the night before. So, with Norman I would take charge of who goes on television and John Wakeham would be released. We would try to coordinate better and have the assault next week on Kinnock and the Labour Party.

Well, as everything else had been agreed I thought that was the least of our problems. Stephen said the Prime Minister appeared to be very well satisfied. I hung round for a while, waiting while Peter Morrison chaired a meeting I was slightly impatient with. We went through a number of (it seemed to me) fairly routine and tedious things. The message, really, was that the constituencies were a bit restive. When Peter finished the meeting at about 6.35, I went to talk over the position with him. Then I saw Steve Robin and told him about the changes with John Wakeham – i.e. that Norman and I would be handling the television. I went over and waited with Alistair and Michael Dobbs for Norman, who was late because he was with the Prime Minister.

When Norman came in, he was in a very good mood. Rather

mysteriously he said to Michael Dobbs: 'Yes, it's OK.' I'm not sure what it was they were plotting. At the beginning of our meeting he said: 'Yes, we've got to do some things differently. I've just got instructions from the Prime Minister about the next phase in the campaign.' A moment or two later, he said we would be dealing with the television from now on. Alistair told me Sue Timpson, a journalist, was coming in for a drink and asked if I would join them when the meeting was over. I readily agreed.

In the middle of the meeting, I got called out twice – once because Kenneth Baker had telephoned, and I told him about the change of strategy. He was quite content with that. Then a few minutes later I got called again, and it was the Prime Minister on the phone. She told me of her meeting with Norman. She said, 'But since Norman left, I've had Woodrow Wyatt on the phone, and he asked me, "Why are they hiding you from the television party election broadcasts?" He said I should have been on the first, third and fifth.' She told him that she hadn't been on the first and wasn't going to be on the second, so she had to be in the next three.* 'Absolutely right,' I said. 'Prime Minister, I think you should just introduce them or something,' and she agreed.

Then she said that people have told her how appalling our ministers look. She said, 'Nigel's got to get a haircut.'

'Absolutely right.'

'Well, will you tell him?'

---

* According to Wyatt's journal for this date, he had also echoed my message that the party should be more vigorous in attacking Labour.

'No, Prime Minister,' I said, 'you've got to tell him.'

'All right, I will. But what about Kenneth Clarke? He's got to smarten himself up.'

I said, 'Don't worry, I'll tell Kenneth.'

And then she went on about how we've all got to look good, and she said: 'Well, at least I hope I look all right.'

I said, 'Prime Minister, oh yes, you look all right, there's no problem with you and Norman.' I told her I would give her a ring the next night when she came back from her tour.

'Well,' she said, 'I've got to do a lot of work, I've got to finish the speech.'

'Don't worry, Prime Minister,' I said, 'unless there's anything wrong, I won't ring you.'

I went back to the meeting. Afterwards Norman and I carried on talking. I said, 'I must talk to you about the appearances on television,' and we went on agreeing who would be on and what sort of posters we would be having. During the course of the meeting, Norman had explained that he would be attacking Kinnock in a speech on Tuesday night, and the Prime Minister would be attacking the Labour Party in a speech at the same time. I think everyone was cheered by this. The polls looked as if we had levelled out – they'd been catching us up, but we hadn't actually moved very much. We thought perhaps a bit of attack might move Labour down again.

We hadn't been there for very long before a message came through that Sue Timpson was with Alistair. We wandered in and Alistair opened another one of his bottles of champagne.

We chatted for about three quarters of an hour – perhaps even more. It was all quite good stuff. But when Michael Dobbs came in, Alistair slightly ostentatiously got up and put his jacket on for dinner, and we all broke up. I said, 'Norman, let's go and gear up the television performances.' As we stood out in the hall, Alistair sidled up to me – that's the best way to describe it – and said: 'Look, we're going to have a meal at Claridge's, would you like to join us?'

I said, 'I would love to, Alistair – just give me fifteen minutes.'

I went back to Norman, who said, 'Come on, come back to Margaret.* I'm going to be in terrible trouble, we'll have a jar.'

I said, 'Norman, I'd love to. But I've really got a commitment I must go on to.' Norman is really treating me more and more as a partner, which is very good. I did go back with him and pop up to see Margaret – it's the first time I've been to their highly modified house. I gave Margaret a quick kiss, and she gave me a brochure for Lita. Then I went on to Claridge's and had a rather jolly dinner with Alistair and Sue, who seems very nice. We agreed what we would have to do about television for the rest of the campaign, and I suggested some ways in which we could help. She agreed totally with the sort of strategy we were proposing to adopt and obviously approved of the sorts of names we were going to put forward on television. She agreed that Nigel is an estimable character but isn't the best person to put on television. By the time we left, I thought life was looking up just a little bit.

---

* Margaret Tebbit.

Monday 25 May

Today was a Bank Holiday, but you could have called anyone at central office because there it was a normal working day. It was also the first day proper of the campaign. I left home at about ten past seven. Norman Dodds drove me into the office, and we got there at about seven twenty-five, going straight into Norman Tebbit's usual morning meeting. That went quite well. The polls hadn't moved very much, although Labour were catching up a bit, and one of the TV-am polls hadn't been too good. In the general discussion, Alistair suddenly suggested that we should have a great big thermometer – the sort of thermometers that churches and other institutions put up to show how much funds they have raised – to show the continually increasing cost of Labour's spending pledges. We discussed it for a few minutes and thought we should put it outside our building, for there was still some mileage to be had out of Saturday's press conference, which really hadn't got as much coverage as it should.

The Prime Minister arrived rather early for the eight-thirty meeting. I thought she was a bit edgy. Nigel, John Wakeham, John MacGregor, John Moore* and Nick Lyell† were there. I wondered when and how she was going to deal with Wake-ham. When we sat round the table – the room was really quite crowded – she said a few words to him about how he must get younger people on television, we must put more attractive faces

---

* John Moore (Baron Moore of Lower Marsh after 1992), 1937–2019. Conservative MP, 1974–92; financial secretary to the Treasury, 1983–86; Secretary of State for Transport, 1986–87; Health and Social Services, 1987–88; Social Security, 1988–89.
† Nicholas Lyell (Baron Lyell of Markyate after 2005), 1938–2010. Conservative MP, 1979–2001; Solicitor General, 1987–92; Attorney General, 1992–97.

forward and it really should be organised from the centre. That was all she said about it. She then passed onto expressing concern about education and other matters. I was, frankly, more than a little bit appalled at this, so I passed a note to Norman saying we really must get together with her after the press conference to talk about John.

We went down to the press conference and all went reasonably well. Nigel put up a very good performance about getting the economy going. The general questions weren't many, and after the conference we went upstairs again to Normans's office. The Prime Minister had a word with Paul Johnson* and then joined us.

I said, 'Prime Minister, we must have a word,' and we all sat down. I continued, 'Prime Minister, you will have to tell John Wakeham the plan,' to which she agreed. After dealing with one or two minor matters we sent for Wakeham and trooped back to her office, John, Norman and me. After a lot of meandering, she finally got to it. She said, 'It really has got to be run from the centre, all the television appearances have got to be run by the three of you.' With that she got up, said she had to go and went off for the day.

We couldn't let things run on, so after that I went upstairs with John. I said, 'Come on, John, let's have a look,' and I went through all the planned appearances with Steve Robin. I just took over, took charge of things and agreed all the appearances

---

* Paul Johnson, 1928–. Editor of *New Statesman*, 1965–70; prolific author of books and articles; formerly a left-wing firebrand and subsequently a strong supporter of Mrs Thatcher.

for the next few days. After that I said to John: 'If there are any changes during the day, I will give you a call.'*

Willie Whitelaw had called in while all this had been going on and said he would come back at about eleven-thirty. We met in Norman's office and shared our concern with the way education had got away at the Friday press conference. We agreed that we would meet later today with Ken Baker, and I volunteered to swap my jobs press conference with Kenneth, so he could have his earlier. We agreed with Willie that we would get the education policy settled at this afternoon's meeting.

Afterwards I got a phone call from *The Sun*, which produced a cutting about Ken Livingstone from two years before, justifying something that had happened on Sunday that no one had really picked up. Neil Kinnock had given an interview to David Frost, and in the course of it he had said that if you don't have nuclear weapons, what you have to do is just let the Russians occupy you first – so advocating a policy of surrender.† This two-year-old cutting from *The Sun* had Ken Livingstone saying exactly the same thing. Norman took this with great glee.

Alistair asked me what I was doing for dinner, as he was entertaining Kelvin MacKenzie, so I agreed to join them.

I went back into Norman's room, finding all the Saatchi people there, and we started discussing the 'iceberg' party election broadcast to which the Prime Minister had given the green

---

* I suspect that that day I laid the basis of personal animosity with John that came to a head in my losing the chairmanship of the party later that year, yet I felt very strongly that the changes had to be made and made that day.

† In one of their most effective posters of the campaign, Saatchis produced a sign showing a soldier with his arms raised, under the heading 'Labour's Policy on Arms'.

light on Saturday, so called because 90 per cent of the Labour manifesto was hidden. We decided we would use either John Moore or myself; we would film both later that day and then decide which of us would be used. They were starting filming at 8 o'clock, but they couldn't take me for some time, so I agreed to come at 10 o'clock. Meanwhile I fixed to meet for dinner with Alistair at 8.45.

After a quick lunch I had another conversation with Norman, and we decided we would give the story on Ken Livingstone to George Younger, who had a press conference that day. Norman then started to sketch out his speech, so I went back to my room, sat down and started telephoning the editors.

I telephoned David English at the *Daily Mail*; Nick Lloyd at the *Express*; Max Hastings at the *Telegraph*; Charlie Wilson* at *The Times*, as I could not get hold of Peter Stothard;† and finally Kelvin MacKenzie at *The Sun*. I outlined our strategy and everything. They all seemed quite happy that we were beginning to get a grip on things.

Then Willie came into Norman's room with Kenneth Baker, Angela Rumbold‡ and Brian Griffiths for our policy discussion. We sat down for about an hour and a half, starting at 6 o'clock and finishing at about seven-thirty, quarter to eight, and got the policy statement on education thrashed out. Kenneth, like me, is

---

* Charles Wilson, 1935–. Editor of The *Times*, 1985–90; managing director, Mirror Group, 1992–98.
† Peter (since 2003 Sir Peter) Stothard, 1951–. Editor of *The Times*, 1992–2002; editor, *Times Literary Supplement*, 2002–16.
‡ Angela (after 1992 Dame Angela) Rumbold, 1932–2010. Conservative MP, 1982–97; Minister of State, Department of Education and Science, 1986–90; vice-chair of Conservative Party, 1995–97.

not awfully good on detail. But we managed to get everything done, and by the end I thought we had a good document.

Afterwards I went into Peter Morrison's room – Peter had gone north for the day and evening – and discussed the teachers' strike with Willie and Kenneth Baker. Willie was very concerned about its likely effect. I was quite firm, saying that I didn't think it would affect us at all, and in fact in many ways it could even be a plus, since the strike would prevent some parents going to work.

Afterwards I went home for a few minutes and had a shower. I was feeling very tired, not helped by all these early starts. Then I left for Claridge's for dinner with Alistair, Woodrow Wyatt and Kelvin MacKenzie, which was very enjoyable. I must say he does lighten up my life enormously in central office, and MacKenzie does seem a nice chap.* At five to ten I left them, got into the car where Howell was waiting for me, and between ten and quarter to twelve we shot and re-shot the video. I don't think I was awfully good at the beginning, although I got into it by the end, and it would be a rather good broadcast to use. Anyway, it was done, and I arrived home at just gone midnight feeling very weary indeed.

Tuesday 26 May

Woke up still feeling weary. I had to be at central office early. In fact, I got a phone call at about 6.50 to remind me that I was

---

* There is an account of this dinner in the first volume of Woodrow Wyatt's published *Journals* (Sarah Curtis (ed.), London: Macmillan, 1998, pp. 348–9). Wyatt thought I was very free in my comments, but I evidently made a good impression, as three days later he told Mrs Thatcher I was a better organiser than Norman Tebbit (p. 351).

on breakfast television at 7.30. I went in, and we did the interview in the press room. The interviewer came on to me and said something like: 'How can you and the government expect to be re-elected when crime is up, unemployment is up, rape is up?'

'What a very facile question,' I said. I don't think I came out of it very well.

Then I dashed across and had a very quick meal at the canteen, which made me feel a bit ill, I think because I ate so quickly. Afterwards I dashed up to the morning meeting, a minute or two late. It seemed to be going all right. We weren't doing too well in the polls but not badly. I think there was a better feeling around that we were beginning to get our act together. It was a Law-and-Order day, so Douglas Hurd was due to come in. The pre-briefing went very well, the Prime Minister came in and we went over her meeting. She seemed more relaxed and seemed to be going OK.

Then we went down into the press conference. Hurd was absolutely fine – excellent, in fact – and presented a very good picture. We wrote a statement too, and that went very well indeed. The press conference went on a bit. I was sitting in the front row. All of a sudden there was a question on housing, and the next thing I knew we were beginning to go off at a tangent. I had a sinking feeling that we were going to make exactly the same mess up of it as we did on education a few days before. It went on for quite a while, and I was beginning to feel very sick. I'm not sure how much damage we had really done to ourselves.

After the press conferences, I had to go down to Gough Square (LBC) to do the Brian Hayes phone-in programme, the programme on which last week Norman was falsely accused of saying we didn't deserve to be re-elected. On the way down, Howell told me he knew Brian Hayes from the old days, and it was true: when we were waiting he gave a cheery wave and introduced himself to me. It was quite a good show, with a tame-ish audience. One good incident really worth remembering was halfway through. One of the matters that had come up in the press conference that morning was political control of the police. Douglas Hurd had produced a Labour Party policy document, only a few weeks old, in which they said they were going to do this, although Gerald Kaufman* was denying it. When I heard the 11.30 news, there was Kaufman denying it. So when we came back on air I said, 'You know, I couldn't help hearing Mr Kaufman deny it, but can I just read this out to you from the policy document,' and I read it out. I thought I'd scored a good point.

Nigel Lawson had been on *Election Call* that morning, and I'm told he did extremely well. I went up and spent some time with Steve Robin to make sure that we knew where we were going on the television briefing. Sally Oppenheim-Barnes came in to see me and started really fretting, saying she thought we were about to lose the election, we've really got to handle things better and just concentrate on three simple messages. I said I'd go and have words with Norman and went to see if I could find him, but he was quietly trying to write his speech. Then I saw

---

* Gerald (after 2004 Sir Gerald) Kaufman, 1930–2017. Labour MP, 1970–2017; Minister of State, Department of Industry, 1975–79; shadow Home Secretary, 1983–87; shadow Foreign Secretary, 1987–92.

David Wolfson, who'd been with the PM this week. Evidently, her speech needed some work, so he'd brought it back with him to London. He said he'd been up until 1.30 the night before helping to write the speech for South Wales. He saw no point in going with her this time; he'd be late back and probably up the next night to write the next speech. So I said: 'Come on, let's have some lunch,' and we went round to Annico's, where we had some pasta, which was very good.

When I came back again, Norman was still seeking inspiration and writing his speech. Paul Twyman came in to see me, and I got him to organise some letters. I decided that, as we were postponing our press conference, we could miss out the short letter and just have the big one. Then I sat down and telephoned all the editors, telling them what was happening. The speeches we were making tonight – the PM's speech in Wales and Norman's speech – were coming over at 5 o'clock, and we were going to have the party election broadcast. They seemed to be much more cheerful because they thought we were getting our act together.

Nick Lloyd of the *Express* told me a correspondent of his had picked up quite an interesting report that had come out of Moscow about three years ago, when Kinnock had been to see Chernenko, General Secretary of the Communist Party, and evidently issued a communiqué late at night, which appeared in *Pravda*. It talked about some sort of non-aggression pact after we'd given up nuclear weapons. That certainly made me feel very happy, and I told him that whatever he did he shouldn't use it too soon.

Alistair had a few punters in for drinks, including John King,[*] and I went and had a cheery few minutes and said a few words. Then I went down to Croydon, where I spoke to a meeting of sixty or seventy people. Howell came with me. Although I was getting quite tired, we'd agreed to call in to Harry's Bar to have a snack with Tim Bell and Brian Griffiths on the way back. Brian had to get back because there was a speech-writing session, but afterwards I sat down with Tim. While we were talking, there was a phone call for Tim, after which he came back to us, beaming all over his face, to say it had been David Hart, who had just seen the *Nine O'Clock News*. It had come over very powerfully and the attacking speeches had been very good indeed.

We decided after our chat that Tim would go and see the PM the following night and try to persuade her to get Norman to go out as much as possible. She would say to Norman, 'Look, David Young can't speak for anything, why don't you go out and make more speeches and let David sort of become the office manager and mind the shop and organise things.' We thought that might work.

Afterwards I went back home. Lita said the television had been very much better, and so it was. David Hart rang. He thought we really were getting our act together and things looked very much better, but he still thought there were some improvements to be made and he knew of my conversation with Tim. So I thought, 'Well, perhaps we should.'

Then the phone went again and it was Norman on the line. I

---

[*] John King (Baron King of Wartnaby after 1983), 1917–2005. Chairman of British Airways, 1981–93; president, 1993–97.

congratulated him on his speech. I think he was tensed up – I'm not sure if he had been celebrating or not. But he was going on that he had come into the office, there was no one there from the press office and he didn't know what was going on on television. I'm not sure if he was blaming me. We discussed an idea Norman Blackwell had had to pare down the number of people in the morning meetings, and Norman said he had dictated a minute reducing the number of people who would be at the PM's briefing meeting. He'd been asked to do Radio 4 at 8.10 and wanted me to come in and take the morning meeting in his place. Of course, I said I would and that I'd see him in the morning. Then I thought I'd ring Tim to tell him this, because obviously Norman must be trusting me more in getting me to take the meeting. Virginia answered the call – this was about 11.30 p.m. – and said that actually Tim was on the other line to the PM. So I said, 'Don't worry, ask him to give me a call when he's free.' A few minutes later he rang back and said the PM was very cheerful – she'd obviously made a good speech – and how well Harvey Thomas had organised the evening. I told him what had happened with Norman, and he agreed he'd do something about seeing the Prime Minister the following night.

I was just about to go to bed when I decided to give the PM a call. She was in a very good mood. I told her what I'd been organising and that I'd spoken to all the editors, who were all going to be very supportive. She said yes, she'd seen *The Times* and they had a very good headline. And then she said to me, 'David, you know you're doing more than anyone else to win this election?' I thought that was reward enough; it certainly kept me going. I told her a number of things I'd been doing and what I suggested she should say to Norman. Afterwards I went to bed feeling that things were very much on the way back.

Wednesday 27 May

I woke up early, at about 6.30, as ever feeling tired. At about 7.05, I left, and I got into the office before half past to start the morning meeting. I said straight away that the chairman wanted to reduce the number of people in the morning meetings, and I'd sent round just previously a copy of the minute. We were trying to make this a shorter meeting and attempting to leave her less stressed. I then said I also wanted to get some changes made to the press conferences themselves, because I didn't think the present format worked very well. We discussed some ways in which we could change that, and I pushed ahead with the idea of getting a thermometer put up.* I told them I wanted to have it put up, have Norman do an unveiling and a few days later to get a mobile ladder along and get the press there when Norman went up and increased some of the red on it to show how much Labour would cost the country.

The PM came in on time, and I had to make sure we excluded quite a few people from the morning meeting. Norman arrived a little later. The polls appeared steady, no big changes. The meeting was very much more relaxed than usual; it certainly appeared as if the reduced numbers worked and worked well.

---

* Like most of the other innovative ideas, this came to nothing.

Kenneth Baker was there, as he'd come in at the earlier morning meeting and agreed his press statement.

As I was expecting a question on unemployment, I made sure there'd be only four people at the press conference. I would be sitting next to Norman, next to Norman the Prime Minister, and next to the PM Kenneth. We went into the press conference with our music blaring away. Kenneth went and did his thing. It was a very well-run, good-natured press conference, with jokes to the PM about a ministry for women and a ministry for men, and it finished on a very good note. We ran a few minutes over time, but there were no questions that caused us any problems.

The PM came upstairs, and we talked a bit about Norman making speeches. She persuaded him to put one or two more in but didn't quite get it as far as I would like to see it go. I decided to see him to nail him down.

A little later on, Chris Lawson came in and we sketched out the changes I would like to see made to the press room. In particular, I wanted a bow to the front so that the PM could sit a little bit back and be able to see all her colleagues, and to change the slogan etc. I must make sure I can get all this past Norman. I went upstairs, where Alistair had Ian Aitken[*] and another journalist having champagne. We had a pleasant chat with them, and I got the conversation round to the Labour Party's rates policy. I said I'd give them a copy of their manifesto. At 11.30, we were holding a press conference, which I'd fixed up

---

[*] Ian Aitken, 1927–2018. Journalist, with the *Daily Express*, 1954–64; *The Guardian*, 1964–90.

the day before for the health minister and four or five doctors. I wandered down, stood at the back and felt quite sure that the changes I was going to make were worthwhile.

I went back to Norman, and we had a conversation with the PM on her plane. This was very unsatisfactory because the telephone didn't work properly. I finally got off the call at about 1 o'clock and went to join Alistair again for lunch. He had David Montgomery* of the *News of the World* at the Connaught restaurant, where they made a fuss of me. It was rather a pleasant lunch but didn't really get us anywhere. I left and got back to the office at about 2.45, fairly relaxed.

In the morning, Norman had voiced considerable doubts about the state of the 'iceberg' party election broadcast. Before lunch I'd been told we probably weren't going to issue it, which depressed me more than a little. I said, 'No, we really must do what we can.' Norman explained there were a number of legal problems. When I came back after lunch, Michael Dodds was there. He told me that Norman had asked that I should see the video at Rushes – the same place where we had made the video for the manifesto. Providing that I was prepared to put my political future on the line, we should release it and let it go. I said, 'OK, we'll go down and watch it together.'

Peter had come back – he'd been up in his constituency overnight – and I told him where we'd be going and everything seemed all right. Paul Channon rang – he'd also rung the day

---

* David Montgomery, 1948–. Editor, *News of the World*, 1985–87; *Today*, 1987–91; chief executive, Mirror Group, 1992–99.

before – and it finally looked as if the trade figures were going to be OK. So, I fixed for him to come in and have a press conference the following morning. We agreed the form that the press conference could take, and then it was time to go down to Rushes, where we saw the final film. It looked very good: I didn't think there were any legal issues, and my political career was the least of my worries. Then we split up, and I went off with Howell to see three of the editors, while Michael Dobbs went off to do News International. Howell dropped the video in to the *Telegraph*, and I went up and saw Nick Lloyd, who immediately got some champagne out. We showed the film, which he liked very much, and we showed it again for Paul Potts, who liked it even more. Then David Stevens came in and we showed it a third time, and I must say each time we showed it, it looked rather better.

At about 7 o'clock, we popped down to see David English, and he too thought it was a good, hard-hitting film. We had a chat with him for a while. At about 7.30, I went back to central office and found out Norman had pulled out of doing *Newsnight*. There was a possibility I would have to do it instead. Norman was going on in the morning with Kinnock. The great disappointment, I have forgotten to say, was that although I'd spent all this time shooting this party election commercial, in fact they had decided to use John Moore instead of me. I must confess that when I saw the film, I thought John did it rather better than I did.

At about 8 o'clock I rang Lita, who wasn't overly pleased that

I hadn't given her any notice. I did see Raine, Countess Spencer;* she'd been in and given me some chocolate cake in the afternoon. You do get an amazing collection of people in central office!

I came home, and at about 8.45, I rang Tim and asked him to watch the broadcast. He thought Labour were still coming over very strongly indeed. When I'd been with Nick Lloyd earlier, Howell had come bustling in and told us that the big Gallup 2,500 poll put us at 44.5 per cent and Labour at 36 per cent. We had been rock solid – in fact slightly gaining support – and although Labour were still catching up, they were still a long way behind us, while the Alliance had dropped down to 18 per cent. Well, we saw the party election broadcast and it certainly appeared strong. But we still didn't lead the evening news. I thought that was very slanted towards Labour.

Later I'd rung Tim back, and he said that he liked the broadcast. He thought it was very strong, but he would have preferred something with a little more humour in it. We talked for a while, and he said he'd spoken to Carol, who had suggested that we go round together and see her on Friday or Saturday night. I must say I certainly had the feeling that everything I had asked the Prime Minister to do on Saturday seemed to be working well. We chatted for a while about things, and I said I'd probably go round Friday night because on Saturday I wanted to go to the country – we were going to Glyndebourne.

Earlier I'd complained about the media coverage to the

---

* Raine, Countess Spencer, 1929–2016. Daughter of the novelist Barbara Cartland; married her second husband the 8th Earl Spencer in 1976; stepmother of Diana, Princess of Wales.

monitoring unit. They rang me back a little later and gave me the comparative times. It was certainly true that we were down in quality, if not quantity, on the *Nine O'Clock News*. A little later, Howell rang to say Rod Tyler had contacted him. He'd been on the battle bus and thought the press arrangements there needed some improvement. Howell also suggested that I should ring the Prime Minister in the morning to see if there were any improvements that could or should be made. I thought this was a good idea.

Howell said he had been up to the research department when the party political had been played, and it brought a round of applause. So at least that's been going well. Well, I'm now going to go to bed, having exactly two weeks to go. It doesn't quite seem all that long since we called the election, but I suppose it will come to pass – it's just very tiring.

Thursday 28 May

Still rather worried about the way things are going, and when I came in for the 7.45 pre-briefing, I popped in first to see Alistair in his room. I asked him if I could borrow his house again, because I wanted to have a word with Tim. I thought it would be sensible to get Gordon Reece as well, and I asked him if he would care to join us. He said no, he was actually busy – I think he was taking Norman and some other people to lunch at the Garrick – but he certainly jumped to agree to it, and I ensured that Howell would make arrangements.

We went in for the pre-briefing meeting, which went satisfactorily. It was Health day, and Norman Fowler had rigged downstairs a most impressive map of the United Kingdom, with lights showing the hospital-building programme. We had evidently had a very good reaction to the party-political broadcast on Tuesday, which was a great relief.

The defence issue was running strongly, and it looked as if there was some hope in the next day or two that we would very much have checked the Labour advance.

The Prime Minister came in for the pre-press-conference briefing meeting. That went very well; the new format of having fewer people seems to work nicely, and we were able to get a short break between that conference ending and the main press conference starting. When we went down, our music was blaring away. It was marvellous – the theme music Andrew Lloyd Webber had written for us – and it was a very good-natured and good-humoured conference. In fact, when Norman Fowler did his bit with the lights there was a spontaneous round of applause – well, I suspect it may have been started by our people, but it at least appeared to be a spontaneous round of applause. The conference wasn't well attended at the start, because this was the occasion when Kinnock was going to have his press conference in London and he was being hounded by questions on defence. We knew that well in advance, but we were determined not to let our conference start any later, and although it was a fairly low number of people in the beginning it gradually filled up. When we came to near the end of the questions on the health service, the Prime Minister asked Fowler to do his lights bit all over again. He did, and thank goodness, the lights worked. Afterwards there was a slightly less spontaneous round of applause.

We then threw the room open to general questions, which went quite well, except all of a sudden there was a question for me on the workings of the community programme. I went up to answer it, and I found to my more than slight annoyance that there wasn't a chair, so I had to start answering standing up. Eventually a chair was brought, and I carried on in a more comfortable posture. So the press conference, I think we can say, went quite well overall.

Howell had some slight difficulty in organising lunch, but that was all done, and we arranged that both Tim Bell and Gordon Reece would come over to Alistair's for a meeting tomorrow. I had also spent some time speaking to Norman about the necessity of him making some more speeches. I said, 'Look, Norman, you and the Prime Minister are the only two people who actually get on the box.' So we started to sketch out a way in which he could be making speeches every day when she wasn't.

I had reported to Norman that that morning, when I'd rung the Prime Minister, she had said something about wanting to appear on every party-political broadcast. I think she'd been receiving advice or felt that she was being hidden in some way. We discussed ways in which we would talk to her about the strategy of the next week of the campaign, because I'd been advocating that we should be attacking the Labour Party on what they were actually saying in their manifesto, which was often ignored.

The chairman's secretary, Shirley Oxenbury, said: 'Look, Norman, why don't you go over and have a quiet supper with the Prime Minister on Friday night? That's exactly what Cecil Parkinson used to do in the last campaign.'

Norman said, 'Yes, well, I think David and I will go over and we'll have a quiet supper – can you fix it up?'

'Oh good,' I said, although my heart was sinking because that's exactly when I had fixed to go over with Tim. Afterwards, I went next door and had a quiet word with Shirley. She immediately picked up the situation and we worked out how to get round it.

There were some stories coming through in central office, and I had one or two phone calls which suggested the press on the bus weren't getting as good cooperation as perhaps they thought was due to them. We were worried about that, and we just had to think of some way in which we could make it better.

I spent some time with Howell working out what it was I would be saying at my employment press conference. Then, with Norman Blackwell, I popped into Christopher Lawson's, where we watched the *Six O'Clock News*. I must say I felt it was totally biased. I got Chris to ring up the monitoring people, who came back to say it was about six minutes and twenty seconds for Labour, three minutes and a bit for the Alliance and only one minute and twenty for us. I went straight on to the BBC to speak to Michael Checkland,[*] who was away in Finland until the following Monday, so I asked for John Birt[†] instead. It was a slightly amusing conversation. I said: 'I want you to understand this is not an official complaint – I'm ringing you in a way in which I would perhaps have rung my brother in the old days to

---

[*] Michael (since 1992 Sir Michael) Checkland, 1936–. Director-General of the BBC, 1987–92.

[†] John Birt (Baron Birt of Liverpool since 2000), 1944–. Director of programmes, London Weekend Television, 1982–87; deputy Director-General of the BBC, 1987–92; Director-General, 1992–2000.

talk about it – but have you seen the *Six O'Clock News?*' He said he hadn't. I said, 'Well, please do look at it.' He said he would go and watch the *Nine O'Clock*. But I said 'No, no, please look at a tape of the *Six*,' which he refused to do. So I gave him the reading. I insisted that the balance seemed to be out, and he said he didn't think they had to balance it. It was my understanding that they did, but he promised me that the next day he would look at all the news bulletins with an eye to balance.

To cut a long story sideways, I later watched the *Nine O'Clock News* and felt sick, because the first *seven* minutes was totally us. I don't for one moment believe it had much to do with my phone call, but it certainly gave some comfort to our people to think perhaps my intervention worked.

I was due to do a television piece later that evening and there was an hour or so to kill before the strategy meeting, so I went home for a snack. When I was there, Shirley Oxenbury rang. Evidently Norman was on to do *Election Call* tomorrow morning – she'd just had it confirmed – and I would be asked to do the morning meetings and the press conference. I said that would be perfectly all right for me, and at 9 o'clock I went back for the start of the strategy meeting, which ended up in a fairly aimless discussion on the content of Norman's speeches. It didn't have very much to do with strategy or with organising what would come next. Every time I mentioned our idea for a 'spending thermometer', Norman seemed to duck the issue.

That carried on for a while, but eventually I excused myself and went with Howell and Norman Dodds to Teddington. We got there at about 10 o'clock, and I went into the green room and watched the end of the news. I was due to be interviewed along with John Prescott – who, I was told, was off having his hair washed – and with one of the Gang of Four; not Shirley Williams* but the other one who didn't get elected.† He seemed quite a pleasant chap. We all shook hands. They were both wearing rosettes and I wasn't, but I suppose that was appropriate in some ways.

We eventually went into the audience. The commentator said, 'Last week's show was very dull' and he hoped to get this one livelier. When I first went in my heart sank, because it seemed that everyone in the audience was either wearing a red rose or else a sort of SDP/Alliance yellow lozenge. But in the end, it worked out to be a marvellous programme – just a pity in some ways that it wasn't national. I think I did quite well, and what was quite interesting was that a number of people wearing roses were actually our people who had put roses in their lapels and obviously got called for questions on the assumption that they were Labour.

I went back with Howell and we got home at 12.15 at night. There was a little note on the front door from Lita – 'Nine and three quarters out of ten' – and I gather that my mum had been watching. Apparently she had jumped up and down and clapped her hands when I told the audience she lived in Brent, so obviously that's gone down well.

So, all said and done not too bad a day, and I've got a feeling now that we've really got Kinnock on the back foot. During the

---

* Shirley Williams (Baroness Williams of Crosby after 1993), 1930–2021. Labour MP, 1964–79; Cabinet minister, 1976–79; SDP MP, 1981–83.
† Bill Rodgers (Baron Rodgers of Quarry Bank since 1992), 1928–. Labour MP, 1962–81; SDP MP, 1981–83.

evening he had given an interview to Dimbleby* in which he talked about three things: first, he said how much he endorsed Pat Wall and Dave Nellist† as official members of the party; second, he actually said he was going to make secondary picketing legal again – which was quite amazing – and reverse all the other labour laws we had brought in since '79, as well as giving the unions back their privileges; and third, he talked about lifting the upper level of the National Insurance limits. Well, I'm sure there is a lot of capital for us to make our next charge on this. So, I'm beginning to get a lot more optimistic about the whole campaign.

There is one thing I haven't yet mentioned: I am becoming increasingly concerned that we haven't got our housing policy right, and the relevant press conference is due tomorrow. Yesterday, I had telephoned Nick Ridley, who was very reluctant to come up. But eventually I insisted that he had to give up his constituency engagements and come to London in order that he might have a meeting with Willie, Norman, Brian Griffiths and myself, to anticipate all the possible questions and answers on housing. He had turned up at 11.15 on this morning. Norman was busy writing a speech, but the rest of us talked in the Prime Minister's room at central office. In the end, we got everything agreed. There is no doubt about it – we have gone into this election with our two most exciting policies not really worked out.

---

* Jonathan Dimbleby, 1944–. Broadcaster and author.

† Pat Wall, 1933–90. Labour MP, 1987–90. Dave Nellist, 1952–. Labour MP 1983–91; independent Labour MP, 1991–92. Both controversial left-wing MPs, whose endorsement as official Labour candidates was cited by the Conservatives as evidence that Kinnock had not fully purged his party of extremists.

They came at meetings at No. 10 when people were tired and rushed, and we should have got the detail really worked out a lot, lot better.

Friday 29 May

I woke up early. This was the day I was going to chair the early meetings, and I suppose sit on the Prime Minister's left at the press conference, so I wanted to get there in good time. Despite yesterday's meeting, I was still very worried about the position with Nick Ridley and housing corporations, and although I'd asked Brian Griffiths to slip a note to the Prime Minister, I thought I would ring her early, as I have been doing for the last few days. I rang at about ten past seven, to find to my great surprise that she was still asleep. I rang back at about 7.40 and told her how well things were going, but I also expressed this point to her about housing corporations, which she took immediately. Nick Ridley declined to come to the very early conference – I understand that he wanted to get his notes in order. I chaired it, and we went through all the necessary points. I'd arranged over the past day or so to get the press conference room reconstructed and that seemed to be going ahead all right. I cut the meeting short after about twenty minutes. Nick Ridley and John Patten had arrived, and so had the Prime Minister, so we went into her pre-briefing meeting.

It appeared right away that things weren't going too well on the tour. I know that Christine Wall had arranged for the Prime Minister to have a chat with the travelling press, who were getting a bit bolshie because, in their view, they had paid the £3,000 for their tickets and didn't seem to be getting much value for it. When the PM had gone to see them on what she thought was an off-the-record chat, they wanted it on the record and started to really push her for that. She was very apprehensive indeed. The press were trying to press her on exactly where we would extend VAT, and she was very reluctant to give way.

Then we moved on to the main matter, and she raised with Nick the point about private landlords for council house tenants. Nick agreed that he would restrict it in the first place to building societies or housing corporations. We went into the press conference. On the platform that morning was the Prime Minister, with me on her left, and Nick and John Patten were on her right. It went very well indeed, although Nick in his usual languid way just sort of waved his hand in the distance rather than getting up and referring to his graphics.

It was all very good natured, and we restricted it to just over the half-hour. Just at the very end Bevins from *The Independent* and John Cole from the BBC raised questions about VAT, which Margaret managed to fudge her way through. I had arranged that after this press conference we were going to let Sally Oppenheim-Barnes have a few words with the PM about pacing herself and slowing herself down. I was going to speak to the travelling press. Well, just as I was about to do so I got a message: would I go upstairs? Margaret was in a right state about what to do about VAT. Norman was there too. We got Nigel on the phone and eventually it was fixed that she was going to see Nigel over the weekend in order to settle what was going to happen on the matter. I know Nigel wanted to avoid limiting his options for the future, and she was very keen that we shouldn't allow the story to run and build up into a scare.

She left at about 11 o'clock. I got hold of Howell. I thought we should have a few minutes with Tim, and we fixed to see Gordon Reece and Alistair at Alistair's house later on that afternoon.

I was with Norman, going through the words he would be using in his speeches, when suddenly there was a new development. A Scottish Nationalist chap who had once been a Tory had that morning at a press conference played back a tape which turned out to be a party-political broadcast, which had Margaret saying in 1977 that if the Conservatives let unemployment go to 1.3 million then we deserved to be drummed out of office. I said I would deal with that on the *Six O'Clock News*. While the meeting was going on, I was called to the phone, and I had to think of a statement. I merely said that Margaret was as far-sighted as usual – the Labour Party was drummed out of office in '79 and we were returned in '83 and we will be in '87. I don't suppose it's going to be a real problem, but it was a slightly inconvenient thing. I said the same sort of thing for the BBC, and that made me slightly late for getting over to Alistair at the Garrick. We had a very cheery and champagne-fuelled lunch with him, and I met quite a few people there.

Over lunch, when we were by ourselves, we talked about the future of the party organisation. A lot of people are assuming more and more that I'm going to be the next chairman. I certainly wouldn't do it unless Alistair wanted to continue, but he told me about his idea for pulling down central office and re-building it. The more I think about it the more this makes sense to me. We could end up with a small, better-paid core of professionals and buy in all the services we actually need at election time.

I came back to the office. Howell's been trying everything agreed to make our press conference go smoothly on Monday. I agreed the wording of what would be there on the cards and dreamed up the idea of having a dead rose on the side of it when we came to Labour's policy. Then, having cleared all the other bits and pieces, I went over to Alistair's house, where they were all assembled, including Gordon Reece. Two more bottles of champagne were opened, and Tim produced the cards he was going to use for the meeting with the PM tonight. All that seemed to be quite well set.

It looked to me a slightly ambitious presentation, but I thought the strategy was absolutely right that we be attacking Labour for the next three or four days. I'm much keener on tackling Labour for its trade union policies than anything else. Then, we will go on and become positive towards the end of next week. Tim's idea involves changing the press conferences from departmental conferences into ones that are more themat-ic. Anyway, we'll just have to see how we get on.

Tim then said he wanted to go home for a quick wash, and Howell fixed for his car to go to Downing Street. I went back to the department for a quick wash myself, then took my car over to No. 10. When I got there, Stephen told me that the PM was still worried about VAT and other matters. He had heard and approved of our strategy, but he said he was taking the night off and he was going to leave us. We promised to ring him and let him know what actually happened.

We went up to the flat, and Margaret was there with Denis and Carol. The five of us sat down to talk. Quite obviously she was very tired – she'd also had a drink or two, and she was in a very fractious, irritable frame of mind. She was kind enough to say that when we met a week ago, we got the strategy right, and things do look very different now. I expounded to her where the strategy should be now and where we should be going in the next week. Then Tim got out his cards and started going through his presentation. I think we got to her, although it was quite difficult to say. However, we did go through how the policy should be changed, what the next party-political broadcast should be, and how we should go very much on the attack.

We went in to have dinner, and at the same time, we managed to discuss the whole policy. Denis and Carol were very kind about my performance on the Thames television show the night before. Crawfie was there.* She was fussing a bit over Carol, who was due to go off at 9.30 (I think she had a date), and the Prime Minister was very much a mother about her. Carol insisted on waiting, although she did slip away towards the end of the meal, and the more food she ate the more the Prime Minister actually settled down. After dinner, we went back into the other room

---

* Cynthia Crawford, Mrs Thatcher's personal assistant.

for coffee, and Margaret's eyes kept on closing. She was very tired indeed.

When Tim and I got into the lift we just looked at each other, shook hands and said: 'Thank God we've got the strategy set right.' And I think we have. I promised the Prime Minister that we would get a speaking note for her, so she would have that when she went to see Tim the very next day.

I came back at about 11 o'clock, absolutely worn out. But at least tomorrow we have Glyndebourne, and it promises to be spectacular – the first night of *La Traviata*. I am looking forward to it very much indeed.

One other thing I should mention: Crawfie told me that she is moving into No. 10. She wants the Prime Minister to sleep a bit later in future, and if I want to speak to her early in the morning I should actually speak to Crawfie first. I said I would do that.

Saturday 30 May

I slept a bit later and got into central office in time for the 9 o'clock strategy meeting. First, I popped in to see Alistair and asked him if I could borrow College Street for a meeting with Tim a little later on. Then I went into the strategy meeting, which lasted for about half an hour, and all seemed to be going well. Afterwards, I spent a few minutes with Norman. The polls look a lot better. I managed to talk Norman into agreeing the general strategy line which we'd agreed with the Prime Minister yesterday evening. This will certainly make our life one hell of a lot easier. I said I had to go down to the country – I was going to deal with 'the marginal constituencies of West Sussex', I said. I told Shirley where I was really going, and they knew where I'd be and what time I would be back.

Then I walked over to College Street. Unfortunately, they weren't expecting us, but that wasn't too great a problem. Tim wasn't there, but he turned up a few minutes late. It was evidently the day for Trooping the Colour rehearsals, and it had taken him forty minutes to get there. We quickly worked out a speaking note. I had suddenly thought up a line for the Prime Minister to take on VAT, and I rang it through to Stephen, who thought it was very good. It was quite simply this: 'Don't ask me about raising money on VAT, you go and ask the Labour Party. We've got enough money, we've got our spending plans set for the next three years, we don't need to raise more taxes. But *they* do. Where are they going to get it from?' Stephen thought that was a very good idea and promised to ring it through to the coach.

Anyway, with Howell and Tim we worked out exactly the line we would have to take. I left the two of them at it to get a note to put it in to the Prime Minister.

I then walked back to the office. Because of Trooping the Colour, I thought I would go south. I got caught up in the Milk Race and eventually got home. We packed up all the gear, then drove down to the country. On the way down, I realised I'd left my bow tie behind, so we rang up the Harmers (our neighbours in the country), who said they would bring one round. Before they could do so, the phone went and it was Michael Dobbs, who said, 'David, we've just got the script of the new party election broadcast. It's going to be attacking the trade unions and all sorts of things, we'd like you to be in it.'

'Oh good,' I said.

'But we've got to shoot it tonight,' said Michael. After a few expletives I asked if they could put it off until tomorrow, but as soon as he put the phone down, I knew I'd had it. John Sharkey, managing director of Saatchis, rang a few minutes later and said they couldn't do it tomorrow; they were shooting it on film and had to do it today. I agreed. I made him go and get a hire car to send Lita to Glyndebourne and back. Then, in the midst of all this, the Harmers came round. I got the bow tie and thanked them very much, then off I went, back again to London.

Got home just in time to freshen up – rang Tim, rang Howell. On the journey back Ken Baker called me in the car. He's been ringing me most days to see how it's going on. He couldn't stop laughing when I told him my story. I went to some studios in Blandford Street, where we shot and shot and shot again the last part of the party election broadcast, which I didn't actually think was particularly good. It was all about somebody – the Labour Party – doing conjuring tricks which always failed, and I was part of the audience. Anyway, we'll see how it all works out. I must confess, though, that for the past few days I've been feeling more and more nervous and despondent about the outcome of the election.

Afterwards I took Howell off to a local Chinese restaurant, and we had a very good meal. But when I got back at about 11.30 and went to bed, I was feeling no better.

Sunday 31 May

I slept late, not really waking until gone 9 o'clock, and rang Lita. Happily everything seemed to have gone off OK at Glyndebourne the night before. I messed around for a while, then David Hart telephoned, full of despondency and alarm. He started telling me all the things we should and shouldn't be doing. I told him about the letter we've been trying to get twenty-five top industrialists to sign. It had been delivered, and Frank Johnson of *The Times* had rung me on the Friday. Evidently the editor, Charlie Wilson, was refusing to sign it. I said to David: 'You've got good contacts, see what you can do.' He agreed, but he was pretty aggressive about all the things that were wrong in central office.

A little later on I was still clearing up all my bits and pieces. I rang Tim Bell, and we talked about where we were going. I told him I didn't know what had happened at the meeting between Norman and the Prime Minister, which had been scheduled to take place at 7 o'clock on the previous evening, and I said I would ring him as and when I heard what had actually happened. He sounded a lot more cheerful than I did – I was really quite depressed about prospects. He told me to give Gordon Reece a call and gave me his number. I rang Gordon, who was really full of good cheer. He thought things were going very well, that the impact of Defence was yet to come through in the polls. There had been one very bad poll in *The Observer*, which had showed us at forty-one against Labour's thirty-seven, but he told me that had been conducted on the previous Wednesday, and he was really quite relaxed about where we are going. I had rehearsed both with Tim and with Gordon the line that I was going to take, and they thought it was quite splendid.

I'd rung Howell a bit earlier, but he'd been out. I'd left a message on his answer phone, and he rang back just before lunch. Tim had said he was expected over there, but in fact he was still at the department. He sounded slightly more cautious and indeed told me (which I later accepted) that I was raising too many different points in one press conference. I am finding as time goes by that Howell's advice is more and more valuable on political matters, which is really quite interesting, since deep down I don't believe for one moment that he totally supports what we are doing.

Just before I was due to go and have lunch with Karen and Bernard, Robert Atkins rang and started to fill me with doom and gloom about the situation. He'd had conversations with Ian Lang and other chums but I refused to let him depress me, and eventually I cut him off. Then I went off to have lunch. I came back about 3 o'clock and settled down to do more work – principally to bring these notes up to date. Then David Hart telephoned through and told me he'd got the letter sorted out. With a bit of luck that will appear on Tuesday.

By the time I finished my work, Lita had come back. Then I got a message that the meeting at No. 10 had been brought forward to 7.15, so I went speedily into the department. One matter I had forgotten is that Keith Joseph had rung in the morning and said he had some advice for the PM about words to use on caring. I asked him to let me have these and said I would deliver them to her.

I went into central office and Keith's notes were there. I picked them up and went upstairs where Norman's meeting was just starting. Alistair wanted to see me, so I went in there first. He anxiously asked me what had happened on Friday night and Saturday. I told him that as far as I knew it had gone all right. Then I went into the chairman's meeting, and that seemed to be going well. I told Norman I was slipping off to see the Prime Minister about the tour. I asked about the meeting on Saturday night. He said, 'Very good indeed, I'll tell you all about it later.' Then a moment or two later he said: 'Well, we're going to change some of the press conferences for the week to come – David, yours is all right.' Then he led me to believe that in fact he'd accepted the strategy Tim and I had outlined on Friday night.

I left after about ten minutes and went over to No. 10. Peter Morrison, Christine Wall, Roger Boaden and David Wolfson were there. We all went in to Stephen Sherbourne, who seemed to be fussing a little bit about her, though that was fair enough. We waited for a while, and then I heard she was on the telephone to Woodrow Wyatt. I said, 'Look, I've got a lot of things to do.' Alistair had invited me to have dinner with him and Sue Timpson and I'd agreed to meet them at the Connaught at quarter to nine. I said I would go upstairs and see her on my own first.

I asked her how she had got on with Norman, and she said only 80 per cent well. She started telling me about Woodrow, who had just mentioned to her some book on postal ballots. At this point I got the others to come in, and then she wrote out a card with the postal ballots book, and also some quotation or other from Kinnock. I said, 'Prime Minister, the thing I want to deal with first is the *Jimmy Young Show*.' I got settled who was going on the show and then said I needed to go and make arrangements for tomorrow.

After leaving her, I went back to central office and discussed the arrangements for the next day with Howell, Paul Twyman and Norman Blackwell. I showed Paul the card the Prime Minister had written out. 'Oh,' he said, 'that chap came in only the day before yesterday. I think I've got his book.' He popped out and came back with it. 'Good,' I said, 'I'll earn a brownie point or two, I'll pop it in for her on my way back.'

I'd been invited downstairs as soon as I came back to look at the alterations they were making to the press room. It really did look good – a great improvement on before. So that pleased me immensely, and I thought, 'Well, I'll be there doing it tomorrow and be the first one to get it going. It's going to be a big day.'

Howell knew I was going off to have dinner, so on the way back I went into No. 10 and found out the others were still with the Prime Minister in the study upstairs. I went in and gave her the book. 'Oh,' she said, 'how marvellous, how on earth did you get it in time?' 'Oh, well,' I said, 'I don't know, just luck. I'll get some more copies from the research department.' And off I went, thinking to myself I really had earned a few brownie points purely by luck.

At the Connaught, Alistair and Sue were still having a drink in the bar. Sue had a number of points. Jon Snow had become so effusive over Kinnock that they are really thinking about taking him off *Channel 4 News*. Alastair Burnet (whom she called

Brunette) was of the opinion that it would cause more trouble to take him off than continue with him. I said to her very decisively that I felt he was doing so much harm where he was, it didn't matter what trouble it would be if we got rid of him. She wanted in particular to have an opportunity for the Prime Minister to see the television newsmen for five minutes early each day, so she would make the 5.45 news. I promised that with Alistair I would speak with her tomorrow morning. But I think Sue was more relaxed than she had been last week. I think the general feeling all over the place is that things are going better.

Incidentally, at 6 o'clock when I was going off to my meetings, the phone rang and it was Christopher Soames,* who had rung me the week before. He raised one or two points, but by and large he was much happier with the way the election is going. We fixed that we would have lunch or dinner sometime when the election is over. But the view of Keith Britto and other statisticians at central office is that the polls really are showing us 9 per cent in the lead, and with a bit of luck the next two days will show Labour continuing to go down. I think I've got home my belief that what we've got to do is attack them and attack them hard on trade union policy.

Monday 1 June

Today is the day of the press conference. I arrived at 7.30 and first went to inspect the conference room. While I was there, Howell

---

* Christopher Soames (Baron Soames of Fletching after 1978), 1920–87. Son-in-law of Winston Churchill; Conservative MP, 1950–66; ambassador to France, 1968–72; Leader of the House of Lords, 1979–81.

was putting up the title behind the podium. I was very pleased with the way the room now looked, and I agreed the title he put up without any difficulty. I thought the graphics I had seen the night before had come out very well indeed. At 7.45, I went upstairs to the morning chairman's meeting. Everyone was there, and the polls had not changed very much. It was getting slightly worrying, going on Defence all week without much effect, when Defence was possibly our most positive policy.

We carried through the usual routine businesses. I told Norman exactly what the title was and what the graphics were, and then at about twenty past eight the Prime Minister arrived. At the PM's meeting we agreed the press notice – there was no dissent on it. But Margaret, I thought, was in rather a tense mood – slightly tetchy. We went through all the questions that had arisen overnight and there seemed to be far too many points of detail – she does want to master every single point to show that she is on top of everything.

We went into the press conference at 9.30. I must confess, for the first time in a very long time I was feeling more than a little nervous. I'd organised that I'd have a tie mic so I could move round rather than hold anything. That all went extremely well. When we had the visual with the dead rose there was a titter around the audience of fairly hard-bitten press men. The questions were quite slow in coming, but in the end I thought I managed to get nearly all points through. At about five past ten I passed a note to the Prime Minister and we finished it off.

I went into Norman's room and Willie was sitting there with

John Wakeham. Norman and I went in, and Willie said, 'Ah, David, now you're here I'll tell you to your face what I've just said behind your back.' He said, 'I've been in politics fighting elections for thirty years, but I could never have handled any press conference as well as you've just handled that. I don't know how you've done it – you're only a beginner – but congratulations, it was marvellous.' I thought John Wakeham looked more than a little sick, but there you are.

I went back into the Prime Minister's room and thought I would just check with Sue Timpson whether she would give the interviews each day. She agreed to do that. Then I slipped into Alistair's room to ask Piers to ring ITN and tell them that would be done.

I went back into my room and Howell was there. He started to speak to me about a Southampton public meeting. Now, I'd been approached by Tony Garner on Thursday or Friday last week to take up an invitation that had originally gone to Nigel Lawson. I thought it had been for a television programme down in Southampton, and I'd gladly agreed. In actual fact, it turned out to be a public meeting. Eventually I told Tony that I would do it, and he came back and told me they'd now made arrangements and increased the size of the meeting from 300 to 350. I thought that perhaps we could get some television there.

We started the strategy meeting at 12 o'clock. It went quite uneventfully until I got called out to watch the *One O'Clock News*. To my joy we were well up in the news and making the headlines. It looked as if it had gone very well indeed. I went off with Howell for a very pleasant lunch with Rod Tyler. I think we talked about all aspects. He does know an enormous amount about what is actually going on. He showed me the introduction to his upcoming book, which is written very well. Quite looking forward to it coming out – I just hope for heaven's sake it has a happy ending!

Got back to the office at about three. It was a fairly quiet afternoon, and I sat down thinking about the speech I'm going to have to make in Southampton on Wednesday night. I was slightly concerned that there had been no requests for television, but then I was asked to do the debate at the end of the *Nine O'Clock News*, which evidently I was going to do with Shirley Williams and John Smith.

I wandered on to Alistair's office, and he told me that he had just received a film from David Hart, which was about left-wing infiltration into education. We watched the film and it really was very powerful stuff – I thought very powerful indeed – and we thought that perhaps we should use it in some way. Michael Dobbs came in and saw it. He thought we should go and see if we could get permission to use it. A little while later Howell came in to see me absolutely aghast. He said Dobbs had just told him that he had the film months ago at Saatchis. Howell had sent it on to Saatchis and they were just going to check to see if they had got the rights. Well, I must say, what a waste after all those months!

I went in to watch the *Six O'Clock News* and was delighted

that we seem to have the initiative. Eventually I slipped off home, where Karen made me an enormous omelette. Then Howell came round, and we went off to do the *Nine O'Clock News*. I went up into a green room, and Shirley Williams had just arrived by helicopter. She came in looking much more glamorous than she usually does. We sat and watched the news. I got more and more irate, because all they showed was an odd throwaway remark that I had made at the morning press conference about unemployment and the Prime Minister apparently disagreeing with me. And so I was not uncritical in my remarks while Ron Neil, who is the head of BBC News, was sitting opposite me. Eventually I went into make-up and then into the studio.

I was tired, and a bit angry, but it went absolutely splendidly. Afterwards I had a quick drink. Norman Dodds was waiting downstairs next to another Rover, and on driving away he told me he had spent the hour with Kinnock's driver. Kinnock had been upstairs doing *Panorama* that night – I'd watched part of it. He had laid down an enormous verbal barrage and it had been very difficult to get any meaning out of it. But Norman told me to my amazement that Kinnock's driver had confided in him that Kinnock himself actually expected to lose the election. I think it is rather good psychology that the enemy expects to lose, but we will still see. When I got home there was a note stuck to the front door from Lita: 'Nine and three quarters out of ten.' She thought it had been really excellent. I went to bed that night feeling tired but a bit more relaxed about the polls since I'd spoken to Gordon.

Tuesday 2 June

Went into the 7.45 strategy meeting much more relaxed as this was not going to be my day. It was Nigel's turn, because we were talking about the economy. Before the Prime Minister came in, Christine Wall came up to me – I thought in a slight temper – and said, 'What's all this about Martyn Lewis on the BBC?' Well, the day before Howell had told me that Lewis, the BBC interviewer who is a supporter of ours, said he would love to have a five-minute interview with the Prime Minister before she left her tour. All he wanted to talk about was her vision for the future. 'Well,' Christine said, 'I'm not having it, they are only trying to trip her up.' She really was very defensive about what was going to happen. So that worried me very much and I said (in a rather cowardly way): 'Well, you'd better go and speak to Howell.'

The Prime Minister came in for the pre-conference briefing a minute or two late. Nigel is really quite impossible in some ways, but eventually we agreed the press notice and went through the items. The polls didn't look very good, although perhaps there was possibly a chance of Labour moving down. I sat on the front row at the main press conference, so I was well out of it, but I thought in actual fact that it went rather well – quite relaxed and good humoured.

Afterwards I saw the Prime Minister for a few minutes. She looks worried and certainly not very relaxed. I had a quiet chat with her and Norman. Eventually she went off on her tour. Then I had to go down to the Ritz to meet BT chairman George Jefferson about a slightly difficult matter. I had a long chat with him – he told me that he was looking for a new chairman, and I'm not sure if he was actually canvassing me, but in any case I told him that I was committed for the future.

By the time I came back I suddenly realised to my horror that I had missed the strategy meeting. In fact, it had started early, at 11.15, and was still going on just after midday, but I decided not to go in for the later stages. I went back to central office and Howell came in. He said I should have a word with Tim, so I rang him up and agreed to have lunch with both Tim and Howell at Mark's Club. We had a rather pleasant but inconclusive lunch in which we discussed strategy without coming to any really firm conclusion. What we did say was that we would meet with the Prime Minister on Wednesday night when she came back from that day's tour.

Then I saw Michael Dobbs, who told me the party election broadcast was ready. So we went up to watch it with a crowd of friends in John Desborough's room. I must confess to being very disappointed with it indeed. It started off with the theatre scene and went on to show the Labour Party as a magician failing all his tricks.* It ended up with just about fifteen or twenty seconds of me sitting in the audience watching the tricks being performed. And then just at that moment my phone went. It was Kenneth Baker, and we stopped the tape while I chatted with him about what he was doing and the problems from his

---

* Whether consciously or not, this idea was stolen from a great parliamentary speech by Neil Kinnock's predecessor as Labour leader, Michael Foot, who had compared Sir Keith Joseph to a conjuror who forgot the end of his main trick.

point of view. When I had finished, we put the tape back on and it immediately switched to film of about three minutes, which, with a musical background, was all about the Prime Minister and how she's an international statesman and everything else. I couldn't quite believe it – I think for two reasons. First of all, it was clearly two entirely separate films; and secondly, I'd given up Saturday night, Glyndebourne etc., for something which was only fifteen or twenty seconds long. It did seem a slightly bizarre sort of film.

A few minutes later there was the *Nine O'Clock News*, which announced a poll on *Newsnight* showing that, on a marginal poll, we could be heading towards a hung parliament. Now, the difficulty with this poll was that quite frankly it wasn't a recognised poll company, and we didn't quite trust it.* But nevertheless, the prospect that Labour was somehow catching up with us in the marginal seats was rather disconcerting to put it mildly. It was certainly quite a check and was rather depressing, particularly as I had to go over to BBC for *Newsnight* and had to think fairly seriously how I would react to it.

Norman started another strategy meeting, which wasn't going very earnestly, so I excused myself and went over to *Newsnight* with Howell, getting there a little bit early. John Prescott had turned up. I do find him a terribly awkward individual – he really has got an enormous chip on his shoulder. We waited while he made some excuse about phoning his wife – it's about the

---

* The poll had been organised by the journalist Vincent Hanna, who was criticised for using students to canvass opinions.

second or third time I've heard him do that – and then he came in with his rather jolly female assistant and two or three other fairly earnest young people. When we got to do *Newsnight*, we first had the poll. They mentioned all sorts of health warnings, but even so they said that it looks as if we are heading towards a hung parliament. I just said, 'Well, of course, we take all polls seriously. It's going to make us work harder.' John Prescott went very upmarket and started to talk about victory, while the Alliance's Malcolm Bruce, who was down the line from Aberdeen, was reasonably cautious about it all.

After that we went onto *Newsnight* proper, and I found to my absolute horror that the film they had prepared featured Prof. Story of Newcastle, who is allegedly a small businessman who is avidly against small business, and Richard Layard, the professor of labour economics who of course is really an Alliance politician and who had written a letter about me in the *Financial Times*. It was really a very loaded film stacked all against us. When the film finished, they came to me and asked me a question. I just said that this film was totally bizarre and went on with all the reasons why. Then we went into the discussion generally. Of course Bruce, being up in Scotland at the end of a line, was at a disadvantage, but I thought Prescott was rather better than usual. I still managed to have the upper hand – it really went rather well. It eventually finished at about half past eleven, and when I got home Lita said it had been very good. It took me some time to settle down – I always find that after evening television it takes a while to relax – and we finally went to bed about quarter to one.

Wednesday 3 June

Well, this was the day when the Prime Minister was not going to be around, and we only had to have one pre-briefing meeting. The first meeting was fixed for 8.15, so I had a slight lie-in, although Norman Dodds was very anxious I should get there in time so he could have his breakfast before the canteen closed. Norman Tebbit was in the chair for the press conference, having said during the pre-briefing that he intended to act just as a chairman and to pass the questions over to all of us. It started dead on time at 9.30 and was reasonably well attended – though perhaps not quite as well attended as normal. At about five past ten, I passed Norman a note. Up to that point it had gone very well indeed, but he did tend to carry on and on and on and hogged a lot of the questions himself. Actually, it ended up with people walking out because it went on till just after half past ten. I'm not sure how much of it really got over. I went upstairs, and Willie and John Wakeham were sitting in Norman's room. Willie went right off the top about it, and criticised Norman for taking the limelight and letting it go on far too long. Willie certainly appeared very close with John Wakeham.

Then Chris Lawson came in to me and gave me a note. To my horror, it said that Norman Fowler was going to have a chart made with a sort of dying rose on it and a statement by Hattersley which talked about how big the pension was going to be under Labour. Well, I thought, that was absolutely mad because it would appear on television and really give time for the other side. I hit the roof about it. Peter Morrison said he would deal with it. I went and had a quick word to find out what time Alistair was going to come back to central office. As I was passing Peter's room, he suddenly called me and said, 'I've got Norman on the phone.' When I picked up the phone, I assumed it was Norman Tebbit, and I almost said, 'You see what that idiot Norman Fowler's doing?' But I suddenly realised it must be Fowler, and I just avoided putting my foot right in it. Thankfully, Norman saw the point of what I was saying about the chart, and he said he would look at it again.

I'd agreed to go to Southampton that evening for the speaking engagement, but I hadn't really got my speech done. So, when I came back, eventually I sat myself down, got my machine out and started to write. I spent from ten to one until 2 o'clock writing what I thought was quite a good speech, and I printed it out. It was about the choices that are facing us. We agreed to get Norman Blackwell down to put some finishing touches to it. Then I promised to go down to Colin Moynihan's constituency to do some canvassing, I thought, or some kind of help for him. I really didn't like the idea of this very much, but when I got down to Colin's place what he really wanted was to show me how he is running his campaign. In fact, I found it a very interesting half or three quarters of an hour. He is very optimistic. I could see he has built his campaign very much on local issues, and I thought it was actually going rather well.

Then he brought me to his next-door neighbour, who is fighting the next seat. For some bizarre reason, he just wanted me to go to meet one particular local employer who couldn't get employees. So, I go along to some chap who works in the dry rot industry – an enormous man with a great big pot belly. He was very bigoted about the country being full up with black people and that's why you can't get jobs, why there is unemployment etc. He went on and on about how the job centre wouldn't send him anybody. After a while I began to suspect that actually he was offering to pay cash for people, but that's neither here nor there. After the hour was up, I went back to the office thinking it was a bit of a waste of time and still slightly panicking about my evening speech.

When I went back, I found that Norman Blackwell had really made a lot of modifications to the speech and at first I hit the roof. Then I looked at them and realised it now made a pretty marvellous speech. So, you can imagine my horror when I suddenly found out the press office had issued the old speech before it had been amended! To make matters worse, I discovered that there were rumours going round the City about a rather bad poll that was coming out, showing our lead down quite a lot. I went over to Keith Britto and he said the poll showed us only four points ahead of Labour, but this could vary quite a bit and we would really have to see.

Now, I'd actually found out during the day that Tim and I were to go and see the Prime Minister, and I'd been in touch with Stephen on the bus. We fixed that when I came back to London from Southampton, which would be at about 10 o'clock, we would go over to see her. We rang to say there was a possibility I could be a few minutes late to Southampton. The arrangements I'd made were that Norman was going to go ahead a bit earlier to avoid the rush hour, and then I would get a pool car to take me to the station. I rang Tim and fixed where I would meet with him, but just before I got to the pool car there was an enormous to-do about getting my real speech out to the press. So Howell, who was due to come with me, agreed to stay behind and also work on the graphics which Norman Fowler was to use. Anyway, I was told that Margaret Bell would have a proper copy of my speech, and so I got the pool car to take me round opposite Caxton House near Victoria station. It was pouring down with rain. Margaret gave me a copy of the speech, and I went back to Waterloo and got there in very good time.

I got on the train and thought I would ring the office just to be on the safe side. I got hold of Margaret to make sure the full version of the speech would go out to the press, including the extra bits. Suddenly I noticed that there was a train next door to us at the platform, and all the people were looking through and pointing. As they came into my carriage, people sort of nodded, and later as they left they wished me good luck. Obviously I'd been on so much television recently I'm now really quite well known.

Down to Southampton and the agent is waiting for me. In the car he tells me how Michael Heseltine was there a few weeks ago and got a standing ovation. 'Oh well,' I said, 'Michael Heseltine is a good speaker.' I got to Bitterne School, and it was all a bit shambolic. I went in and saw the hall, and the television cameras were all set there. And then I went in and had a press conference. There were a couple of fairly aggressive local reporters and I gave a radio interview – oddly enough, as I was giving the press conference, they were recording what I said for the radio interview.

By 7.30 we had a good crowd – it must have been close to 300 – and I went into the meeting. I really got carried away by the whole thing. There were hecklers there in good measure, but I think I gave as good as I got – in fact, I think I probably ended up on top. At the end of my speech, to my complete amazement I got a standing ovation – actually, they gave me three standing ovations, because the chairwoman got up and said she wanted to show their appreciation to me, and everybody stood up again. Then I realised that the other MP still had to give the vote of thanks, and so they all sat down again. He gave the vote of thanks, and when I got up to leave, to my amazement everybody got up again for the third time. So, I can safely say it was a great hit.

I left at about 8.30. It was still light and all the BBC cameramen and technicians with their big vans outside the school waved at me and called over to me and wished me good luck. Obviously things were really going very well indeed.

Norman Dodds lost the way a little bit going out of the town on the way back to London. I had been dreading getting on the telephone, but eventually I rang central office. I spoke to Keith Britto, who told me very bad news and my heart really did sink. Evidently the new poll showed us that we were 40.5 to Labour's 36.5. We *were* just four points ahead, and obviously they were catching us up fast.

Well, we got back to London in very good time. Because we were a bit late leaving Southampton, I rang up Tim, and Howell was there. We agreed that Howell would ring through to No. 10 for them to expect me at 10.15. Actually, we got into London rather earlier, so I thought I would call in for a hamburger – I hadn't eaten anything that evening. I got to No. 10 at just about quarter past ten.

Stephen saw us and told us she was very tired – in fact, she had been suffering from a very bad toothache. When we went upstairs, Denis was there and she was obviously very weary. She was tetchy, she was very depressed and, worst of all, she knew the poll result. She started talking about the prospect of actually losing. We said, 'Look, what we've really got to do is to change what we are doing, get a coherent thing, get everything coordinated.' Tim gave his plan for the way in which the whole campaign should be run, which she seemed to take in.

Then I said, 'Look, why don't you persuade Norman to go and spend all day out, and then say, "David, you go and coordinate things while Norman is out."' She talked about the complaints she was getting about Norman being on television the whole time, so I said, 'Prime Minister, one way to do this, why don't you say: "Norman and David – the pair of you – I don't want you to be on television. I want to get the younger faces there."'

She said, 'Yes, *yes*, that would be a good way.'

And I said, 'Prime Minister, we will organise something for you. We'll do it tomorrow morning and it will all be done, just leave it to me.'

At this point she looked very tired indeed. She had some more things to do, and she started work on a box. It was about half past eleven/twenty to twelve. Tim and I walked out with Denis, who said she'd had this terrible problem with an abscess, and she was very tense at the moment. As we went down, the chap at the front door showed us tomorrow morning's *Times*, which had headlines about the bad poll results. He also showed us the *Telegraph*, which seemed to refer to the meeting we had just been having upstairs – which was either very amazing or else they had guessed very well indeed. Anyway, I got home and went to bed feeling very depressed and very, very nervous indeed.

Thursday 4 June

I woke up feeling very worried and apprehensive – I hadn't slept too well. I went into central office for the 7.45 meeting. The atmosphere was a bit tense as we went through everything. The poll was undoubtedly a shock, and there were further polls due. The bitter irony was that this Thursday was 'Wobble Day' – the day that Alistair McAlpine had been forecasting for the past three weeks. Early on in the campaign, I went into Alistair's room, where there was a big chart on the wall, and they were plotting the likely trends in the polls. Towards the end of the chart, on one date there was a pencil line all the way down, and I asked what it meant. 'Oh,' said Alistair, 'that's Wobble Day.'

'What's Wobble Day?'

He said, 'Well, we had it in '79, and we had it again in '83. You see, they'll be above us on that day – they were in '79, they moved to half a point above us. In '83 that was the day when the campaign was going wrong, and we met and thrashed it out and we changed this and we changed that – it will all work out all right, but you just wait and see.'

And, of course, Labour have certainly been gaining on us. We got closer and closer to Wobble Day, and lo and behold we were in it. It was certainly a great big wobble, only I wasn't sure at all that things would change for the better this time.

The Prime Minister came into the meeting at just before 8.30 – she looked very tired and very strained. She immediately turned round to Norman and said, 'We have really got to change some things – we've got to have younger people on television. You and David, you've been on too much and you're too old. We must have younger people.' We went on through all the points and had the report on the polls. She was very tetchy and nervous and became obsessed with all the detail.

We went downstairs to the press conference, and she just was not good at all. It went on and on. She got caught out on a question dealing with private healthcare.* There somehow seemed to be a feeling around that we were on the run. Kinnock had had his press conference before ours. The press all came in, and they were pushing the PM with questions arising from things that had come up in his press conference.

When the meeting ended, we went upstairs and had the meeting I had fixed the night before. This time Willie was there with John Wakeham, which annoyed me slightly.† She went on about the advertising, which she didn't like at all. She wanted it more aggressive against Labour's left-wingers, more along

---

* She said she was treated privately 'to enable me to go into hospital on the day I want, at the time I want and with the doctor I want'. The implication – that the state health system was not delivering an adequate service to less affluent people with an equally urgent need for treatment – was only too true. This unconscious indictment of her own government's stewardship of the public services would have cost Mrs Thatcher the election if the electorate had been sincere in its stated preference for improved healthcare over further cuts in taxation.

† Wakeham had not been invited.

the lines that we had discussed the night before. She went on
again about television – how neither of us was to be on television. Norman said he had been fixed to do the *Granada Five
Hundred* and one or two other things. It would look very bad
if he suddenly got called out of it. She agreed to let him go on.
She told Norman that he must go out to more constituencies,
which was what we had agreed the night before, but she didn't
say anything to me or ask me to do anything. I slipped a note
to Stephen, asking 'Has she changed her mind?' He looked at
me and shrugged his shoulders. I was getting more and more
desperate until eventually I said, 'Prime Minister, what do you
want me to do?'

And she just exploded. She said, 'I can't do all this myself; I
can't tell you.'

'No, no,' I said, 'I know, Prime Minister, you just tell me
what you would like me to do' – really to give her an opening
to tell me to go and fix this or look after that. But she didn't
say anything at all. Then she went on about the party election
broadcast, and the meeting broke up without anything being
resolved. I felt very depressed. I really thought for some peculiar
reason that I was being left out in the cold and being blamed
that things weren't going very well.

After the meeting, I went out into the hall. She was standing
there with Stephen. I said, 'Prime Minister, this really won't do. I
want to help you, I'm willing to do things, but you must give me
the authority, I have no position.'

She said, 'I know, I know, it's very difficult.'

'Look Prime Minister, let me take over the party-political

broadcast – I'll run it and take it over with Stephen and we will get it all done, but you must give me the authority.'

'Yes,' she said, 'all right, you do it with Stephen.'

'Just come back, come and tell Norman and I'll get it done.'

'No,' she said. 'I've got to go now.' After she left, I went back and told Howell all about it. I really felt awful. Stephen stayed behind to fix up one or two things, then he went back to No. 10. I spoke to him on the phone later. He said, 'No, no, she really does want you to do things, she just feels it's a very awkward position and she doesn't know how to deal with Norman. She's very worried that there might be a great big bust-up.' Very strange, I must say, that here we have the 'Iron Lady' – the toughest woman in Europe if not the world – and yet she cannot actually go and tell one of her people what they should do!

It was really getting very depressing and very worrying. But we had to get the party election broadcast meeting arranged. So, I got hold of Howell and said, 'Come on, let's fix a meeting this afternoon.' With Stephen, we fixed a meeting for 3.30 at No. 10 with Tim, Tony Jay, Stephen, Howell and Ronnie Millar.*

Amidst all of this, I had to give a formal lunch at Lancaster House for the Chinese minister for aeronautical industries. All the people were there from my other life – in government – which now seemed so remote. The Chinese ministers received me very warmly – remarkably warmly, in fact. Eric Sharp told me he had just come back from China and my standing was

---

* Ronnie (after 1979 Sir Ronnie) Millar, 1919–98. Playwright, and contributor to many of Mrs Thatcher's most important speeches.

enormously high. The aeronautical industries minister was very effusive – we exchanged presents, we made the speeches, we finished lunch. I told Eric that I was rather worried about the campaign and after a while began to get more than depressed. I began almost to wonder if this wasn't going to be my very last government meeting. I began to think semi-seriously about what I would do or would not do in the event that the inconceivable happened and we lost the election.

I went back to central office and saw Keith Britto. I heard there were more rumours about the state of the campaign going round the Stock Exchange, and I had two or three phone calls in as many minutes saying there was a new poll coming out that evening and Labour had moved within 2 per cent of us. Well, I had that sickening feeling that normally when you expect bad news it always comes to pass. I recalled how the day before there had been a rumour and that had absolutely been confirmed. So, I was very depressed and very nervous and tetchy – rather like the Prime Minister, in fact.

At half past three I went over to No. 10. In the waiting room on the ground floor, we had a long meeting and went through everything. I outlined an idea for the party-political broadcast – the PM's last one – which was about paths and choices. Really, I suppose what I suggested was a little bit coloured by my speech the night before. To my slight surprise, I found out when I finished that it was almost exactly the script they had already written, so we agreed to take it further. Tim said he had prepared a programme of advertising on the theme of 'Britain's Great Again, Don't Let Labour Ruin It'. It was on the lines that unemployment's been coming down for the past six months, but every Labour government there has ever been has put unemployment up. I told him this was fantastic.

'What will you do with it?' he asked.

Well, I jumped up and said, 'I'll tell you what I'll do with it. If she doesn't take it, I'll walk out – I'll resign because we'll lose the bloody election!' Tim looked at me, startled. The Prime Minister was due to come back at 5.30 or 5.45. I told Stephen that what I wanted to do was show her Tim's campaign and the campaign Saatchis had put together. Then she would have to decide which of the two she wanted. We would have to do one or the other, because we really had to go into this advertising campaign if we were to save the election at all. I really felt we were on the point of actually losing it, and I said so. And Stephen, to his great credit, agreed.

I waited for a very nervous three quarters of an hour, pacing backwards and forwards and really worrying. Then Howell came back and brought with him the boards for Tim's campaign. It started to rain then – a torrential downpour. He put the boards out and they were fantastic – only roughs, but they really did look very good indeed. Howell stayed behind and we showed them to Stephen, who loved them. I kept on ringing my office every twenty minutes, but there was still no news to confirm or deny this rumour of the 2 per cent poll. The market had gone down enormously. Eventually we heard that the Prime Minister had landed in her helicopter – she was on her way back. I rang through to the car and said what I wanted to do.

When she came in, I met her down the corridor. I said, 'Prime

Minister, come in here and look at this.' And she looked at it, and I said, 'Tim did it.' She loved it.

'Well,' she said, 'what do I do now?'

I said, 'Prime Minister, look, it's very simple. I've got Saatchis waiting for me with their campaign. I'll bring them over, you have a look at it, and if you like it, we do it. If you don't like it all you've got to say is, "No, I don't like it, David's got something better. I've got to go off and do my Dimbleby interview. David, you sort it out." Then you just walk out, and I will deal with it all.'

She looked very relieved at this thought and said, 'All right, I must go and get briefed up.' Off she went. I've learnt one vital lesson – that she cannot do anything unpleasant; I've got to do it for her.

I rang through to Michael Dobbs to tell him to come over. Norman answered the phone. I said, 'Norman, could you bring all the stuff over and get Saatchis over?' He agreed and thought we could do it for 6.30. I said, 'Norman, would you mind coming over five minutes earlier?' He sounded a bit puzzled but said he would. So, I paced up and down some more and waited for what would be a very, very difficult time.

Outside, the rain was really coming down in torrents. Eventually John Sharkey came in, together with Maurice Saatchi. We were waiting for the Prime Minister outside the Cabinet room for a few minutes. Eventually I said, 'Why don't you take the stuff upstairs, and when Norman comes, we can pop in?'

Maurice Saatchi said, 'I don't mind starting without Norman, he can catch us up.'

So I said, 'No, no, let's go upstairs.'

While we were going upstairs, a commotion started at the front entrance. I went back down and was told that Norman would be there in two minutes. 'Norman,' I said when he appeared, 'I must see you – there have been one or two developments.' He looked at me and I said, 'Come on, I want to show you something. Look, she's asked for some other things to be done, come with me.' I take Norman into the waiting room and show him Tim's programme.

'Who did this?' he asked.

'Just look at the programme.'

'No, no,' he said, 'tell me who did it.'

I said, 'Tim Bell.'

He said, 'Well, that's it then, that's it.'

I got him by the shoulders and said: 'Norman, listen to me, we're about to lose this fucking election. You're going to go, I'm going to go, the whole thing is going to go. The whole election depends upon her being right for the next five days, doing fine performances on television – she has to be happy, we have got to do this. Now, look at this campaign, look at it.'

He looked at it, and said, 'It looks very good.'

'Yes,' I said. 'It's very simple – we'll look and see what they've got from Saatchis, and if that's better we'll use that. One way or another, we'll get it done. But if this is better, we'll use it.'

'All right then,' he said.

'But you've got to,' I said. 'Norman, it's your future and my future and all our futures and the future of this flaming country.' I went on quite a bit.

The Prime Minister is still in her room. Norman has one look at their campaign and his face gets longer and longer. He says, 'This won't do, this won't do at all, it really won't. I don't know… she'll go mad when she sees it.'

So, Norman and I looked at Tim's programme again, and I said, 'We've got to use this one, haven't we?'

'Yes,' he said, 'we have, I can't possibly show her the Saatchi programme. Send Maurice down to me.'

I go upstairs, and there's David Wolfson wandering around with Stephen. I say, 'Maurice, could you go down? Norman would like to have a word with you – we're getting a bit mysterious, I know, but if you could do that, if you would just go down and see Norman.' I got Wolfson to take Maurice down. Then we asked John Sharkey to put all the boards away, as I was worried she might come and see them.

I took Stephen into the next room and told him what we were going to do – that we were actually going to get the Saatchis to adopt the other programme. He said, 'David, you would do a marvellous thing if you could get the whole thing done without even going to her. Just tell her it's off her hands.'

I wandered downstairs, and there was David Wolfson coming along the corridor, waving a piece of paper and looking cheerful. He said, 'We've got the poll results.' It was forty-four, thirty-four, twenty. So obviously yesterday's poll had just been a rogue. Immediately, I knew we had the election won after all, and everything was going to be all right.

Norman, I assumed, was still in the waiting room with Maurice. So I walked in there, put my head round the door and said,

'The polls have come through,' and gave him the figures. He looked pleased and asked me to come in. I looked and suddenly realised John Sharkey was there as well as Maurice. Maurice said, 'I can't possibly do this, I can't possibly take it, it won't go.'

So, I still had to convince two mortal enemies to accept and use the work of the other without upsetting the PM at a critical moment. I went up to him and said, 'Now look, Maurice' – and again I got him by the lapels – 'you've got to do it.'

'No, no, we can't possibly…'

I said: 'Maurice, how much are you worth, how much are your companies worth? Do you know how much you'll be worth this time next week if we lose this election? You'll be broke, I'll be broke, the whole country will be broke – now forget your bloody pride, this is the programme she wants, and this is the programme you're going to do.'

I literally shouted at him. He looked very sulky and said, 'Well, it's all amateurish.'

I said, 'Look, forget it, leave it – just do something similar, it's what she wants, it's a positive upbeat message that she wants.' He said he could prepare it and I said, 'Work all night, bring it round at 10 o'clock tomorrow morning after the press conference, and we will get it done.'

Well, he hummed and he hawed and they looked at each other. Eventually, they agreed to do it, and they got their boards together. I walked out with Norman, who said, 'Well, I want to go and tell her.' Stephen tried to stop him, but I held him back. Norman went upstairs to wait for her. A few minutes later they came down, and obviously he had told her. She looked very relieved that they were going to do this programme, and really, to be fair to Norman, he genuinely realised Tim's idea was by far the better one. After he left, I went up to the Prime Minister, who was about to record an interview with Dimbleby. I said, 'Prime Minister, don't worry, I will get everything done, you just forget about it – you can see it tomorrow if you want to, just relax and go and sock it to them.'

I went back into the private office, where David Norgrove, one of the PM's private secretaries, was sitting reading a magazine, and I teased him a bit about having nothing very much to do. I asked the duty clerk for a piece of headed notepaper and scribbled a note to the Prime Minister, telling her exactly what I'd arranged. I left it with the front desk to give to Crawfie. Then I went and telephoned Alistair and told him that all had worked out well. I fixed to have dinner with him later, and also to borrow his house yet again, and then I rang up Tim and fixed to meet him there.

I'd had two very, very emotional meetings – they had really drained me… I don't think I have ever put more into two meetings than those, and I felt worn out. So, I went out to Norman Dodds, who had been sitting patiently waiting outside since about 3.30. We rang Howell, picked him up and went round to Alistair's house. We got there just as Tim arrived. Alistair's man opened a bottle of champagne, and I think I drank half a bottle before I could even speak. I told him the whole story, and I think Tim was a bit shaken that I had disclosed to Saatchis that he had prepared the work, but in the end he just accepted it. After about an hour's chat celebrating the results of the polls, I left and went over to Claridge's, where I met Alistair for dinner and told him the entire story all over again from the beginning. I must say, I was living every second of it, but it really was for me a tremendous achievement. Stephen, whom I'd rung before, told me it was the greatest thing in the world I'd done to take the burden away from the PM and get all the decisions made.

The dinner with Alistair was very pleasant. We sat at his usual table, which was the third one along. I was just enjoying a rather good steak when the head waiter came over and whispered in my ear that there was a call for me. I went to take it at his stand, and it turned out to be Norman Tebbit. I couldn't hear too clearly, but he appeared to be going on and on and on – he sounded a little bit as if he was tired and emotional, and it worried me slightly, as I couldn't quite make out what he was saying. I went back to discuss things with Alistair and got his commitment that if I were offered the chairmanship after the election, we would rebuild the whole of central office, transform it, bring it up to date and turn it into something good. So, I went back home very tired but feeling that we had made a step forward. I'd had quite a bit of drink. I went to bed but woke up at about 4.30 and immediately started worrying about what my next meeting with Norman would bring. I found it very difficult indeed to get back to sleep.

The Final Friday, 5 June

I went to central office for the 7.45 meeting, more than a little apprehensive. At the beginning, Norman was rather withdrawn and a bit surly. But after five minutes of joshing from me, he warmed up and it went quite well. We looked at the polls with a great sense of relief all round – they were much improved. So, the meeting finished in relatively good heart. The Prime Minister came, and we went into her pre-meeting briefing. It was going to be pensions that day, so Norman Fowler was there, as were both his ministers of state. I showed Norman the graphic we had had prepared for him after the enormous argument about his dying-rose chart, which repeated in full Hattersley's promise to increase pensions by £5 and £8 a week.

I took the opportunity to tell the Prime Minister that Saatchis were coming round at 10 o'clock to look at the advertising. She said, 'No, no, I've got a tremendous amount to do, I've got to do television and all sorts of things, I can't possibly do it.'

'All right, Prime Minister,' I said. 'Leave it with us and we will do it.' After that it was a much better atmosphere. She said to Norman that she wanted Gordon Reece to help out, and Norman said he would be delighted – he always wanted Reece about. It was agreed that Norman would ring him to ask him to come in.

The press conference started. As I wasn't in it, I watched upstairs. Fowler began to do his two graphics, both of which fell down, so it was a bit of a shambles. I was told that he was pointing with a hand microphone, so no one actually heard any sound. Nevertheless, it went quite well. I went in for the question part. The press conference, ostensibly on pensions, moved over to the NHS, and again the Prime Minister gave an over-full answer to a particular question. She was once again asked why she went to be dealt with privately. She mentioned Shirley

Williams – or Barbara Castle, I think – and said, 'I'm a very busy person and a minister, therefore I had to do it at a time that would suit me rather than to suit the hospital.' She went onto a long, fairly moralistic defensive of the health service. I fear this is an issue that will run for a little while.

When the press conference was over, I spoke to Norman. We agreed that we would wait until she left, and we asked John Sharkey and Maurice Saatchi to wait in Michael Dobbs's office until then. But first we went into Norman's room and looked at the advertising. It was very good – not quite as good perhaps as Tim would have it, but really good. Maurice was also a bit sulky and a bit withdrawn, but by the time we finished he seemed more cheerful. Maurice or John said they've got three pages of advertising booked for Sunday. I said, 'Come on, Norman, let's have three pages every single day – Sunday through to Thursday – don't worry about the cost, because I've spoken to Alistair and there's plenty of money.' So, we sat down to do it, and they raised the question of the *Mirror*. I said, 'Yes, even the *Mirror*, because it's their voters we're after.' We agreed on all that, and with a bit of luck it should be all right. So, I left that meeting actually quite relaxed about the way it would go. The advertising looked good, and at least we got the whole idea in without causing the PM any particular trouble.

I went back and spoke to Howell. We played around with the idea of having a press conference and writing an open letter to the TUC. I left him with some ideas about what we should do about that.

Lunch at the Connaught with Alistair again. This time it was with Mr Taubman, who owns Sotheby's. To my great delight, when I got there Sotheby's chairman Grey Gowrie was there as well. It was quite a pleasant lunch. Taubman's an unusual sort of chap.* He didn't quite seem to me to be the sort of person who would own Sotheby's, but there you are. In the course of the meal, Grey turned round and said to Taubman: 'David's daughter works for us in New York, and we don't even pay her a salary.' I said, 'She's back in a month or two,' and Grey said, 'Oh well, yes, and when she comes back she's going to be working for me.' This was quite encouraging, I thought.

After lunch I went back to central office, where I messed around with one or two things and planned a press conference, which I eventually thought I would hold on the following Monday on the lines of 'Whatever happened to the TUC?' This was an idea I put in at the last minute for the speech I did on Wednesday in Southampton.

I had an appointment to go down to Saatchis at six to look at the extracts for the Prime Minister's broadcast. I got there a little bit late, at about seven. Howell drove me there, then he went to get the graphics ready for our press conference. When I arrived, Jeremy Sinclair[†] and John Sharkey showed me the film they had prepared which the Prime Minister had rejected. It was four extracts of her speeches at conferences, ending up with the most recent. They had put the music from Holst's 'Jupiter'

---

* Part of this conversation is related by Alistair McAlpine in his memoir *Once a Jolly Bagman* (London: Phoenix edition, 1998), p. 121. After leaving Sotheby's in 2000, Alfred Taubman was sentenced to ten months in prison and fined $7.5 million for price-fixing.

† Jeremy Sinclair, 1946–. Joint founder of Saatchi & Saatchi, 1970; director, 1973–95; partner, M&C Saatchi since 1995.

behind it, and it was very powerful stuff. They showed me a whole lot of market research they had done, which showed the reaction from a group of people. The reaction really did appear quite good, but I argued for a long time against it. That carried on for quite a while, and we got a bit more work done. I then looked at the wording Tony Jay had prepared for the video, and we looked at some extracts from some other speeches. I came back at about 9 o'clock.

Alistair had had Shirley and Alex* in his room watching the *Nine O'Clock News*, which was quite good for us. They had already ordered a big Chinese takeaway, and I had a few cold spareribs. I went back and got some work done and eventually went home at about 11 o'clock. It was very pleasant to think that this was the last Friday of the campaign.

The Final Saturday, 6 June

There was to be a special press conference today – a Defence conference Norman had fixed up the day before. As the Prime Minister wasn't there, there was no need for the two pre-briefing meetings, so I only had to be in at 8.15. I drove myself in. When I got there, there was no one around and I found that there was some confusion. Eventually the meeting started at 8.30, and I had a quick word with Norman. He still hadn't reached out to Gordon Reece following our meeting with the PM yesterday, but he said he would.

Nigel Lawson and John MacGregor came in. We raised the

---

* The chairman's secretaries.

tax issue. There wasn't very much for me to do, but I thought they did very well. The questions were good, and there was a more relaxed atmosphere around the place. Later I cleared up a few papers and spoke to Tim Bell and Gordon Reece, who was still waiting to hear from Norman. Eventually, at about 12 o'clock, I decided I would disappear. I was feeling very tired indeed. I went home to lunch and spent a pleasant hour or two just tidying up some odd papers at home.

Well, I got back a little after 4 o'clock. Tony Jay was there with Gordon Reece, Howell, John Sharkey and Jeremy Sinclair. We were talking about the script of the Saatchi speeches film. It was a fairly inconclusive discussion, but at about 6 o'clock I thought we had something that looked quite good when it was typed out. Then Gordon and I went over to No. 10, where we sat down with the Prime Minister, Stephen and David Wolfson. I had previously arranged with Sharkey that we would get the cleaned-up version of the speeches video without all the grain on it. The Prime Minister looked very much better in it, but, unfortunately, when they played the tape the sound wasn't as good. That was because of a chance remark I'd made to Jeremy Sinclair, who had followed my instructions exactly and reduced the level of the sound. I'm afraid that this slightly spoilt the effect. But still, we can always change it.

We went through the script. The Prime Minister looked at it and said, 'No, this won't do at all. David, where on earth did you get this from?'

'Well,' I said, 'Prime Minister, I wasn't actually there.'

'Good lord!' she said. 'I had two meetings to discuss it with

Tony Jay. Well, time changes and of course the campaign goes on.'

She had simply changed her mind. She then started to dictate her thoughts to us. Gordon, Stephen and I took down what she was saying, then we all trooped upstairs. Denis was there and we played the tape. We had the first speech cut out of it – the Prime Minister had been very conscious of how much her appearance had changed since 1979 – but then she played the others and it had a tremendous effect. It really did knock everybody out. She confirmed that we could take those films for the start. After a while I left her and went back to the office. I rang up Jeremy Sinclair and we got John Sharkey and Gordon and told them the good news and the bad news. The good news was keeping the first start of the film and that the 'two paths' idea was definitely lost. The bad news was that we had to do a complete rewrite of the text. By about 10 o'clock we had got as far as we could go with the beginnings of a new script. We decided we would call it a day, and I went home, getting back at about 10.30, I suppose. Lita had left some food out for me. Eventually, I went to bed feeling very tired indeed.

The Final Sunday, 7 June

It was a chance to have a reasonable lie-in and I didn't wake up, I suppose, until half past eight. Then Lita put on the television, and we watched the Prime Minister with David Frost. She was very good indeed. The health thing had still been running, and at one point he was pushing her about private health. She turned round and said rather sweetly – when she is certainly at her most dangerous – 'But tell me, Mr Frost, don't you use private health yourself?'

'Yes,' he said, 'but when I do I feel guilty.' Well, that absolutely got him, and I thought she came away from it looking very good indeed.

I spent a quiet-ish morning tidying up some papers and trying to get myself up to date. Kenneth Baker rang through, and I had one or two other phone calls to Tim and to Gordon Reece. Eventually, at about 11.30, Lita and I left to go up to Wembley for the family rally.

I got rather caught out going up Edgware Road, and the traffic was terrible. But eventually, I saw a little yellow car ahead of us with four or five people in it and recognised the 'I LOVE MAGGIE' caps on the back. I followed them through a peculiar back-route way up to Wembley.

We arrived at about quarter past one. There was a mix-up or two over getting the right sort of seat, but eventually I sat with Peter Morrison near the front. The photographers took all sorts of silly pictures of us. The atmosphere at the rally was absolutely tremendous. Entertainers Bob Monkhouse and Jimmy Tarbuck told some excellent political jokes, and all the flag waving Harvey Thomas had arranged gave it a very warm, clean, cheerful family atmosphere. Couldn't have been better really. When the Prime Minister came on she was absolutely tremendous, and as she spoke I could see the makings of the party election broadcast. I knew that whatever happened we would have to go back and rewrite it further.

After the show was over, we slipped upstairs for some tea. The

PM was there and didn't spare herself, going round speaking to all the stars. Bob Monkhouse came up to me, and I found to my rather considerable surprise that he knew exactly who I was. I always find that slightly amazing – I'd seen him for the last God knows how many years on television.

I got away in time, dropped Lita home, then went on to No. 10. Gordon was there, with Tim, Tony Jay, Stephen, of course, and David Wolfson. We went in to the Prime Minister and showed her the new script. Right away, I'm afraid, it was obvious that this script wasn't good enough. She gave some ideas of how she would like it to be rewritten. We fixed that we would get this done, and then we would go on to the studios in Lower Regent Street. She decided to go down there before us to get ready. In the waiting room Tony Jay was busy redrafting with Tim. When we got the first sheet out, we sent it on down ahead. Eventually they drafted the whole thing, part in longhand and part in shorthand. By now it was about 6 or 6.15, and we got a phone call: would we go down to Lower Regent Street now? Oddly enough, we were told that it would be very embarrassing if Tim actually came down to the studios. I said of course, there was no question of Tim ever appearing there. So we had to leave him behind us.

It turned into quite a long saga. She looked at the new script and said, 'Yes, that's very good indeed.' But when she came in just before the final make-up, she said, 'Mind you…' and started looking at a word here and a word there. The next thing I knew, we were into a session that ultimately lasted about three hours or more – it was gone ten before the final, final version of the script was ready. And then we went down to the first floor to photograph it. The first shot failed after about a paragraph. Gordon was saying, 'No good, no good, that's good, that's good...'

Anyway, to cut a long story sideways, by about 11.30 at night we got the last shot in the bag. We did one more shot on video tape, just in case. They professed to be pleased with it. I eventually got home at midnight really quite worn out just with the nervous strain of seeing everything done. I had hardly got in when the phone went, at about ten past twelve. It was David Wolfson. He said, 'Have you seen tomorrow's *Times*?'

'No,' I said. 'I never get it – well, not till the morning.'

'Well,' he said, 'she has.' He started to read out headlines. Evidently it had a big picture of Kinnock and all sorts of headlines about a marginal poll that was going to make it a very close-run thing. And David said, 'Look, she's not that keen on seeing Robin Oakley tomorrow. If you aren't careful, she won't see him at all, go and see what you can do.'

So, I promptly picked up the phone, rang Oakley and said, 'Robin, for God's sake this headline has made her very upset – we've got enough problems already getting her to do interviews. Be a good lad and see what you can do.' He promised he would, and I went to bed feeling that tomorrow would produce yet more problems. It was, I suppose, the last Sunday of the campaign, but even so it seemed to have been going on a hell of a long time.

The Final Monday, 8 June

The last Monday of the campaign. I got up slightly groggily and went in for the early meeting at 7.45. Norman was there.

The polls looked all right, but Norman wasn't awfully cheerful. I mentioned the Robin Oakley position and he immediately went up somewhat, apparently because of a problem with the *Mail*'s David English. At about 8.30, the Prime Minister came in. She was terribly tired and very tense, and obviously she had a lot to do. She was going on to Venice, and she had to do the Dimbleby interview. She said to me, 'I don't really know if I should do the Robin Oakley interview.' Norman immediately butted in, saying that it would be very embarrassing if she did, because he'd promised the other interview to David English. She asked me what I thought, and I said, 'Well no, Prime Minister, you've got a lot to do. May I suggest you don't do it, but you go and leave at 10 o'clock sharp?' She agreed to this. I think Stephen got Peter Morrison to speak to Oakley.

We went through all the usual pre-briefing. I had my own press conference a bit later on with Kenneth Clarke, so we agreed I would pull myself out of this one. John Moore was there with Nigel and Paul Channon. It was a very competent press conference. I think Nigel got the tax story running very well – the graphics Howell had made for him looked very good. After it finished, at about 10 o'clock, I saw Robin Oakley. He was very worried about what he would do. I said, 'Leave it with me.' Charles Wilson also rang from *The Times*, and he was very concerned about the Oakley interview. I made it very clear that it wasn't Robin's fault, it was just pressure on the Prime Minister, and that I would see what I could do.

Then I did the briefing about employment issues with Kenneth Clarke, Jonathan Hill, Howell and Norman Blackwell. We went downstairs to our press conference at 11.30. Surprisingly, it was reasonably well attended, and it went well. I used our new graphic. Kenneth had a few good lines, and I was told later that it ran all day, even to the news bulletins that night. In fact, in many ways we got as much coverage from our employment press conference as we did for the main one.

Early on in the day I'd seen Rod Tyler at the morning press conference. We had lunch together, and I told him all the rather eventful incidents of the previous week. On the way back, Howell showed me a chapter of Rod's book which is quite racily written. I suspect I'm going to be figuring fairly prominently in the second half of it.

After lunch I was busy chasing up to see how the party election broadcast had got on. I popped into Alistair's rooms and asked if he was free for dinner. I fixed to take him out and eventually, thanks to his office, we managed to get into the Connaught Grill.

One thing I've forgotten to mention: after the morning press conference, I had seen Alistair, and he told me that Y. K. Pau, one of the biggest businessmen in Hong Kong, was coming. When he came, he presented Alistair with a really large cheque. I said, 'Y. K., that's a marvellous thing to do. The one thing we need is lucky money, and your money is lucky money.' Well, that pleased him immensely – I'd remembered that the Chinese have a thing about luck. I told him I was going to go straight to the Prime Minister and tell her about the gift. Afterwards, Norman Tebbit told me that Y. K. had come and greeted him very warmly on the way in and said goodbye to him very warmly on the way out. The whole time he was surrounded by journalists, and he was just hoping they didn't recognise him and ask what he was doing there.

The afternoon wasn't too busy. I always find that slightly amazing. I spent some time ringing round Tim and Gordon Reece and John Sharkey. A little later, I was called into Norman's room. We looked at the advertising and approved it for the next day or two. I must say my relationship with Norman remains distant at times, but not that bad. Eventually I got the message that we should go down to view the new film, not to Rushes this time, but to a little place somewhere in Soho. It was a very battered, tatty sort of place. The film was shown, and we went through everything. I thought it looked quite good – in fact very good, so I got quite keen. Gordon was with us. In the street outside, I asked him what he thought about it, and he thought it would be OK. Then I went back to the Connaught Grill, where I waited a few minutes and met Alistair. Meanwhile, Norman Dodds took Gordon and Howell back to the offices.

In many ways, it was a great pleasure going back to the Grill because every time I go there now, they automatically give me the very best table they can find and make a tremendous fuss about me. There is no doubt that my profile is enormously higher as a result of the election. I had a good dinner with Alistair. We talked over the future, agreed more and more on the policy to be adopted and discussed what job I should do. He told me Norman had been speaking to him during the course of the day. He thought Norman was certainly trying to carve something out for himself. He suggested that I should go into Education, which I thought was a slightly surprising thought. It suddenly occurred to me that chairman of the Conservative Party and Leader of the House of Lords would be rather a good position to have – maybe those jobs could be done together. But in any event, he recommended to me that in fact I don't need to ask for anything. He told me he was going to have lunch with the Prime Minister on 24 June, and I should leave everything in his hands – although he did warn me she had a great gift of not really appointing people properly, just letting them get at it.

We went back to central office afterwards. Norman was there, and after looking through the advertising, he threw everybody out and asked me what I wanted to do after the election. He made the surprising suggestion that I should go on to Energy and clear up the privatisation of electricity, which I thought was very odd. That would be very much a demotion – bit bizarre actually.* And then he asked me if I was interested in going to central office. I was very non-committal – in fact, all I kept on saying was I would go back to Employment, although I wouldn't mind doing the DTI. But he said that he and I and Alistair and Cecil – and Willie, I think – could really clear up central office and reform it and get it going well. The more I heard about it the less interested I became in it, but I just kept being very non-committal. I told him – in fact, I wrote out on

---

* After the election, Cecil Parkinson was brought back to handle this job, so although it remained fairly low profile (and Energy eventually ceased to be an independent Cabinet position), it was clearly seen as a vital position within government.

an envelope – that I knew what he was going to do. He just told me he would let everyone know as soon as we knew the election results, and we just left it at that.

I went back at about 12.15 after a lot too much to drink. Back home I thought, 'Well, one day less.'

The Final Tuesday, 9 June

We had an 8.30 start. I went into central office. As the Prime Minister was away – she was in Venice – we were starting late. Norman was going to chair the meeting. I had taken myself out of it. It went well, and Norman finished it off after about twenty minutes. Nothing very much had particularly changed in the polls, but there was beginning to be an end-of-term sort of feeling about the whole campaign.

After it finished, we went upstairs. I looked a bit at one or two things I had to do. Then at about twenty to eleven, I suddenly found to my horror that Jimmy Young, which I was due to be on at 11 o'clock, wasn't just an ordinary *Jimmy Young Show* – in fact, of all bizarre things, I was to be on yet another programme with Prescott, and Malcolm Bruce was going to be down the line from Scotland. We were on for an hour, between 11 o'clock and 12 o'clock. I think it was probably my least satisfactory performance ever.

It was very odd. First of all, Prescott was his usual bullying self, but halfway through I suddenly got absolutely and utterly bored with all the stale old arguments I had been using for the past five years. I knew it was unsatisfactory, and I knew it wasn't very good, but there you are – that was it. I just couldn't wait for it to end. Afterwards I went downstairs, and I said to Howell that I didn't think I was very good. He was too polite actually to agree with me, but I think he thought the same thing.

I went back to the office just for a few minutes, then we went to the Ritz, where I was to lunch with Tim and Gordon, Howell of course, and also Tim's partner, who looked very much like Doctor Who but was a splendid chap. You could really tell we were slowing down because we were taking longer and longer to do less and less. But we had a very jolly lunch and an enormous amount to drink – mainly good champagne. I think we were fairly relaxed at that time. We were still just a little bit twitchy, but all the polls looked good, and we talked a little bit about the future. Again, wherever I went people made more than a slight fuss about me. It must have been three or three-thirty by the time we left. I went back to central office, and we started ringing round waiting for the party election broadcasts to be delivered, because tonight was the night the PM was going to do the broadcast.

The Prime Minister went up to Harrogate after she got back from Venice. I heard afterwards that Stephen, who faxed the speech out to her, had received the shock of his life when she arrived, and Charles Powell came over with the speech. He found to his utter amazement that she had accepted the whole speech and only altered a word or two. Anyway, we sat and waited for some time, and then eventually the Saatchis came over. They showed us the final version of the tape. I thought the music in the introduction was still far too loud, but we approved it, and then we waited and waited and waited until we received over half a dozen video tapes. Then Howell and I got in the car and we went off to drop a copy at the *Telegraph*. We popped into the *Mail* as well and played it to David English. Between you and me, I don't think he liked it that much. Then we went over to Nick Lloyd, who gave us some more champagne – never drunk so much champagne in one day! We showed it to him, and I think he thought it was terrific, although just at the peak moment the telephone went, so I think it lost some of its impact. At about 9 o'clock we decided to call it a day and I went home. I arrived just as the party election broadcast was starting. I don't think Lita was awfully impressed with it, but there you are, there it is, it's happened. I had a snack and watched *Newsnight*, where Vincent Hanna came out with a poll that went into considerable detail. Although he quoted all the health warnings, it could still be inferred pretty strongly that we were heading towards a hung parliament. That got me very depressed indeed, and I began to wonder whether or not our last-minute charge was actually working. On the other hand, I looked at all the advertising that was going on and all the issues were going our way, except perhaps trade unions. Even so, I was getting more and more nervous and even more twitchy.

The Final Wednesday, 10 June

The last day before the election. This was the wrap-up press conference day, and it took a great effort for me to go in yet again for the 7.45 meeting that Norman wanted first. It was fairly uneventful. The polls still seemed to be carrying on with two fairly parallel lines and we looked at all the press statements. They then produced a shorter press statement for the Prime Minister. My original idea was that everybody should say a few words, but that didn't really seem to be too popular.

This was the morning the PM was going to do *Election Call* – the Robin Day programme – which was going to be done from central office from five past nine till 10 o'clock. Then there was going to be the press conference at ten-thirty.

Willie turned up for the last meeting with John Wakeham. Shortly after 9 o'clock, I went into Alistair's room and sat and watched *Election Call* with Willie and John. She really did perform magnificently.

In that morning's *Independent*, there had been a great big scare story about our supposed intention to privatise the job centres. I was quite furious with this story, which was uncalled for and unprovoked. That passed the time until about 10 o'clock, when the Prime Minister came upstairs and we all congratulated her. We went through the plan for the press conference. She said she was going to make a very short opening statement and then leave it open to questions. Norman said he had invited all the press corps for drinks, and there was very much an end-of-term feeling about the whole thing – it was more than a bit unreal.

We went into the press conference, and after her short statement she threw it open to questions. The second question was on job centres. I answered it very firmly, saying unequivocally that there was no question of the centres being privatised. We carried on until 11 o'clock, and then she went to a studio to do some interviews. One of the *Independent* journalists asked me to clarify some of the points I'd made. Then I went into Alistair's room, where I found Willie with one or two of the senior hacks having some champagne. So, I joined them, having quite a pleasurable time until 12.30, when the party was starting.

On the previous day, we'd agreed that Saatchis could have a meeting at one-thirty, ostensibly to agree the advertising. I'd asked Norman if he wanted me there. 'Well,' he said, 'it wouldn't be a bad idea.' Shirley Oxenbury told me that for some reason Dobbs wasn't invited to that meeting, from which she inferred that it might be quite important.

In the morning, I'd asked Howell to book a table because I would like to take Norman Blackwell and Jonathan Hill out for lunch and have a farewell celebration. I went wandering in at the appointed time and there was Maurice Saatchi, who said he just wanted me to know how much he appreciated what I'd done. I made some pleasant noises about working together in the future. Then Norman came in with Michael Dobbs. Saatchi said, 'Now, what I'd like to do is to show you something.'

Dobbs said, 'Is it all right if I'm here?'

'Well, as a matter of fact, Michael,' Maurice said, 'I would just like to deal with this with the chairman and with David.' This was an amazing slap in the face. Dobbs just got up and left.

Maurice then produced a very unusual piece of paper which, I suppose, ended up as a rationalisation of the campaign, making out that it had all been marvellous. In fact, it was a request for a vote of confidence for his agency, suggesting a line they should take with the press in order to make the Sunday papers OK. Well, I listened to all this and got him to change a word or two.

Because I wanted to go off and have lunch, I agreed I would meet with them the morning after the election and brief the Sunday papers on what had actually happened.

I went off and had a very jolly lunch. I thanked the boys very sincerely. We'd run the best press conference of the campaign – I can certainly say that. The way the polls are going, I think we will be there with forty or fifty seats. All the press is running our way, the stories are running our way and it looks very good.

The lunch finished rather late. I went back to the office and cleared up my papers. I hoped I would get away at 6 o'clock at the latest. I was just waiting around, talking to Alistair and the others, when all of a sudden there was news of some more polls. I sat down in Alistair's room, had a drink or two, and it was 8 o'clock before I finally got away. There were a variety of polls. The minimum showed a lead of seven and a half points; the maximum showed twelve points. It did look as if we were heading for a victory. But some of the marginal polls gave our victory as being very slight indeed, and there was still talk about a hung parliament. That made me more and more nervous, and I went home that evening rather more worried than I cared to admit.

I had rung Lita at 8 o'clock from central office and said I would take her out to dinner at Mr Kai, a local Chinese restaurant. I picked her up and took her there, and we had a very pleasant meal. Everybody in the restaurant and the owners made a great fuss of us and wished us luck. I made sure they were all going to vote.

Later that evening I spoke to Tim and Gordon and one or

two others. The more we spoke the more nervous I was making myself. At least I could be secure in the knowledge that tomorrow is Election Day, and I don't have very much to do any more. I'm not going to go in – I'm going to take it easy, because on Election Night I have the big round of all the television. So, I rang up Karen and booked her for lunch, and then I took myself to bed.

Election Day, Thursday 11 June

I had consoled myself with the thought that I could have a lie-in on Election Day – it was the first day I didn't have to be anywhere. But at 6.30 the phone went, and it was David Li* ringing from Paris to wish me luck. By ten past seven, I'd had my fifth telephone call and it was absolutely impossible to sleep. I stayed in bed until quite a bit later, speaking to people and feeling all the old nerves about the whole thing. In fact, as the day went on, I started talking myself into there being not much of a margin at all in the election.

I was messing around until 12 o'clock, when Karen came round. I had booked to take her to a Japanese place to make a change from the night before, and Lita came and joined us. We drove down to St Christopher's Place and had a very pleasant meal. I was told afterwards that I was quiet and withdrawn, but I really was extraordinarily worried about the way the election was going. In the morning, everybody who spoke to me was worried, and we were beginning to talk ourselves into some of

---

* The chief executive of the Bank of East Asia in Hong Kong and a family friend.

the most difficult, depressing sort of feelings about the whole thing.

I came back home at about 3 o'clock. Walking back slowly with Karen, I bought some magazines and decided that I should go to bed. I slept very intermittently – I kept on getting phone calls to wake me up, and I was really feeling worse and worse and worse. All I could think of was that by this time tomorrow I would know where we were. Eventually, at about 6 o'clock, I got up out of bed still feeling extraordinarily tired. We had agreed to meet at San Lorenzo at 7.30. Alistair was giving a dinner and they were all there. It was a very nice party, and we all thoroughly enjoyed it, except I couldn't eat very much. I had a first course and salad, and then in the middle of it Alistair got called to the phone. When he came back, he said, 'I've got the ITN exit poll from Sue Timpson.' He gave me the figures which looked something like forty-four, thirty-two, twenty, which really was an enormous lead. That gave me a tremendous boost of confidence and I exclaimed: 'We've got it, we've got it!' We made a toast to the Prime Minister.

I was due to leave at 9.15, so they quickly gave me some spaghetti. I really didn't eat very much of it. Then Norman Dodds came to pick me up. I'd promised to pop in to see David Hart, just to say thank you to some people who had given him support. Then I went on up to Wood Lane to the BBC studio, where I was the first one on *Election Call*.

As I went in, I asked BBC journalist Barbara Maxwell what their exit poll looked like. 'Ooh, it's grim,' she said, 'could be seventeen seats short of a majority, or at the very best probably a majority of just twenty-six.' Well, my heart sank a bit, but not too much because I knew what the other exit poll was. I went into the programme and David Dimbleby and all of them were as cheerful as could be, and they really did think they had a great story on their hands. But also, I think they were quite happy that we apparently weren't doing that well. They interviewed quite a number of people, and Julia Somerville had a rather aggressive interview with Jeffrey Archer, I noticed.

Jeffrey had bitten the bullet earlier that day. There had been a slightly bizarre incident the day before – on the Wednesday – when somebody told me that Jeffrey had been invited to the election-night party. I wondered if that was sensible. I went in to ask Norman, who thought it was a terrible idea. We were work-ing out what we could do about uninviting him when Shirley came in and reminded Norman that he'd actually authorised the invitation! Earlier today, Jeffrey had telephoned me about something or other, to wish me luck and say the whole thing was going well. I said, 'Jeffrey, please don't take this the wrong way, but if you are coming to the party tonight, when the Prime Minister comes please don't be photographed with her.'

'Oh,' he said, 'yes…'

I just said, 'Until the court case is over…'

'Does that mean I won't be getting a telephone call from her this weekend?'

I could hardly believe the question – he actually thought he was still in line to get something. I said, 'No, Jeffrey, I'm afraid until the case is over there is nothing here.'

Anyway, Jeffrey was interviewed quite rudely by Julia

Somerville, who asked him all sorts of questions about whether Thatcher would hang on if she hadn't got a proper majority and things of that sort. They were getting so worked up that about five minutes before the first result was due, I turned round and said to Robin Day, who was sitting next to me: 'Do you know what they are saying on the other side?'

'No,' he said, so I told him what our exit poll was forecasting as well. 'Oh my God,' he said and picked up a phone. They started to moderate their attitude a bit after that.

When the first result came through from Torbay, they said on the programme: 'Now, if our forecast is right, the Conservative candidate will have 26,000 votes.' Well, when it was announced – and I had my fingers crossed – it was 36,000. As soon as that happened the whole attitude changed – I mean, they went into deep depression. Within minutes they changed the majority from twenty-six to forty-four, and it carried on climbing up all evening.

At about quarter past eleven they released me, so off I went upstairs to a party the TV producer Bill Cotton was giving. Shirley and Leslie and Dennis* were there and a whole host of people. You could see that a lot of the Beeb people were very glum and a lot of our people were very cheerful. By then the estimated majority had gone up to about fifty-five or sixty.

I spent a few minutes there, then I went off down to Wells Street to do something for ITN. While I was sitting waiting, the estimated majority had gone up to sixty or seventy. I said my

---

* My brother's widow, her daughter and her son-in-law.

bit, then went off again and did something for radio, and then to Gough Square to do something for IRN. Then I was off to central office, where everybody was getting more and more cheery. I was there until 2 o'clock, by which time the estimate had gone up to eighty-eight. Back to Wells Street, and the estimate had gone up to over 100. I was sitting there with the cameras when it finally went to over 326 seats and we had officially won. I thought it was marvellous to actually be there for that moment.

Then I went back to central office again. I finished all the media, gave a little interview outside, got a little cheer and there was a marvellous feeling – all sorts of people up there. Lita had come along by then, and the Prime Minister arrived and there was great fuss and joy and everybody was very happy indeed.

At about 4.15 a.m., I left for home. I had Breakfast Television and a whole host of other things to do a little later in the morning. I got to bed about 5 o'clock, very tired but very happy.

Friday 12 June

First day of the third term. It seemed I had only just put my head on the pillow when the phone went at five to six. Of all the odd things to happen, it was Steve Robin, who said he was still in the office and tried to show me that he was working. He thought the chairman had some early morning interviews and would like to spare him those and would I come down and do it? 'No bloody way,' I said, 'this is the chairman's day of triumph and no one's taking that from him. You let him go and do it.' I was pretty short with him and put the phone down.

I could hardly get to sleep again. After a while I got up and was getting ready when Norman Dodds and Howell came round. I went off to do TV-am with Diane Abbott, who had just won Hackney.* I found her very difficult – in fact, the whole conversation was difficult, and I began to realise the new parliament would not be an easy place to work. It wasn't an awfully satisfactory interview, and I found myself getting even more bored with the unemployment figures.

When we finished, I went off to do some more television. In the studio at Wells Street, I suddenly found to my enormous astonishment that I was back with the same people only a few hours after I'd left it. All of a sudden, Prescott turns up larger than life, then Ken Livingstone. The whole thing was a bit of a waste of time, but it was all right, and I suppose it went quite well. When I came out of that, I was due to go over to do Jimmy Young again.

I thought Jimmy Young went rather well, and I got back into the old swing again. He certainly gave me a good time. Then Howell said we were going to do Radio 4 next, but he said there was some time pressure. I asked him why, and he said that a message had come through that the Prime Minister wanted to see me at ten minutes to twelve before she went to central office. So, we went dashing up to Channel 4. They weren't quite ready for me, so we excused ourselves and disappeared back to central office. Howell said, 'What you've got to do now is think what it is you actually want to say.'

'Well,' I said, 'let me go straight back to No. 10,' and I waited

---

* Diane Abbott, 1953–. Labour MP since 1987.

there. All the lights were up, because the Prime Minister was going to make a triumphant march over to central office. I went into the private office and sat talking to all the lads, teasing them a bit that their holiday had come to an end.

I was told to go upstairs and saw the Prime Minister in her study. I said to her, 'Prime Minister, look, in all the euphoria of our win – whatever it is, 102 seats – let's not forget that eight days ago we thought we were losing it, and that happened because of two things. One was health – now unemployment isn't an issue, health is. I think Norman Fowler did a disastrous job. I spoke to him when I started Action for Jobs and tried to persuade him to do something similar for health. That's what we should have done. But he refused point blank to do it. Secondly: central office. I'd like to make some suggestions.'

'Fire away,' she said.

'Well, Cecil...'

'No,' she said, 'I can't possibly take Cecil there because of his background with the child.* So we discussed whether Kenneth Clarke could go there. She said, 'Would you like it?'

'Oh no, Prime Minister, please not. But of course, I'm a soldier; I'll do whatever you ask me to do.' We went on for a few minutes, then I said: 'You know, we really should do something for Tim Bell – he couldn't be at central office last night.' Well, that got her totally furious. She picked up the phone and asked to speak to Tim. As it happened, she couldn't because he was

---

* A reference to Cecil Parkinson's affair with Sarah Keays, which resulted in the birth of a daughter and precipitated Parkinson's resignation from the Cabinet in October 1983.

out. I subsequently found he had gone down to a tennis tournament he was hosting.

Charles Powell came in and said there was some sort of story that Norman Tebbit had resigned as chairman.* This got her very worried indeed. The time came for her to go, so I excused myself and went downstairs and waited. It had been a very unsatisfactory sort of meeting because she hadn't said a word about where I was really going to go. We hung around the private office until she came downstairs, then she went outside and made a great fuss of everybody. One of the things I had said when we were upstairs was that 44 per cent of first-time voters voted for us – 'I really think you've changed the whole face of the nation.' When she went out and gave a statement, that was one fact she really used – that young people are voting for us and the revolution had taken real hold – a revolution in attitudes, that is.

I waited till the Prime Minister left and went back to central office. I got a little bit of a cheer from the crowd outside. The PM was there with all the staff in the press conference room. Norman, to his credit, called me over. 'Ah, David. David's here!' He gave me a nice tribute, and Norman and the Prime Minister and I had our pictures taken together. We presented her with a cake. It was a really tremendous triumphant feeling.

I didn't belong in central office any more. So, when Howell and I eventually took our leave, I cleared everything out. I suppose it was about ten to one. I said, 'Come on, Howell, let's go out for lunch.' On the way, I asked where we should go. He got

---

* This was confirmed later in the day.

his book out and plumped for Simply Nico. I thought they'd be booked up for months, but we rang through. I said, 'Lord Young here, could we have a table for two?' – 'Yes,' they said, 'of course.'

They made a tremendous fuss of us, and all the people in the restaurant offered their congratulations – all the world loves a winner. It was a lovely atmosphere. At the table next to us there was a couple from up north who kept on interrupting us. I was full of doom and gloom and preparing Howell for the fact that we might be going to DHSS. Then we went back into the department, and I sat down feeling more and more tired.

I saw Roger, John of course, and Peter Makeham hinting that I might go to DHSS. Peter said he would come with me, which I thought was tremendous. I went home at about 5 o'clock, so very tired that Lita made me a snack and I was in bed before nine. I couldn't even be bothered to look at the television.

There were a couple of phone calls which woke me, and I had a real anxiety attack – I just couldn't sleep at all. Eventually, at about 11.30, I hunted around for a sleeping pill, went back to bed and slept like a log.

Saturday 13 June

I slept all the way through until about 7.30 this morning. Then the phone calls started again with congratulations. Finally, at about 9 o'clock, I rang the Prime Minister and got put through. I said: 'Prime Minister, before you make your dispositions, I wonder if you could spare me a few minutes just to talk about what I can do.' I went on again about how I thought the real key issues were health and central office, and maybe I could do this, that and the other.

She said, 'Well, David, I have made up my mind. It's all settled now. I've had the best night's sleep I think I've ever had. I'll
see you later on – I don't want to do it on the phone, but don't
worry, you're not going to the DHSS.' I thought that was really
marvellous news. We had been invited to Trooping the Colour,
which was in morning dress. The PM said to me on the phone,
'Well, you're coming in later but... Nigel, are you on the line?'
Nigel Wicks said he was listening in. So she asked him, 'Can we
have a time for David?' He said, '2.30?', so I said, 'Done.'

'All right,' she said. 'We'll do it at 2.30.' So I went off to
Trooping of the Colour all agog, wondering what on earth my
new job would be.

It was the most marvellous ceremony, but there had been a
security warning, and I couldn't help being distracted by the
large number – literally two dozen, I suspect – of both plain and
uniformed security all around us. They had arrested two people
with CS_2 canisters. On the way back, I walked behind the
Prime Minister and she said: 'David, perhaps we will have our
chat after the reception.' So, I went into the reception thinking
all the time of what I was going to be doing.

To interject at this point, I had been furious about a story which
had appeared in *The Times* this morning giving Young and Rubicam*
all the credit for the change in the campaign, which was absolute
nonsense. I had been speaking to David Hart and Tim and Gordon
about how best to kill the story, which seemed to be taking all the

---

* A rival advertising agency to Saatchis, which had provided the party with the results of some
 research into attitudes that was highly sophisticated but marginal to the conduct of the
 campaign.

credit away from Tim and giving it to other people. I had got hold of Stephen, who confirmed it, but I didn't say a word to Ronnie Millar, who I suspect had been responsible for leaking that story.*

David Norgrove had, slightly indiscreetly, said 'Congratulations on the move,' and I'd said, 'Thank you, David, that's the first time I've heard I was going to have a move.' He looked very discomforted. 'Never mind, forget it,' I said. Then the Prime Minister summoned me to her room, and we sat down.

She said, 'David, I would like you to go and take Inner Cities, together with Trade and Industry. I'd like you to take Kenneth Clarke as Chancellor of the Duchy.'

'Oh dear,' I said. 'I'm delighted to work with Kenneth, we work very well as a team. But does this really mean I have to have a minister in the Commons?' When she confirmed yes, I said, 'Oh well, all right, I'll certainly do it.'

I went on to tell her that whatever she did, whether she decided to stand again or not, it's clear that without a better organisation in central office we will never win the next election. I said, 'I've never asked anything before, but I'm going to ask to do this after the conference.' And I think I've got some measure of agreement with her, but we will have to wait and see. She said she couldn't refuse Norman anything after this, and I said, 'No, let him go and have his valedictory meeting, but after the conference this is the time to really go and do it.'

We left it at that. I thanked her very much for the confidence she showed in me. It was a total bombshell to me having Trade

---

* A more likely source for the story was Geoffrey Tucker, a veteran of numerous campaigns who could have given lessons in skulduggery to Machiavelli himself.

and Industry – I hadn't really thought about it. I wasn't even sure how keen I was on the idea, but anyway, I had it. It would no doubt be seen as a great big step up.

I went back to have lunch, which was very pleasant, before leaving for home. I got home at about 3 o'clock and waited, looking at some bits and pieces. Then at 5 o'clock, I got a phone call – 'Would I go to Buck House for 5.45 for a Privy Council meeting?' What I gathered was that Peter Walker was going to go to Wales, which I thought was absolutely brilliant, and that we had lost one or two people, but Paul Channon had not gone out of the Cabinet – he was going to Transport. We had lost Michael Jopling* and the Welsh Secretary, Nick Edwards – that's why Peter was going there. But I didn't know the other changes, and I tried to ask Nigel Wicks who would be my successor, but he didn't tell me. The Prime Minister did tell me that John Moore was going to the DHSS, so I wondered if Norman Fowler was going to get my job.

When the assistant or deputy clerk of the Privy Council rang through, he said that the new Lord Chancellor would be there. I suddenly realised that Quintin† must have gone. Anyway, through an appalling rainstorm, I drove through to Buck House, getting there in time to piece all the changes together. John Major‡ was going to come in as chief secretary and John MacGregor was going to Agriculture.

---

* Michael Jopling (Baron Jopling of Ainderby Quernhow since 1997), 1930–. Conservative MP, 1964–97; Chief Whip, 1979–83; Minister for Agriculture, 1983–87.

† Quintin Hogg (Baron Hailsham of St Marylebone after 1970), 1907–2001. Lord Chancellor, 1979–87.

‡ John (since 2005 Sir John) Major, 1943–. Conservative MP, 1979–2001; Minister of State, Social Security, 1986–87; chief secretary to the Treasury, 1987–89; Foreign Secretary, 1989; Chancellor of the Exchequer, 1989–90; Prime Minister, 1990–97.

Norman was there, and he went in first for an audience, in which he gave in his seals of office. I didn't see him again. Then we went into the Privy Council. We swore our oath of allegiance, kissed hands, and I got my new seals of office. Afterwards, Willie invited us all back for a drink.

We had a jolly good drink and celebration. I was more than slightly amazed that Peter Walker should have taken Wales – it just shows you what people do to keep in office. I had a chat with Willie afterwards, and I gather I'm not to be told who my junior ministers are as yet. I agreed – I'm not sure if I agreed too quickly – that Ken Clarke would take inner cities and perhaps regional policy. We will have to have a look at that when we get into the department. Certainly these are areas that I know quite well – it will be rather good going back to places I haven't been to for a long time, and it certainly legitimises my trips to China.

After a while, I sat back and had a chat with Norman Fowler. I think I was slightly reckless in telling him my ambitions about central office, but he will probably back me all the way. I agreed I would do more work to help him in the general running of the department, and that I would settle for the best of the young whips. I've got young Maxwell Beaverbrook,* which makes me more than happy. He will have a lot of work to do, and I'll certainly bring him in as a Lords whip, but what I can't do is have another Lords minister. So, there's no question that I'm going to be doing a certain number of questions and so will he. I am going to spend a bit of time in the House, just to see what

---

* Maxwell Aitken, 3rd Baron Beaverbrook, 1951–. A hereditary peer.

happens next. I suspect that this is only a job for a year or two. Indeed, thinking ahead, I would love to get chairmanship of the party and then see where we get with those two together.

After I came back to the office, I spoke to Gordon Reece, who sounded delighted and thought inner cities was the key appointment. This made me begin to think that perhaps I should do more about it – perhaps I'd been slightly rash in giving it to Kenneth. I spoke to Tim, and, lo and behold, he'd had a phone call from the Prime Minister at 8 o'clock that morning. David Hart rang and tried to pretend that the story in *The Times* had actually been accurate, but I think we got the truth around for enough people. I spoke to John and told him he had an immediate transfer to the DTI if he ever wanted to go. I think he was grateful, but I don't think he will ever take it up.

Then I rang Brian Hayes, the permanent secretary at the DTI, and he offered to drop the box round. I invited him in for a drink and we had a chat. I feared that there might be some difficulties there, but we will just have to see. It's a department with twelve deputy secretaries – we had two in the old department, so it really does make me wonder. If I'm not careful it's going to be a department that causes nothing at all but headaches. 'It's a no-win department,' Hayes said. Well, that's a challenge. I'm going to have to show that it's going to be a *win* department, so I've got to think of some way of getting out the good news.

The only problem is that when I went to the Department of Employment, I knew in advance what it was that I wanted to do. I wanted to turn it into a department of enterprise – I really wanted it to be about employment creation and everything else.

But I can't take those bits back again. What I've got to do now is to see what we can do about getting industry growing and working better.

Here we are at D-Day+1: a majority of over 100; a new Cabinet being formed; me going into a new job, tired out but victorious; some vistas for the future. It's probably time to stop keeping a regular diary. I've now got ten hours-plus of this tape of notes telling the story which started way back six or seven weeks ago. I will piece it all together with the other papers I'm going to get. They are all important. It was, after all, a remarkable period. It was, I suppose, an election that has broken the mould in some peculiar ways. It's made me very tired but triumphant. After a day off tomorrow, I start a whole new world and a whole new job.

AFTERWORD

I can still remember, all these years later, being completely exhausted at the end of the election, but as soon as the Prime Minister told me I was going to the Department of Trade and Industry as their Secretary of State, the adrenaline kicked in and my tiredness suddenly vanished.

The department I returned to was very different and very much larger than the old Department of Industry that I had left to go to the Manpower Services Commission in 1982. No longer were the nationalised industries the heart of the department, for they had all gone, leaving only the basket cases of Rover and British Steel. I finally managed to persuade British Aerospace to take Rover, which had lost money for each of the past seventeen years, along with a dowry of three quarters of a billion pounds, while British Steel, which by now was in much better shape, we were able to float off on the London Stock Exchange.

We turned the DTI into the 'Department for Enterprise' and focused much of its work on helping small- and medium-sized firms to grow and embryo technology companies to get established. I was delighted that I still had Kenneth Clarke with me as my Minister of State, and he had responsibility for inner cities, which were a real problem with high concentrations of unemployment. It was rather odd, since Ken was well known as being one of the leading 'wets' in the Cabinet, and yet we got along like a house on fire.

Shortly after we arrived at the department, we were finishing a rigorous review of the budget for 'pay and rations' when my permanent secretary, Brian Hayes, said that he understood I had a lunch appointment, and if I liked he would be quite happy for Ken to finish off the review. I said 'with pleasure', and departed smiling inwardly for lunch, for I knew Ken well. On my return, I met an ashen-faced permanent secretary, since Ken had been far tougher on the overheads than would I!

I still kept my weekly slot with Margaret, who was as ambitious for change as ever, but the balance of the Cabinet had changed, and I believe that she was the only one who did not know it. I came into Cabinet in 1984, towards the beginning of her second term, and it was only after the '83 election that she had a real majority in her own Cabinet. After Michael Heseltine walked out, and following the '87 election, she had a comfortable majority of the Cabinet but there were times when she did not seem to realise it, and she would sometimes try to force something through when there was no real need.

Occasionally, when there was an item on the agenda which she was concerned to get through, she would start by summing up, and then looking round the Cabinet table saying, 'Is that agreed, then?' At first there was silence, and she would jump in and say, 'Well, that's agreed, let us go on to the next item.' After a while that stopped working.

Enterprise was now becoming well established in the economy and entrepreneurialism was coming back into the vocabulary. When I first came to the department after the election, I realised I was now dealing with a far larger sector than the employment department, and I was going to have a problem keeping communication going between so many ministers, and whips particularly, as I was in the Lords and therefore did not have the chance to spend time with my colleagues during the long, late hours in the Commons.

I then decreed a three-line whip for all my political colleagues in the department, that we should all meet for lunch in the office after Cabinet, which in those days was on a Thursday. There could be up to a dozen at our lunches, which, as they included both Kenneth Clarke and Alan Clark,* together with all my other ministers and whips from both Houses, were often rather enjoyable occasions and served to keep us all in step. Right at the far end of the table, far below the salt, was a young man from central office.

In the meantime, pressure was growing from Europe to join the European Monetary System (EMS), and in addition there was a movement for greater integration of all of Europe led by Jacques Delors. The Prime Minister was due to make a speech at Bruges on the future of Europe, and one day we were discussing

---

* Alan Clark, 1928–99. Clark was a junior minister with me in Employment and was destined to come with me to the DTI.

it at the end of one of our weekly meetings when she asked me to come to lunch the following Sunday at Chequers.

When I arrived, there was only the Prime Minister and Charles Powell, her principal private secretary. I was inherently distrustful of any further integration into the EEC, largely because of the bureaucratic systems made even worse by the regulatory nature of European law. I was convinced that this led to the very high levels of unemployment, particularly amongst the young, which they all seemed to tolerate as a fact of life. Over lunch, we agreed that the best model for the UK would be an association of independent states that would cooperate together when it suited them and not when it didn't.

When she made her speech at Bruges a week or two later, it attracted considerable criticism, not only in Europe but also at home and by more than a few members of our party. I little but realised it, but that was the opening skirmish in the Brexit wars that divided our nation in a way none had seen before. It was possibly the most split we have been since the time of Charles I; the argument became quasi-religious in nature and almost a matter of belief that cut across party and family lines and created long-lasting divisions that ordinary politics rarely achieves.

As I write these lines, now over a third of a century after Thatcher's speech, on the very first weekend that marks our final exit from the European Union and the beginning of a new global relationship (in the middle of a pandemic), I am convinced that we will look back at this time as the rebirth of our entrepreneurial economy.

During my time in Cabinet, as I was in the Lords, I would

have to take questions not only for my own department but for Treasury and Employment as well. There were always four questions a day while the House was sitting, and there were some days when I had to answer all four, which served to keep me up to date on much that was going wrong in government!

One Thursday, in the late spring of '89, I had to leave our usual lunch in the department early to go to the House for questions, and as I left, I heard Alan Clark say: 'All political careers end in tears.' As I hurried down the corridor, the thought first occurred to me that I did not want my career to end that way, and that made me think about what else I had hoped to accomplish for government. I had gone as far as any unelected person could in today's world, but even more important, the economy was in the process of being transformed and almost all the conditions that had so held the country back were either going or gone.

By the following morning, I had made up my mind that I had done as much as I could, and almost exactly ten years after I'd had that first appointment with Keith Joseph, it was time for me to return to my own world and go back to making a living.

I waited until my next meeting with the Prime Minister, and at the end of it I told her that we were approaching the tenth anniversary of my time in government and I was long overdue for my return to my own world. She quite understood, and we agreed that I would go at the next reshuffle.

The date was eventually fixed, and two days before, I attended my last meeting with her in government. It was a Cabinet subcommittee concerned with passports for Hong Kong government employees in the event of a Chinese takeover, and the

Foreign Office had proposed that the passports should go to police and government officials and their families.

I was, I am afraid, a little demob-happy and could not resist putting in a paper suggesting that they should go to any Hong Kong resident who would like to come to this country and set up a business with a quarter of a million pounds of their own capital. I, of course, loved the idea of bringing Chinese entrepreneurs into the UK, and so did the Prime Minister, who ended up having quite a go at Geoffrey Howe – it became obvious that their relationship was not what it once was.

At the end of the meeting, she asked me to come up to her study, and we sat there talking about what had been achieved during my time. Eventually, she said to me: 'David, do you really have to go?' I sat there, silent for a moment, realising that the next words I uttered could change the course of my next few years.

I thought for a few seconds and then told her that I would stay if it were possible for me to have a particular job and she told me that, regretfully, I could not do that from the Lords, and so we agreed that it was the time for me to go.

I returned to a very different world; so different it was hard to recognise. First, the Big Bang had transformed the City, and so many of the institutions had changed that often the only thing I recognised was the buildings themselves! The Big Bang had remodelled the way the banks and the stock market worked, but there was no doubt that it was a much more entrepreneurial City.

The second surprise, which I had not really realised while I was still in government, was that it was now thought retiring ministers would take an unfair advantage with them when they returned to private life, and they should therefore wait a year to fifteen months before taking up paid employment. In no department was that more believed than in the DTI, as it was assumed I would know everything that was happening or going to happen in the financial world! Nothing could be further from the truth and I was probably less well informed than the average, but there was no arguing and I had to leave well over a year before I could take a paid job.

I did not waste my time and took a number of voluntary jobs, including as president of the Institute of Directors and chair of council of my old college, UCL. And as there was no inhibition on my working overseas, I went on the board of Salomon, the New York bank, and chaired their executive committee. I also took on a number of charitable jobs and bided my time until I could really get back to work.

I could see Margaret only very occasionally now, and of course, since I was now out of government, there was far less that we could discuss. Gradually, particularly after my period in purdah was over and I started running Cable & Wireless with all the overseas travel that that entailed, I stopped seeing her. However, the government began going through some rocky patches, and the papers would increasingly run stories of intrigues against her.

A serious rocky patch was caused by the effect of the community charge, better known as the poll tax, and demonstrations around the country continued to grow. I had been at Chequers at the Sunday Cabinet meeting when Ken Baker laid out the community charge for the first time. It was going to be introduced at £140 a head and then, depending on the increase or otherwise of local authorities spending, it would vary up or down.

This community charge had first been introduced into Scotland, and from the first it attracted enormous criticism for its perceived unfairness. The original concept was that it would be introduced over a number of years by equal instalments, and at the same time rates would be reduced each year, so there would be a gradual transfer from the old tax rating system to the new community charge.

At the party conference immediately after the '87 victory, such was the heady atmosphere as we celebrated our third election victory that at the debate it was suggested we should stop messing about with instalments and have the confidence to introduce it in full right away. Unusually for a Conservative Party conference, a resolution was not only listened to but acted upon, and the government decided to have a straight transition from rates to the community charge.

Unfortunately, when it was finally introduced, it came out nationally at about £1,000 a head (although it varied enormously from area to area) and was devastating for many in less affluent areas. I, on the other hand, lived in Westminster, and for some byzantine reason our charge came out at nil, nor were we ever asked to pay anything for the whole time this charge was in existence. This was clearly unsustainable, and the government's popularity suffered accordingly. The administration was beginning to suffer from the disease all governments suffer from when they have been too long in power: they stop listening and begin to take the electorate for granted.

The inevitable finally happened, and an obscure backbencher, Sir Anthony Meyer, challenged Thatcher for the leadership – she won easily, but the ice was broken, and she no longer appeared completely invincible. Geoffrey Howe finally had enough and resigned, delivering a devastating resignation statement to the House. Finally, Michael Heseltine came out of the shadows and challenged her for the leadership.

Meanwhile, the world was changing fast, and the governments of the eastern European communist states began falling, one by one, to internal revolution. Europe, which had been divided since the outbreak of war in 1939, now appeared to have a chance of returning to some sort of normality, and in 1990 there was a final peace conference called in Paris to celebrate the end of that devastating war which had started some fifty-one years previously. Unfortunately, if Margaret was to attend it would mean leaving London the evening before the parliamentary party vote on her re-election, but as a member of the wartime generation there was never a chance she would not attend.

I was only a spectator and could play no part in this election, but I could see the way it was going. I marshalled letters of support in the press, and the evening before the election I rang Peter Morrison. He sounded like he'd had too good a dinner and was quite dismissive of any need for help, saying to me that it was 'in the bag'. I put the phone down and began to worry.

The election took place while she was still in Paris, and although she won, the margin was so slim she realised she had lost the confidence of the party. If only, and the world is made up of ifs, she had spent the afternoon and evening in the House, fraternising in the tea rooms and bars, she could probably have improved the result to make it convincing enough that she could have survived – but in all probability this would only be postponing the inevitable.

She not only changed the country; she had changed the Conservative Party even more. The paternalistic party of old, the party that had lost its self-confidence in the post-war world and thought its role was to delay, because it could not defeat, the inevitable rise of socialism, was gone. Instead, the party now believed in enterprise, in wealth creation as well as the provision of a health service and all the social security benefits that had been brought in post-war by a Labour administration.

In a somewhat surprising turn of events, John Major became Margaret's successor, proving once again that timing is all. John had only come into the Cabinet as the chief secretary (later becoming Chancellor) during my last year, which proved to be a great advantage over the tired old faces who'd been around for many years.

I went to call on him in No. 10 within a few weeks of his taking office. We met upstairs in Margaret's old office, where nothing had been changed, and we sat in the same chairs she and I always used to sit in when I would meet with her. I suddenly realised that there was silence; I had obviously been asked a question. I was so used, in all my meetings, to sitting still and listening for the first ten or fifteen minutes, but John not only asked questions but listened to what I had to say.

Somewhat to my surprise, John seemed something of a Euro-sceptic, which misled me for a while until I realised he was non-confrontational and liked to appear to agree rather than disagree. At the end of the meeting, he saw me to the door, then down to the front door of No. 10 and then walked with me to the iron gates at the top of Downing Street. I could not help thinking what a very different meeting it had been and what a different Prime Minister he would make.

My concern was always with enterprise and encouraging new firms and start-ups, but the big political question of the day had rapidly become Europe. Under the leadership of Jacques Delors, the European Community was embarking on a path to create a single currency, and the United Kingdom had recently joined the EMS while John Major was Chancellor and blessed by a very unenthusiastic Margaret Thatcher.

Of course, our membership of the EMS would end in tears two years later when we came crashing out, but that did not in any way reduce the enthusiasm for further European inte-gration, a passion that, as with Euroscepticism, cut across both party and family lines.

I was to find out during the course of the next few months that John was, in fact, a passionate European, and he experi-enced continuing difficulty with the anti-European wing of the party. This reached a peak when, a few years later, we were both at a garden reception at the British embassy in Kuala Lumpur. We were standing together when he complained aloud to the gathered press gallery about the bastards in his own party who wanted him not to sign the forthcoming Maastricht Treaty. As you can imagine, the press took that remark up with enthusiasm, and afterwards there was much comment about the 'bastard' wing of the party.

It would be a tall order to expect any political party to win four elections in a row, and in 1992 all the polls had Labour, still led by Neil Kinnock, comfortably on course to win. They were a transformed party, using all the latest marketing skill, but they still retained many of the extreme policies that had beleaguered the party for many years. That they lost marked the final death knell for the hard-left policies and for Neil Kinnock's leadership, which was then taken up by John Smith. Then, following the sudden death of Smith, Tony Blair was elected leader in 1994, and the party took a turn towards the centre.

As Labour gradually moved towards the centre, so did the Conservatives, and although there were still substantial differences between them, politics was rapidly becoming more about personalities than policies.

As the Conservative government approached the 1997 election, it was quickly running out of steam and had lost its reputation for economic competence, particularly after we had to crash out of the EMS on 'Black Wednesday' in 1992. There was now a very active anti-Europe wing of the party, and John Major had precious little chance against a fresh, young, new candidate in Tony Blair. The result was inevitable: a landslide for Labour, ending eighteen years of Conservative government in their worst defeat since 1906.

The figures were startling: the Conservatives suffered a net loss of 178 seats in what was the first of three consecutive

Labour Party election victories. However, it was no longer the Labour Party of the post-war years that had nearly destroyed the UK economy in the '70s. Their belief in nationalisation as the panacea for all ills and confiscatory taxes to equalise society had long since gone. Now, they had no desire to increase taxes and were comfortable with the private sector and the need to create a prosperous economy. They now held the middle ground, and the Conservatives were beginning to look as if they could even turn into a fringe party. In many ways, I thought this was Margaret Thatcher's real victory, for she had not only transformed the Conservative Party; she had changed the Labour Party even more, and both were changed for the better.

I knew Tony Blair and Gordon Brown quite well, for back at the time when I was at the DTI they were joint shadow ministers for Labour, and although in the House they would face Ken Clarke, I would occasionally come across them either in television studios and elsewhere, and I liked them both. Alas, they were not too keen on each other, and this was the beginning of the Blair–Brown wars.

Denis Thatcher passed away in 2003, and Margaret began to pay the price for years of only two hours' sleep a night. I was invited to a small, private lunch in the Royal Chelsea Hospital where she was also a guest. She was, I thought, a little quiet and subdued over lunch. Afterwards, I sat with her for a coffee and suddenly the old spark was back and she put the world to rights in short order, but it did not last too long.

As the years went by and the atmosphere between No. 10 and No. 11 continued to deteriorate, Gordon Brown staged a dawn raid on the DTI and moved the sponsorship of the City and of the insurance industry from the DTI to the Treasury, where they remain to this day. How the Treasury can be both the sponsoring department and the regulator of both the City and the insurance industry is a mystery I have not yet solved, but the really bad outcome was the emasculation of the industry department. Today, it is no more than a shadow of its former glory, and it resides in a now little-noticed department called BEIS. Yet now, as we work our way out of the coronavirus pandemic, we need a strong trade and industry department like never before.

My term as president of the IoD was due to end after ten years and the 2003 annual convention at the Royal Albert Hall would be my last. This was always a tremendous occasion, and the hall would be packed to the rafters. Margaret would no longer accept speaking engagements, but she readily agreed to attend the convention for a short while, and I really wanted to show her how we all felt about her. It got off to a good start, and just before lunch I slipped out and greeted her at the back door and walked with her into the wings.

Before the lunch break was announced, I walked up to the dais and said: 'I would now like to introduce the woman who made my life and who has made the lives of each and every one of us in this hall today: the Right Honourable Margaret Thatcher.' With that, she walked on the stage and I joined her. The whole Albert Hall stood as one and clapped and cheered. It was completely overwhelming; we were literally battered by a wall of applause that never seemed to end and there were tears in her eyes. I was sent a photograph afterwards that showed us, completely to my surprise, standing hand-in-hand for support. On the way out, I said to her that this was how we all feel about her and what she has done for our country.

Tony Blair's popularity, which had shot sky-high at the time of the death of Diana, Princess of Wales, never reached those heights again, and following the intervention in Iraq it dropped to depths from which it never recovered, even to this day. After ten years, in 2007, Gordon Brown followed him as Prime Minister and turned out to be the right man in the right place, as the global financial crisis struck in 2008, and Brown spent much of his time and effort struggling with the crisis. It meant he did little to improve the popularity of the government.

In the meantime, David Cameron had become leader of the Conservatives and brought the party further back towards the centre. By now I had long finished my time with Cable & Wireless, and I was back working for myself funding start-ups. But I still had the ambition to help to encourage entrepreneurialism, which had faded but not entirely died in the intervening years.

One day, I got a call to go and see Cameron, whom I had assumed up to then I had never met, until we did. I recognised him immediately from my after-Cabinet lunches at the DTI as the young man from central office who had sat at the far end of the table well below the salt. Now he was young man no more but the leader of the Conservative Party and on his way to No. 10, which he achieved by winning the next election. It was not a clear-cut victory, and he had to be satisfied with a coalition with the Liberal Democrats, with Nick Clegg as his Deputy Prime Minister and the Lib Dems with some seats at the Cabinet table.

I was invited in again as a volunteer to deal with problems arising out of health and safety legislation, which had been interpreted far too bureaucratically and was rapidly becoming a scandal that filled the papers day after day. At a time when companies were struggling to establish themselves, it gave an opportunity for the unscrupulous to charge large fees for completely unnecessary work on the grounds that they were complying with the law.

On my first day, I was given meeting room A, one of the large rooms in the Cabinet Office. It was a very large room, with a meeting table that would seat at least thirty-six, and in the corner was a solitary desk. I couldn't help smiling when they showed me the room, for there was a story, which may be apocryphal but I suspect not, that when Michael Heseltine had agreed with John Major that he would become Deputy Prime Minister and went to see the Cabinet Secretary in his office about suitable accommodation, when there was some question about how long it would take to find somewhere for him, he looked round the secretary's office and said that he thought this would do quite well. He was hurriedly told that they would have accommodation by the next morning, which they did by emptying out one of these large meeting rooms and furnishing it accordingly. Since I was not Deputy Prime Minister, the meeting table would remain.

I accepted the accommodation, built a small team of civil servants and spent the next few months finding my way round the intricacies of the health and safety legislation, which was a real minefield and had been much complicated by European law. In the end, we found a very simple way out, and I produced a paper called 'Common Sense, Common Safety'.

All too often I had seen papers published that eventually ended up pigeonholed and ignored, so when I had agreed to work for David Cameron, I had made only one stipulation: that the papers I produced would first go to the Cabinet for approval and acceptance by the government before they were published and would not end up in some dusty pigeonhole. I duly presented the paper at the next meeting of the Cabinet, and it was enthusiastically endorsed. Within a day or two of publication, the problem disappeared in real life and from the press.

A week or two later, Jeremy Heywood, later Cabinet Secretary but at the time in charge of No. 10, appeared uninvited in my office and mysteriously said: 'Follow me.' He took me through the door that separates the Cabinet Office from No. 10, up the stairs to room 123 on the first floor, which sits over the entrance, and told me that this was now my office. It was the only other single-occupant room in No. 10 besides the PM's.

Within a day or two, I had agreed with David Cameron that I would now become his enterprise adviser and set about ways to make it easier for new companies to start and small and medium companies to grow. I was appalled at what I discovered, for everything I had introduced in the '80s had gone and left no trace. Of course, the Youth Training Scheme had gone with the fall in unemployment, but to abolish entirely technical and vocational training in the school system was completely ignoring all the technology that was becoming a necessary part and parcel of everyday life.

It did not take me long to recruit a new team of civil servants, and initially there was plenty of low-hanging fruit to deal with. For example, we found that if you started a new business from home, and more than half of new businesses are started from home, it was not only a breach of planning laws but also you could incur capital gains tax on the value of the room you used for your business. I did not take too long to put this right.

I had been away from the small business scene for over twenty years, and the difference was remarkable. Whereas all those years ago the problem was to persuade people, particularly young people, that they had it in them to work for themselves, now the problem was quite the opposite. So many young people had been inspired by the stories of the new tech billionaires – quite often people who were young themselves when they started a new business in a new technology and made a great success very quickly – that the problem now was almost how to slow them down. I visited areas like Shoreditch and Hackney, which back in the '80s had been depressed, almost slum areas, which were now full of technology companies with new restaurants and bars.

One day, a small group of young entrepreneurs came to call on me with plans to set up an organisation to be called Start-Up Britain. I liked the people, and I loved the idea, and within three weeks they were before the Cabinet. Over the next two or three years they made a real difference in the way people, particularly young people, thought about working for themselves.

But as good as the scene was, it had suffered grievously as a result of the financial crash of '08 and the almost complete withdrawal of the banks from helping new start-up companies. When I had started in early 1961, I had gone to my local Barclays bank, and it was the manager who lent me the money to start. But now that was no more.

When the banks had computerised many years ago to save overheads, they had taken the managers out of the branches and replaced them with call centres, and the personal touch had gone. Today, managers only existed for medium and large companies, and start-ups now depended on money from family and friends. I remembered the Enterprise Allowance Scheme of the '80s, and I was determined we should do something similar again, but now not to solve any unemployment problem but to encourage the birth of more small firms.

Initially, the Treasury turned me down, so I applied again with the same result. At the third time of trying, the Treasury capitulated, realised I was not going away and finally agreed.

The scheme I proposed was simplicity itself, and I knew it worked because I 'stole' the idea from the Prince's Trust. I had worked for the trust for many years and had been responsible for fundraising and also for the business programme, which ran a very similar scheme although for smaller loans, and so I knew it worked. A five-year loan of up to £5,000–£7,000 at a modest rate of interest, and most important with a mentor. This was no more than an individual they could telephone if they had a problem or wanted some advice, for I remembered how lonely it was when I first started and how important advice was then.

The Prince's Trust themselves were delighted, because from the beginning they became one of our partners in distributing the loans.

I approached James Caan, a high-profile, successful entrepreneur, to chair the Start-Up Loans Company and he took to it with great enthusiasm. He set up the first offices in his own headquarters until we could establish our own, recruited well and started the business. He ran the business for the first few years, and when it was running well, he stood down.

Today the company is run by the British Business Bank, and Start-Up Loans have been responsible for over 75,000 new businesses. But what is even more important is that the internet is today used to advertise a whole host of bodies that help new start-ups to get funded.

In the midst of all this, Margaret Thatcher passed away, on 8 April 2013. On the day of the funeral, the cortège, which we joined, went from Westminster to St Paul's Cathedral. All along the way the crowd, three or four deep, clapped respectfully. In the star-studded congregation were the Queen with Prince Philip – the only other former Prime Minister's funeral she had ever attended in her long reign was that of Winston Churchill. All I could do during the service was to remember how the world had been during the '70s, after decades of decline, and how much we all owed her.

In my time with David Cameron, I initiated a whole host of programmes designed to help small firms: from installing a compulsory database of every public sector contract over £25,000 which could be readily searched by any small firm, to recruiting business schools to start helping small firms in their area, to in 'Enterprise for All', looking at enterprise in education and giving every school in the land an enterprise adviser, often a local small businessman or woman, to bring local firms and large companies into the school to play a role in the education system.

At the end of the coalition government's first term, I stood down. I could be reasonably pleased with the way the economy over the decades had morphed into an enterprise one. The election came, and David Cameron and the Conservatives were returned with a clear majority. Yet, there were dark clouds on the horizon, as the issue of our membership of the European Union was coming ever closer to the fore. Cameron decided he had to take the issue head-on and announced that there would be a referendum on our membership after he had renegotiated fresh terms for our continuing participation. The referendum duly took place after he returned with some new, immaterial concessions; the government lost; and Cameron resigned. We now had a headless government with little or no enthusiasm for carrying out the result of the referendum.

In the resulting Conservative Party leadership election, all the parties fell by the wayside, leaving only Theresa May, the Home Secretary, as the sole candidate, and she was left with the unenviable task of negotiating an outcome she did not support. What was even worse was that the Labour Party, in a reaction, perhaps, to losing the past three elections, had retreated to its comfort zone: Jeremy Corbyn was their leader; the most extreme left-wing leader since Michael Foot in the early '80s. In a purported attempt to strengthen her hand in the upcoming EU negotiations, May managed to get the necessary two thirds vote under the Fixed-Term Parliament Act to call a snap general election in June 2017.

When the election started, the Conservatives had a 21-point lead, but that did not last long and steadily began to erode away under May's listless leadership. As none of the young had any memory of the '70s, nor even believed what they were told about that appalling decade, Jeremy Corbyn's ideas appeared fresh and novel, and he began to receive a rapturous reception whenever he appeared.

As the campaign went on, the Conservative lead diminished, and at the end, despite winning 42.4 per cent of the vote, the Conservatives made a net loss of thirteen seats, while Labour made a net gain of thirty seats, with 40 per cent of the vote.

Now Theresa May found herself with a substantially reduced majority in the House, increased opposition from within her own party from the Eurosceptic wing, as well as increased opposition from Labour. Her negotiations with the EU bore little fruit, and she could get none of her proposals through the House. Eventually, on 7 June 2019, she announced she would resign as leader of the Conservatives once a successor had been chosen. There followed a somewhat complex election process, in which Conservative MPs chose a shortlist which was then put to the party membership, and as a result Boris Johnson was decisively elected.

Boris had no better luck than Theresa, for after renegotiating the new withdrawal agreement, the House still rejected it. It had, by now, become an impossible House, and Labour thought they saw their chance, agreeing to legislation for an immediate election, which was duly held on 12 December.

Jeremy Corbyn excelled himself by producing a manifesto that, while professing a Green Revolution, produced a Red one, reintroducing much of what we had changed over the decades since the '70s. Swathes of the economy was going to be renationalised; rather surreptitiously, the unions were going to be given back much of the privileges they had lost in the '80s; and taxation would be made 'fairer', which meant substantially increased: in other words, back to the '70s.

But by now, the youthful infatuation for Jeremy had cooled, and adoring crowds were no more. When the results were in, it was a landslide for the Conservatives, at least in comparison with their last few elections, and they had a majority of eighty. But even more important, even than their recorded share of the vote (43.6 per cent), were the gains they made in the 'Red Wall' – long-standing Labour seats that had voted Leave and essentially voted for Johnson and Vote Leave, which the Conservatives vowed they would complete.

In many ways, this was still Margaret's victory: victory for the enterprise economy we worked so hard to introduce in the mid-'80s, which had been consolidated by that long ago election victory in 1987. Since then, there has not been any government, irrespective of party, that did not pay at the very least lip service to enterprise as a concept and a goal.

In the early part of January 2020, we were looking forward not only to a new decade but to a new entrepreneurial future – we had succeeded in our efforts to finally leave the EU, although it would not actually take effect until the end of the year. We could start to focus on all the new trade agreements we were now free to make that would focus on bringing joint benefit to all parties. There were also forty years of EU legislation that littered our statute book, and we could now streamline, use those parts that suited our economy but rid ourselves of Civil Code remnants that simply slowed us down.

Then, in the wet market in far-away Wuhan, people started getting ill from an unknown disease...

ACKNOWLEDGEMENTS

I would not have considered publishing without the encouragement of Michael Hayman supported by Sir Anthony Seldon, nor would I have survived the events described in these pages all those years ago without the active support of Howell James and the late Lord (Tim) Bell.

I would like to thank Charles Moore for so readily agreeing to write the Foreword and James Stephens and Lucy Stewardson at Biteback for making the process of authorship so agreeable.

Finally, I would like to thank Jacky Bell for giving me the opportunity of speaking about her late husband at his memorial, where I conceived the idea for this book.

INDEX